DESIGNING WITH ILLUSTRATION

DESIGNING WITH ILLUSTRATION

STEVEN HELLER AND KAREN POMEROY
DESIGNED BY SEYMOUR CHWAST
A PUSHPIN EDITION

VNR VAN NOSTRAND REINHOLD
NEW YORK

PUSHPIN EDITIONS

Editor
STEVEN HELLER
Art Director
SEYMOUR CHWAST
Designer
GREG SIMPSON

Library of Congress Catalog Card Number 89-14723

Printed in the United States of America

Van Nostrand Reinhold
115 Fifth Avenue
New York, New York 10003

Van Nostrand Reinhold International
Company Limited
11 New Fetter Lane
London EC4P 4EE, England

Van Nostrand Reinhold
480 La Trobe Street
Melbourne, Victoria 3000, Australia

Nelson Canada
1120 Birchmount Road
Scarborough, Ontario
Canada M1K 5G4

16 15 14 13 12 11 10 9 8 7 6 5 4 3 2 1

Library of Congress Cataloging-in-Publication Data

Heller, Steven.
Designing with illustration.

"A Pushpin edition."
Includes index.
1. Illustration of books—United States. 2. Design—United States. I. Pomeroy, Karen. II. Title.
NC975.H4 1990 741.6′092′273 89-14723
ISBN 0-442-23277-2

CONTENTS

ACKNOWLEDGMENTS

This book would not be possible if not for the cooperation and support of its participants. Heartfelt thanks to all the illustrators, designers, and art directors who gave us their time and work.

Sincere gratitude and respect go to Lilly Kaufman, our editor at Van Nostrand Reinhold, whose enthusiasm, editorial savvy, and patience have made this a pleasurable experience. To Julie Lasky, our copy editor and project manager, whose insight and skill were invaluable. To Sandra Cohen for administering the design and production. To Edward Spiro for additional photography.

PREFACE

Illustration is not simply a narrative art; nor is it divorced from the total design process, as some practitioners would have us believe. Designers who illustrate and art directors who know how to use illustration effectively have a greater capacity to make exciting graphic work. Likewise, illustrators who have an understanding of typography and design fundamentals are better equipped to present their work successfully. This book has two goals: to show designers and illustrators that drawing, specifically the practice of illustration, is a viable part of the design process; and to encourage art directors not to forsake illustration during this era of high-tech trickery.

Our title, "Designing with Illustration," signifies an aspect of contemporary practice that suffers from years of prejudice. However, it stresses that drawing is important to the design process (a notion that fell into disrepute at many art schools during the past three decades), and that over the past century design practitioners have used drawing and illustration for decorative and conceptual purposes. Hence, *Designing with Illustration* focuses on three distinct but sometimes overlapping methods:

■ *Illustration as a separate activity used in an overall design.* This practice is represented in the section called "Illustrators Who Design," which includes such artists as Dugald Stermer and Steven Guarnaccia, who often provide the visual pieces to a larger design puzzle, sometimes integrated at the drawing stage, but usually pieced together by an art director or designer afterward. These artists also may incorporate design forms in their work under the auspices of an art director.

■ *Illustration or drawing as the integral element of design.* This is represented in the section called "Designers Who Illustrate," which includes, among others, Michael Vanderbyl and Milton Glaser, for whom the distinction between drawing and graphic design is blurred.

■ *Art direction as a primary organizing function.* This is represented in the section called "Art Directors," which exemplifies the creative collaboration between designer and illustrator. Featured among other products of this collaboration are examples of Louise Fili's book jackets, Paula Scher's record covers, and Kit Hinrichs's book designs.

The work herein, selected from illustrators, designers, and art directors, demonstrates a broad range of illustrative design in various media, from corporate annual reports to packaging and shopping bags to animated television identification. The practitioner is the primary focus, but sometimes a speciality is highlighted (e.g., book jacket, poster, advertising, promotional display, and so on), while at other times a range of endeavor by the same person is featured. Each participant has been asked a customized set of questions about his or her specific work and about the process and philosophy by which it was created. The answers have been edited, but remain true to the individual's voice.

The marriage of type and image is essential to the definition of the design process. In fact, scanning recent Art Director's Club annuals one finds that although a high percentage of work involves photography and typography as principal elements, a healthy percentage includes drawing, painting, and even sculpture. This might suggest a revival, but more accurately it is a quiet rebellion against a curious yet prevailing view that drawing as a final product is old-fashioned. *Designing with Illustration* underscores the viability of drawing, and particularly of illustration, as both a design tool and a primary transmitter for ideas in today's communications environment.

—Steven Heller

INTRODUCTION

Priester

(*right*)
THE CIRCA 1906 POSTER FOR THE PRIESTER MATCH COMPANY WAS A *TOUR DE FORCE* AND A MILESTONE FOR ITS MAKER, A 16-YEAR-OLD BOY NAMED LUCIAN BERNHARD, WHO CAME UP WITH THE DESIGN QUITE BY ACCIDENT. ORIGINALLY BERNHARD HAD PAINTED A MORE ELABORATE SCENE: A PAIR OF MATCHES ALONGSIDE AN ASHTRAY THAT HELD A LIT CIGAR WITH DANCING GIRLS WAFTING FROM THE SMOKE. BERNHARD ASKED A FRIEND HOW HE LIKED THE PAINTING AND WAS SHOCKED WHEN THE FRIEND SAID IT WAS A GREAT ADVERTISEMENT FOR CIGARS. HE IMMEDIATELY PAINTED OUT ALL EXTRANEOUS PROPS, LEAVING ONLY THE RED MATCHES WITH YELLOW TIPS. AT THE TOP HE HAND-LETTERED THE NAME PRIESTER IN WHAT WAS TO BECOME A CHARACTERISTIC GERMAN ADVERTISING TYPEFACE. WITH THIS THE OBJECT POSTER, OR *SACHPLAKAT*, WAS BORN, USHERING IN A STYLE OF SIMPLE AND DIRECT ILLUSTRATIVE ADVERTISING ART.

The Union Torn Asunder

Once design and illustration were totally integrated; now they are disturbingly fragmented, resulting in an unhealthy stratification of the designer and illustrator. Indeed, the union of type and drawing into one composition was deemed unholy by dominant twentieth-century design theoreticians who proffered a machine aesthetic. Codifiers of the Modern graphic design canon in the 1920s—key among them Laszlo Moholy-Nagy and Jan Tschichold, whose 1928 book, *The New Typography*, set the standard—argued against hand-made in favor of machine-made (e.g., photographic) imagery. A schism subsequently developed between what we shall call "pure" designers and narrative pictorialists. Though less pronounced in this Postmodern era, the dichotomy still exists.

Routes of Change

The reasons are based in a Modern aesthetic, the consequence of the critical industrial and commercial revolutions taking place at the turn of the century, at which time artists adopted a reactionary stance against the decidedly nineteenth-century belief that illustration technique and style should be based on the rules that governed academic painting. The illustrators of this "academic" period, like their easel-painting counterparts, chose to re-create their natural surroundings as accurately as possible. Even the illustrators who practiced cartoon and caricature—those who elected to exaggerate natural forms and in so doing criticized the "real" world—drew upon the *beaux arts* tradition. They may have deformed a face or transformed a being into a stereotype, yet fidelity to natural and physical characteristics governed their compositions. Moreover, even the most "expressive" illustrators at that time did not tamper with nature.

The development of the camera as a documentary tool in the late nineteenth century liberated many of these artists from the responsibility of chronicler. The camera recorded details of an exterior environment, allowing the artist to explore the mind and its hidden recesses. Impressionism was the first break from the rigors of academic realism in both the fine and applied arts, and eventually Expressionism stripped the protective covering away from human emotion. By the early 1900s Cubism pro-

510
MASSAG

(*bottom, right*)
INFLUENCED BY THE COMIC SIMPLICITY OF THE GERMAN APPROACH, VOJTECH TESZAR, A CZECHOSLOVAK DESIGNER, RENDERED AN ICONOGRAPHIC AD FOR MASSAG, A TYPOGRAPHER AND PRINTER IN BRATISLAVA.

LA BAIONNETTE
La Légende Héroïque

OSILI
ZOBERBIER

(above)
ALTHOUGH ECONOMY WAS THE KEYNOTE OF GERMAN ILLUSTRATIVE POSTERS, CONTEMPORARY ARTISTS WERE NOT WED TO ONE PARTICULAR DRAWING OR PAINTING STYLE. THE 1924 POSTER BY ZOBERBIER FOR THE WASHING DETERGENT OSILI IS RENDERED IN A POPULAR GEOMETRIC CARTOON STYLE.

(above, left)
FABIANO'S COVER FOR A 1917 ISSUE OF *LA BAIONNETTE*, A WEEKLY FRENCH HUMOR MAGAZINE DEVOTED TO LAMPOONING AND CRITICIZING THE GERMANS DURING WORLD WAR I, PAYS HOMAGE TO THE EARLY POSTERS OF JULES CHÉRET. THE HEROIC ILLUSTRATION, RENDERED IN THE DOMINANT LITHOGRAPHIC STYLE, STANDS ON ITS OWN BUT IS ALSO SUCCESSFULLY INTEGRATED WITH THE MAGAZINE'S LOGO.

vided the fuel that drove the revolution from realism to abstraction. Cubists further developed a distinctly new visual language that circumvented mannerist tendencies of the nineteenth century, avoided the teachings of the Renaissance, and proffered a unique way of perceiving time and spatial relationships. Cubism provided the impetus for Modern visual thinking.

The camera was only *one* extraordinary invention to foster the creative and technical development of the visual arts. Industrial and scientific progress allowed for change in all forms of communication; indirectly, radio, motion pictures, and ultimately television had considerable impact on ambient style. Change in visual priorities was also an outgrowth of the Industrial Revolution: commercialized and industrialized societies produced more goods, requiring intensified salesmanship and culminating in the new field of advertising. Persuasive visuals became the key to advertising art.

The Seamless Marriage

This surge in commerce initiated a stylistic reevaluation throughout the applied arts. In the mid-nineteenth century illustration was primarily used for editorial purposes; but from the 1870s, illustrative design, as we refer to the marriage of type and drawn, painted, or printed image, was championed by Jules Chéret in advertising posters for cabarets and musical revues. His images were exotically colorful and wildly impressionistic; his lettering was designed to conform to the gesture of his art and veritably lit up the Parisian streets with an exuberance lacking in the predominantly typographic ads that came before. Chéret's posters further heralded an Art Nouveau typified by organic form yet machine-made for popular consumption. The seamless union of type and image was the hallmark of this graphic style, of which Henri de Toulouse-Lautrec and, later, Alphonse Mucha also were exemplars.

Other classic examples of illustrative design were produced in the first decade of the twentieth century, when the dominant European advertising form known as the *object poster* emerged, first in Germany and shortly after in England, France, and Italy. As practiced by the Berliner Lucian Bernhard, this method was a rejection of unnecessary visuals and words in favor of a *portrait* of the object being advertised. Such posters usually were presented with the brand name as the only text. They were aesthetically seductive, commercially successful, and demonstrated the profound union of drawing and design. Bernhard's archetypal object poster for the Priester

KEIN TISCH OHNE
MÜNCHENER LÖWENBRÄU

(*right*)
WHILE BERNHARD WAS MAKING HIS CAREER IN BERLIN, LUDWIG HOHLWEIN BECAME THE MASTER OF THE ILLUSTRATIVE POSTER IN MUNICH. LIKE BERNHARD HE WAS INTERESTED IN THE ESSENCE OF HIS SUBJECT, USUALLY FOCUSING DIRECTLY ON THE OBJECT BEING ADVERTISED AND ESCHEWING BACKGROUNDS AND OTHER VISUAL NOISE. SINCE HE WAS THE BETTER PAINTER, HOHLWEIN OFTEN EVOKED A MOOD AND AMBIENCE NOT PRESENT IN BERNHARD'S WORK. THE CIRCA 1922 POSTER FOR MÜNCHENER LÖWENBRÄU TYPIFIES HOHLWEIN'S ELEGANCE AND SIMPLICITY.

(*bottom, right*)
COREY KILVENT'S COVER FOR A 1909 ISSUE OF THE ORIGINAL *LIFE* MAGAZINE (A HUMOR WEEKLY THAT FEATURED REVIEWS, COMMENTARY, AND CARTOONS) IS INDICATIVE OF THE AMERICAN ART NOUVEAU. THOUGH THE STYLE IS NOT AS FANATICALLY CURVILINEAR OR ORGANIC AS THE FRENCH VARIATION, THE COMBINATION OF IMAGE AND THEMATIC LETTERING IS A DOMINANT ASPECT OF BOTH STYLES.

match company typifies the strength of the letter and image designed in tandem. Without the brand name the passerby would have seen merely two matches (a kind of proto pop art); without the uniquely colored matches the name Priester would have been simply another corporate identifier in a sea of common advertising posters. But united these elements were—and continue to be—both functionally and aesthetically beautiful. The poster provided an *aide de memoire* that to this day is still very effective communication. Equally important, Bernhard's poster was a revelation at the time of its inception, since most publicity was overly decorative and ornate.

Realism, Abstraction, and the Hybrid Forms

During the early twentieth century illustration and photography were used on an equal basis depending, of course, on the context, need, and budget. The photograph was best for showing "reality," while illustration was better suited for mythologizing and heroicizing a product or idea. And this, by the way, was a common selling strategy, especially in the United States, where competition for surplus goods raged at a much fiercer pace than in Europe. These methods continued throughout the first half of the twentieth century.

Between the wars realism reigned supreme in American fine and applied arts, while the Europeans veered toward abstract and machine-inspired imagery. However, even in Europe two parallel (sometimes overlapping) approaches emerged, one pure and the other decorative.

The simplification of form was practiced in certain applied arts and evidenced by the fervently ideological Modern art movements and schools. This involved the adoption of pictorial collage and letterform fragmentation as design elements symbolic of the machine age—an approach embraced equally by the Italian Futurists, the Dutch De Stijl, the Russian (and Eastern European) Constructivists, and the German Bauhaus. These groups later developed canons of purity that restricted image making only to photography and available typecase materials. El Lissitzky's illustrations for Vladimir Mayakovsky's book of revolutionary poems, titled *For the Voice,* is an excellent example of unadorned illustration in which graphic symbols were used both to complement the text and define the design aesthetic.

As a commercial alternative to the Modern approach, designers applied stylized mannerisms to a variety of work which was then referred to as "modernistic" or "Art Moderne," or more com-

LIFE
GREAT WHITE WAY
NUMBER

PORTE-T-ELLE
LA DEVISE
TOUJOURS
A
MIEUX
JEAN
CARLU
28

Metallum
DRAHTLAMPE
METALLUM

(above)
Between the turn of the century and World War I the *Berliner plakat* was a primary illustrative advertising style. Noted for relative economy and the use of bold, flat colors, Berlin printers and commercial artists provided industry with stark, eye-catching publicity. One sales tool was the advertising stamp, a postage-stamp-size adaptation of the poster which proved that the best-designed posters—those that could be seen from 100 feet away—also were effective when reduced to one-hundredth their original size. The circa 1903 stamp for Metallum light bulbs by an unknown artist was one of thousands issued.

(left)
From the late 1920s through the 1930s French poster art and publicity was at its stylistic zenith. A. M. Cassandre, the most influential poster artist and typographer, combined cubist forms, decorative typography, and dynamic layouts to define a period style. Among his most talented peers was Jean Carlu, whose style was a mix of surrealist and cubist forms in the cartoon idiom. For the 1928 poster "Porte-T-Elle La Devise," Carlu used a hand-lettered Deco sans serif based on Futura as a major design element with which he perfectly balanced the suggestive illustration.

monly known today as "Art Deco." This was a synthesis of certain Modern characteristics, including geometric patterns as well as Egyptian ziggurats and organic devices, combined with updated decorative ornamentation derived from the nineteenth century. Whereas photography was preferred by the Modernists, sleek and elegant graphic styling characterized the Moderne designer. Whereas austere functional design was the key to the Modern approach, elegant ornamentation defined the cosmopolitan Deco style, for which illustration was extensively used.

During the late twenties and well into the thirties a unique marriage of Modern and Moderne was nurtured by French posterists A. M. Cassandre, Jean Carlu, Charles Loupot, and others. Their particular brand of advertising exemplifies the illustrative design of that age and the limitless ways in which type and graphic and painterly images could be combined.

DEAD MEN CAN'T WALK · A COMPLETE NOVEL
MYSTERY
APRIL
10¢
A TOWER MAGAZINE
LOVE AND DANGER GO HAND IN HAND, IN
THE CASE OF THE RIGID MAN
Also, THEODORE DREISER, LEIGH MATTESON, NORMAN MATSON, and EDMUND PEARSON

Fundamental Misunderstandings

Illustration is a misunderstood form owing to the fact that it is practiced in different ways for a wide range of purposes. Therefore, some clarification of terms is called for. The most conventional definition is that *illustration tells a story.* Some illustration might tell an entire story (such as with graphic novels, comic strips, and illustrated children's books), but more often it is an excerpt from a narrative—a visual signpost. Book illustrations stimulate the reader's imagination by providing portraits of characters and scenes. Illustration, however, must be distinguished from *illumination,* which, as the word suggests, lights up a page of type through decoration. Indeed decorative illustration (borders, spots, or vignettes) are not narrative, although they can help the reader follow a story. Over the decades illustrated books have been either literal translations of texts (N. C. Wyeth's *Treasure Island*), fanciful interpretations (Sir John Tenniel's *Alice in Wonderland*), or abstract expressions (El Lissitzky's *For the Voice*).

Before photographs could be economically reproduced, newspaper and magazine illustration

AIR-FLIGHT
FISK
mileage

(bottom)
Poster art in Europe was more abstract than in America, because posters were viewed primarily by pedestrians moving at a leisurely pace. American billboard illustration, on the other hand, was often layered with stark lettering that could be seen by passengers in a speeding bus, train, or car. The circa 1929 Fisk billboard by an unknown artist is a panoramic tableau boldly featuring the product's name, an urban setting, and an illustration of the Fisk mascot, all rendered with stylized realism.

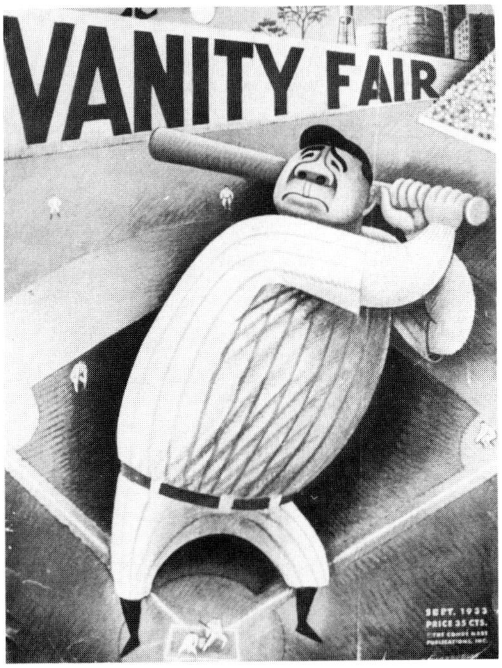
VANITY FAIR
SEPT. 1933
PRICE 35 CTS.

Fortune
One Dollar a Copy
JULY 1937
Ten Dollars a Year

(left and opposite)
AMERICAN ILLUSTRATION WAS USED IN VARIOUS WAYS, AND NOT ALL OF THEM INTEGRATED WITH DESIGN. THESE MAGAZINES REPRESENT THREE APPLICATIONS: THE 1934 COVER FOR *MYSTERY*, BY AN UNKNOWN ARTIST, IS A STRIKINGLY STYLIZED PAINTING SET INTO THE RECTANGLE PROVIDED BY THE DESIGNER (OR PRINTER). NO ATTEMPT IS MADE TO BLEND THE LOGO OR HEADLINE TYPE. CONVERSELY, THE 1933 COVER FOR *VANITY FAIR*, BY MIGUEL COVARRUBIAS, IS A CHARMING CARICATURE OF BABE RUTH SET IN FRONT OF A HAND-LETTERED LOGO WHOSE SHAPE CONFORMS TO THE OUTFIELD FENCE. WHEREAS EACH COVER OF THE MONTHLY *VANITY FAIR* WAS DIFFERENT, ALLOWING ILLUSTRATORS THE FREEDOM TO DO THEIR OWN TYPOGRAPHIC DESIGN, *FORTUNE* MAGAZINE FOLLOWED THE SAME COVER FORMAT EACH MONTH BUT INVITED ITS COVER ARTISTS TO WEAVE THEIR WORK THROUGHOUT THE STANDARD BORDER AND LOGO. IN THE 1937 *FORTUNE* COVER, AUSTRIAN POSTER ARTIST JOSEPH BINDER SUCCESSFULLY USED THAT IMMUTABLE FORMAT TO CREATE A STRIKING GRAPHIC.

"factually" depicted events—at least as remembered by the artist-reporters, who often rendered their finished drawings after the fact from rough sketches. Newspaper artists, called "specials," were assigned to cover critical events where the camera was either too conspicuous or unwelcome. This practice changed with the advent of lightweight "pocket" cameras. And so today's newspaper and magazine illustration is more cerebral and conceptual; and rather than provide objective information, it complements a story.

From the 1870s to the late 1950s the dominant mode of American illustration was narrative. Realism was popular at the magazines aimed at mass audiences. Even when photography became supreme in most general magazines, including *Colliers, The Saturday Evening Post,* and *Look,* illustrators were still called upon to make believable pictures for fiction and other hard-to-photograph pieces. Yet during the late 1930s and early 1940s European Modernists who fled the Nazis and settled in the United States developed new directions in illustrative design. The former Bauhaus master Herbert Bayer often combined what we can categorize as European "objectivity" with an American "narrative" sensibility in his photomontages. Other leading design émigrés, such as Ladislav Sutnar and Gyorgy Kepes, imbued their designs with abstract forms. Before their arrival, however, Americans, including Paul Rand and Lester Beall, were already experimenting with this abstract approach. They invented their own language, building upon the syntax of Modernism. Rand's loyalty to Jan Tschichold's and Moholy-Nagy's dicta for "mechanical art for a mechanical age" was demonstrated *only* as it was appropriate. Many of Rand's *Direction* magazine covers from 1938 to 1942 evidence unprecedented uses of drawing and typography often combined with cut paper and enlarged halftone screens. Rand helped to liberate the contemporary designer from a slavish adherence to a limited workbench of Modern tools.

Contributing to the ideological discourse about the "rightness of form," William A. Kittredge, in the 1940 volume of *The Production Yearbook,* addressed a question posed by the publishing and advertising industries as to whether photographs or drawings were the more effective medium. He concluded that "the average layman and public in general do not notice the difference between reproductions of drawings and photographs. . . . The effect on the public is determined by the interest and dramatic possibilities of their content and composition." Nevertheless, those who were

CONFORMING TO THE EUROPEAN POSTER TRADITION, ARTHUR HAWKINS DESIGNED THIS CIRCA 1935 BOOK JACKET FOR *THE MAESTRO MURDERS* SO THAT THE HAND-LETTERED TYPE ECHOED THE LINEAR QUALITY OF THE EXPRESSIONISTIC ILLUSTRATION.

THE
MAESTRO
MURDERS
FRANCES S. WEES

concerned with making the visual environment more challenging did distinguish between photography and drawing—specifically between realism and abstraction, literalism and illusion. For the progressives the sentimental forms of illustration were much too old-fashioned.

Today, the widespread use of photography has made the consumer skeptical of what might be considered antiquated forms of illustration, but farcical and comic forms remain popular. Indeed the current trend is for three-dimensional illustrative animation like the Domino Pizza "Noid" and the Post Raisin Bran "California Raisins."

Revival, Reevaluation, Rebellion

Contemporary graphic designers are the progeny of the mid-century Modernists, but as with all families, internal rebellion is part of the growth cycle. Today is an eclectic age insofar as no single ideology exists and many distinct methods coexist. Although drawing is again favored in some design courses, there remains a residue of past prejudice. Most university design departments are still segregated from the illustration departments, exacerbating the distinction. While some critics argue that the modern design process is a collage-like puzzle, others insist that design *begins* with drawing. Both points of view are, however, valid. But few would dispute that knowing how to draw increases fluency in the visual language.

Styles, fashions, and tastes have changed over time, but the skills required for good graphic communication remain fairly constant. While the drawing process may now be aided by computers, conventional illustrative design is a long way from becoming moribund. Though graphic designers embrace new technologies in a search for greater creative and technical options, publishing and advertising also demand diversity. *Designing with Illustration* offers options for today and possibilities for tomorrow.

ILLUSTRATORS WHO DESIGN

BASCOVE

Influenced by the Russian novelists of the late nineteenth century, Bascove has literally cut a niche for herself as a book jacket illustrator-designer. Though she takes on editorial assignments, her primary concern is interpreting works of fiction by authors such as Italo Calvino, Primo Levi, and Robertson Davies. Many of her finest jackets have been collaborations with art directors or designers who have provided typographic expertise; but in recent years Bascove has united her talent for cutting images out of wood and linoleum with a skill for creating individualized letterforms. Inspired by the freeform lettering the Expressionists included with their hard-edged illustrations and posters, she now designs unified compositions. Here she comments on the problems and satisfactions of being a painter and an illustrator, as she discusses a few of her recent book jackets.

On her professional identity: I do not consider myself a designer. I do not really design anything except when I do a book cover or jacket. I do illustrations for the *New York Times* on occasion, if there is some political or literary angle. And I will act on my political concerns for magazines such as *Mother Jones* and *The Progressive*, where I am given a wide margin of freedom.

About reconciling the fine and applied arts: I have tried to separate my painting from my illustration, but in the past few years, publishing art directors and editors who have come to my painting shows invariably ask whether they can reproduce my paintings as book covers. I agree to this only on condition that the artwork is credited as a painting, not as an illustration.

On a few occasions I have been asked to do a cover with the same *feeling* as one of my paintings. *In the Skin of a Lion* and *What Is It Then Between Us?* both echo my paintings. However, I cannot really achieve the feeling of a painting if it is done as an illustration. My paintings evolve over a long period of time and are tightly worked out on a grid. Illustration must be specific to the problem that I am solving, and the grid would be a time-consuming constraint. I am afraid it would come off as style rather than integral to the content.

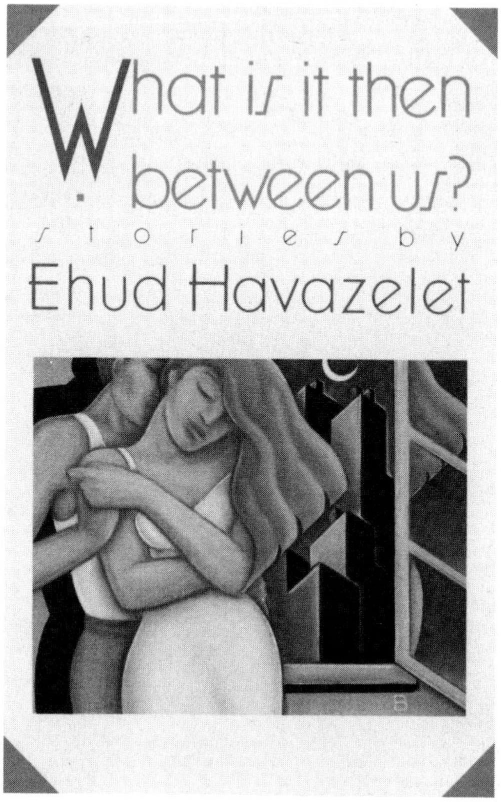
What is it then between us?
stories by
Ehud Havazelet

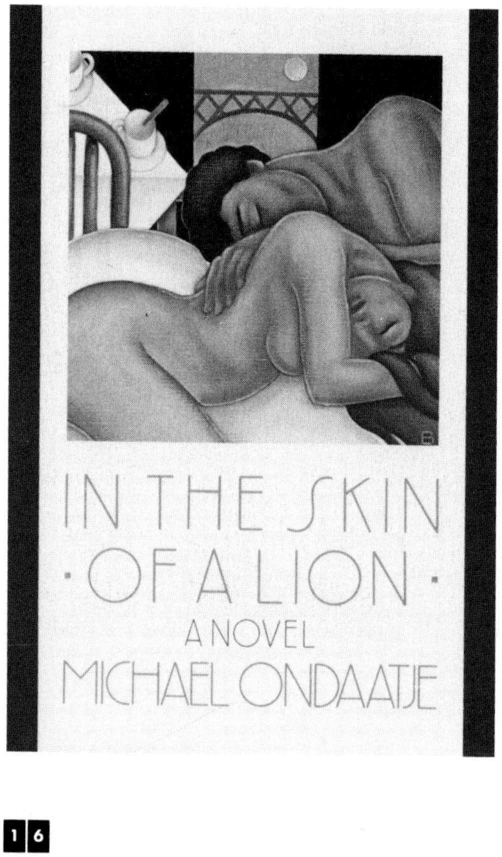
IN THE SKIN
· OF A LION ·
A NOVEL
MICHAEL ONDAATJE

On maintaining the integrity of her images: I like a picture to stand on its own, yet with more decorative pieces I tend to integrate type. Even so, I try to maintain some separateness. Despite the formal concerns, however, my first responsibility is to get a sense of the book across.

About type: Years ago I carved the lettering for my book covers or jackets. If I needed real type the art director would do it. Or when I got jobs where the art director was not interested in carved type and had no desire to do the other, I would ask Louise Fili to be my typographic consultant. Then one of my friends told me that this method was ridiculous. "It's easier to order type," she said—and she was right. It was a little awkward at first, but now I really enjoy speccing, cutting, and manipulating type. To make some-

MEMORY OF
DEPARTURE
a novel
Abdulrazak Gurnah

MEMORY OF DEPARTURE (1988),
Book jacket
GROVE PRESS, *Client*
BASCOVE, *Designer*
BASCOVE, *Illustrator*
KRYSTYNA SKALSKI, *Art Director*

IN THE SKIN OF A LION (1987),
Book jacket
ALFRED A. KNOPF, *Client*
BASCOVE, *Designer*
BASCOVE, *Illustrator*
SARA EISENMAN, *Art Director*

WHAT IS IT THEN BETWEEN US?
(1988), *Book jacket*
MACMILLAN, *Client*
BASCOVE, *Designer*
BASCOVE, *Illustrator*
LEE WADE, *Art Director*

AND OTHER STORIES
JANWILLEM VAN DE WETERING

THE SARGEANT'S CAT
AND OTHER STORIES
JANWILLEM VAN DE WETERING

THE SARGEANT'S CAT
AND OTHER STORIES
JANWILLEM VAN DE WETERING

thing more personal, such as the jacket for *What Is It Then Between Us?*, I am not content to use what is found in a type book, so I just draw and reconfigure until I see some way that I can change it to whatever shape I need, or until there is a way to pleasingly mix up a face. With *Memory of Departure* I ran the type down the side because that sort of thing is common on 1930s travel posters, which relates to the author's dream to leave his country on a long trip.

About color: Color is added to the wood or linoleum cut after it is printed. I paint with watercolor and sometimes use colored pencil because I want a texture or color that cannot be achieved without the combination of media.

About printing: I do not own a press. Instead the printing is done by hand with a wooden spoon. I work the same size and print with very heavy ink flow on a heavyweight watercolor paper that is dampened for optimum absorption.

I give some publishers a black-and-white print in addition to the full color finish so that the printer can ensure a pure black in the final version. Black makes all the difference in the world. Indeed, I use a lot of black in my painting, probably because I am used to using it as the basic color with my cuts.

About composition: Most of my paintings are either square or golden-section rectangles. *In the Skin of a Lion* was itself a square echoed by little squares within the art, which I picked up as a design element. Of course, it means nothing to anyone but me. On *What Is It Then Between Us?* I repeated many 45-degree angles, so that one gets that feeling of continuance all through the piece. But my choice of composition and media depends upon the book. I would not have repeated the solution of *What Is It Then Between Us?* for a book like *Memory of Departure*, because it is a very brutal story.

I cannot make changes with a cut, so I do very tight sketches. I want the editors to know exactly what I'm doing. (Good thing too, for with *Sergeant's Cat and Other Stories* I misspelled the title; I did not realize the mistake until they caught it!) Of course, the marker line will look somewhat different when it is translated into wood or linoleum. I still make small, but significant, decisions while I am making the cut.

Sergeant's Cat was such a strange book. . . . The cat, incidentally, has nothing to do with the story, except at one point when the antagonist threatens it and the police sergeant with violence (the cat is unharmed). But for some reason Janwillem van de Wetering chose to call the collection of stories by this title, and I took advantage of it because I love cats. The whole cover is a fairly decorative solution, from the illustration to the lettering.

On the ways book publishing affects design: It is rare that I have a problem with a publisher or an art director, although I must say that things have changed in book publishing in general over the past ten to fifteen years. It used to be that one simply dealt with the art director and an editor, but now the author is involved—and sometimes the author's family too. And the sales people must be comfortable with the way the book looks and reads. The process of approval is so much more complex now than it used to be. For *What Is It Then Between Us?* I sent in a sketch that the sales people objected to because the characters were naked—so I put some clothes on them. But when I was originally given the assignment, I was told that because of the suggestive title they wanted something, well, more sensual. I sent in a job recently where twenty-five people had to okay it. Consternation began when I showed two figures in the illustration that were criticized as being too confusing. They took a poll: half could see the second figure very well and the other half could not. The result was to keep in the figure but touch it up a little to satisfy those who had trouble seeing it. That situation had less to do with rationality than with someone's wanting to be part of the decision. Many companies are extremely pleasant to work with, but at others the art director is often merely a messenger for all these participants.

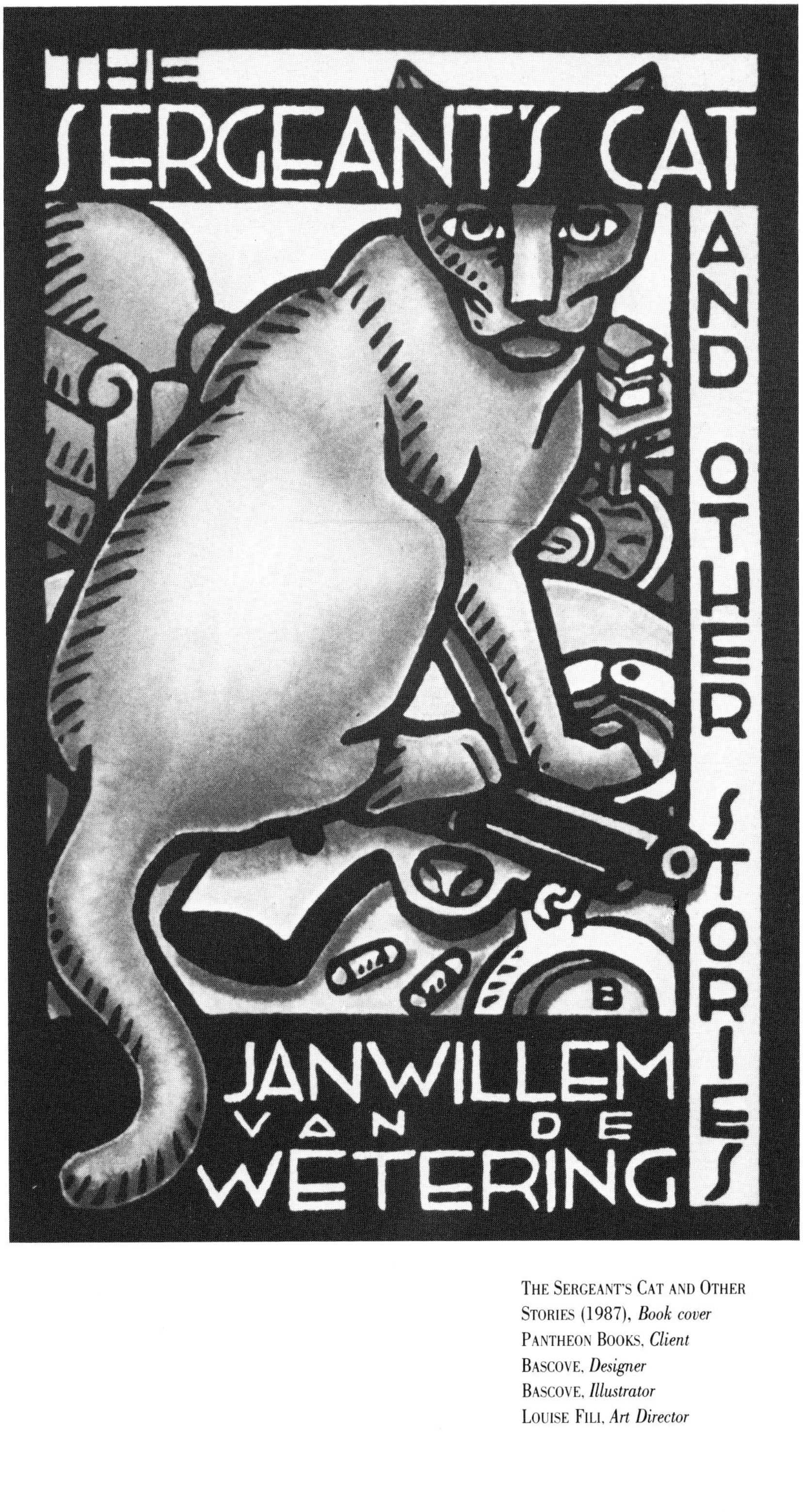
THE
SERGEANT'S CAT
AND OTHER STORIES
JANWILLEM
VAN DE
WETERING
B

THE SERGEANT'S CAT AND OTHER STORIES (1987), *Book cover*
PANTHEON BOOKS, *Client*
BASCOVE, *Designer*
BASCOVE, *Illustrator*
LOUISE FILI, *Art Director*

PAUL DAVIS

Paul Davis began his career in the late fifties as an illustrator at Push Pin Studios, where he developed a distinctive style based on primitive and Early American paintings. An appreciation for letterforms and typography began in childhood when he watched his newspaper-editor grandfather set type by hand and was fine-tuned years later when he began designing scores of theater posters for Joseph Papp's New York Shakespeare Festival. Davis is now proprietor of a full-service design studio that handles a broad range of projects, including the design of bus and subway posters for the New York classical radio station WNCN, and art direction for the literary and cultural magazine *Normal*, the new monthly magazine *WIGWAG*, and the New York Shakespeare Festival. Here he discusses his drawing method and how he art directs the illustration of others.

On the marriage of type and image: A. M. Cassandre [the important French posterist and typographer of the 1930s] used to say that you start with the word. His theory was that you should put the word as near to the center of the poster as possible, then you build the image from there. Though I've never religiously followed that method, I do think he had a good point about making a poster that truly integrates the verbal and visual. If you consider the text first and then reinforce that with the image, the result is stronger than if the combination has no relationship. One of the worst things that has happened to design is that advertising began using a big picture with a small caption or text block underneath. The image, regardless of what it is, becomes cartoon. It's a lazy approach that doesn't harness the power of the word *or* the picture.

On arresting a viewer's attention: The first problem of any poster is to get people to pay attention. They're bombarded with words and images all the time. Therefore I always try to make things that are a little unusual. And recently I have begun to think more about the context in which the work is going to appear. I always thought about it to some extent when, in the past, I collaborated with an art director as an illustrator, but it was primarily his or her job to understand that context. Now that I work more as a designer I realize that in order to make a piece effective and accessible you have to play off both the media and environment. Design is in part *about* context.

the Station for people who have everything.
WNCN
classical 104.3 FM

On *Colored Girls Who Have Considered Suicide*: This was originally intended to be seen in a New York subway station, so the tiles in the image deliberately match those on a subway wall. The theater name is done as little mosaic tiles, and the lettering is intended to look like graffiti, which is of course suggested by context.

About the WNCN bus and subway poster campaign: The side of a bus is an even more special context for advertising. If we get lucky you may see as many as five of the same posters moving in a row.

I got this job because, as a partner in an advertising agency, Davis & Russek, I was the art director for this account. Jim Russek still has the client, and since the idea is driven by my artwork, I am still very involved. WNCN came to us with a small budget and wanted to use it as effectively as possible. They wanted a campaign that would get attention from both listeners and advertisers, so I tried to do something that was stylistically unique. I wanted to give them a *new artist*, in a way.

Everything is hand-drawn, using colored pencil and a little watercolor (they weren't initially intended as bus posters, so the first one is vertical). I had always made drawings like this for fun, but rarely published any. The intent was to appeal to young people who are just beginning to listen to classical music, and to those who understand the art references. This was in keeping with the station's format of "classical disc jockeys." This graphic approach and other strategic changes increased listenership by 25 percent in a couple of years.

I hand-drew the lettering on these posters be-

BOOTH THEATRE
222 W. 45TH ST.
For
Colored
Girls
who have
Considered
Suicide
When
The
Rain-
bow
is
Enuf
Paul Davis

FOR COLORED GIRLS WHO HAVE CONSIDERED SUICIDE . . . (1976), *Theater poster*
NEW YORK SHAKESPEARE FESTIVAL, *Client*
PAUL DAVIS, *Designer*
PAUL DAVIS, *Illustrator*
PAUL DAVIS, *Art Director*

GOLDFISH (1984), Bus/Subway Poster
WNCN, NEW YORK, *Client*
PAUL DAVIS, *Designer*
PAUL DAVIS, *Illustrator*

WNCN'S CULTURE CLUB
WALL ST JOURNAL REPORTS
GUEST DJ'S
WNCN
104.3 FM
BOB EVANS IN THE MORNING
STAR "WAKE-UP CALLS"
TRAFFIC & TRAVEL
NEW YORK'S YOUNGER CLASSICAL MUSIC STATION

WNCN
BILL JEROME IN THE MORNING
NEW YORK'S YOUNGER CLASSICAL MUSIC STATION
104.3 FM

Bill Jerome IN THE MORNING
GUEST DJ'S
WALL ST JOURNAL REPORTS
Elliott Forrest IN THE AFTERNOON
STAR WAKE-UP CALLS
WNCN CULTURE CLUB
104 WNCN FM
NEW YORK'S YOUNGER CLASSICAL MUSIC STATION
TRAFFIC & TRAVEL

Dancers (1987), *Bluebirds* (1988), *The Sun and the Moon* (1988),
Bus/subway posters
WNCN, New York, *Client*
Paul Davis, *Designer*
Paul Davis, *Illustrator*

cause there was a lot of material that had to be included, but I also wanted a result that was casual. If an art director placed lettering like this over one of my drawings without my knowledge, I would object, because this kind of thing must be the artist's decision and execution. In keeping with the format, I also decided to draw the WNCN typographic logo for each poster. I believe this makes people take more notice of it.

On developing new approaches: Picasso said that some artists just turn out little cakes. If I wanted to do that I would have become a baker—that's not why I became an artist. I enjoy change and exploration. I believe style is a voice one chooses for the moment, and I want to be able to use as many voices as possible. Although Cubism has been around for about seventy years it has not been well applied as a contemporary illustrative model. I am therefore using and learning from it. Some of what I've learned about Cubism stems from an essay in *Vogue* by David Hockney, who wrote that the Cubists rejected the idea of camera composition that involves conventional perspective. Indeed, I always had trouble trying to fit everything into my imaginary camera lens. Losing that constraint made my work freer.

The Festival Latino poster is a direct example of this new understanding, and represents a distinct change from my other work: all the type and images are pasted on in a cubist manner. I wanted simply to integrate type and image without any breaks.

On commissioning other artists: With all my years of being at the other end, I am sympathetic to illustrators' problems. I hate having to reject anything. I've functioned best as an illustrator when I've been allowed the freedom, and therefore I try to give other illustrators as much freedom as possible. I do not sketch out ideas for them, but some do prefer more direction and parameters. I try to work with people who have their own ideas and can express them.

Joseph Papp presents
FESTIVAL
LATINO
NEW YORK SHAKESPEARE FESTIVAL
IN NEW YORK
VAMOS
AL FESTIVAL
Oscar Ciccone
and
CeciliaVega
Directors
August 3 to 22 1988
Sponsored by
Philip Morris Companies Inc.
The Public Theater
425 Lafayette Street
598-7155

FESTIVAL LATINO, (1988) *Poster*
NEW YORK SHAKESPEARE FESTIVAL, *Client*
PAUL DAVIS, *Designer*
PAUL DAVIS, *Illustrator*
PAUL DAVIS, *Art Director*

MICHAEL DORET

The idea that letterforms and words can be viable "illustration" is best practiced by Michael Doret, who combines display lettering, ornamental design, and pictorial elements in eye-catching assemblages. His style, though derived from the past—a hybrid of Victorian, Art Deco, and forties conventions—is a fresh counterpoint to the more systematized typographical approaches. Doret effectively integrates disparate and otherwise impersonal elements into playful, humorous compositions. Here he discusses two very effective covers for *Time* magazine, covers for a baseball magazine, and a paperback book cover, all of which convey vital information and an unforgettable form.

GAME

TIME
The
GAME

On the process of doing the "The Oil Game" and "The Selling of America" covers for *Time*: I like the way I work with *Time* because they usually call me when they have no idea what to do. A lot of illustrators get layouts to follow; somehow, maybe because of the nature of what I do—putting lettering and drawing together—they're often at a loss as to how to design a cover. So they just leave it to me. Usually I get a synopsis of the story, and sometimes they don't have the headline yet—they just want me to think about how I would treat it graphically. I can come up with a general notion, but it's impossible for me to proceed without the exact words, because the words are the basis of my design.

The "Selling of America" cover was a hard problem to solve (though when you look at it now it seems like an obvious solution). Initially this was the most deadly boring set of words to work with. *Time* came to me, I suspect, to make the words exciting. I knew they would add a subhead, so I left an open space at the bottom of the design for their art department to put it in.

About the illustration component: I treat most assignments from *Time* as an illustrator would if he were given a blank page or free rein: I write down all the things I associate with the words. An image can be anything from letters that are graphically composed to evoke a certain mood or period, like old signage, to a conceptual illustration, which in the case of "The Oil Game" was an oil pump as slot machine. I usually make a rough pencil sketch to show the idea; then I go to a tighter color comp using Prisma on vellum. The finished art is all pre-separated.

For "The Oil Game" I looked at a lot of old gas-pump references, many of them with raised lettering on the pump itself. The idea for the *O* developed from those glass globes which sat on top of the pumps—and that combination of elements was just a lucky break; if the cover line had been any different it never would have happened. Here the words really determined what the image would be.

By the way, I do not make up the headlines, especially with the editors at *Time.* I'm afraid that had I done so, they would have said, "We love the cover, but if we could just change the words. . . ." It happened once, though it wasn't as critical as it would have been with "Oil." I could have changed the words in "The Selling of America" by doing things like changing the num-

The OIL
GA

MAY 7, 1979
$1.25
TIME
Cable TV
Takes Off
The
OIL
GAME
OPEC
OPEC
OPEC

ber of hangtags to accommodate a different word. With *Time*, however, I've had pretty good success. Unlike the illustrator who just provides a picture, I can control the whole entity (except, of course, for the teaser picture in the right corner and the logo). The only change with "The Oil Game" was made in the way I originally did the *O;* they asked me to change the color so that it would stand out more. It was, needless to say, a small concession.

Reliving his roots: I first got excited about letterforms during the mid- to late sixties, when the psychedelic poster was the rage, and artists like Victor Moscoso, Stanley Mouse, and Rick Griffin were at their peak. It was the first thing that really made me take notice of letters, although now that I think about it, I was aware of letterforms to a certain extent even back in high school, when I did a "Keep the Hallway Clean" poster that combined letters and drawing. It was a crumpled-up piece of paper with the letters falling within the crumples. I don't really know where the impetus to combine letters and images came from. Today my interest is in all the old stuff where letterforms and images were totally integrated. Often there was hand lettering involved, whether or not it was done by the same person as the images; it was a total work. Hand lettering by its very nature is old-fashioned. Contemporary design is characterized by letters in straight lines. People look at my work and say, "It's very Deco," but it's really not, unless I specifically look at Deco influences.

THE OIL GAME (1979),
Magazine cover
TIME MAGAZINE, *Client*
MICHAEL DORET, *Designer*
MICHAEL DORET, *Illustrator*
RUDY HOGLUND, *Art Director*

About his distinctive hand lettering: My lettering does not usually correspond to existing typefaces; it is created to be integral to whatever style I'm working in. Sometimes I may look at some existing typefaces, but more often I'll just make them up. Once in a while it causes prob-

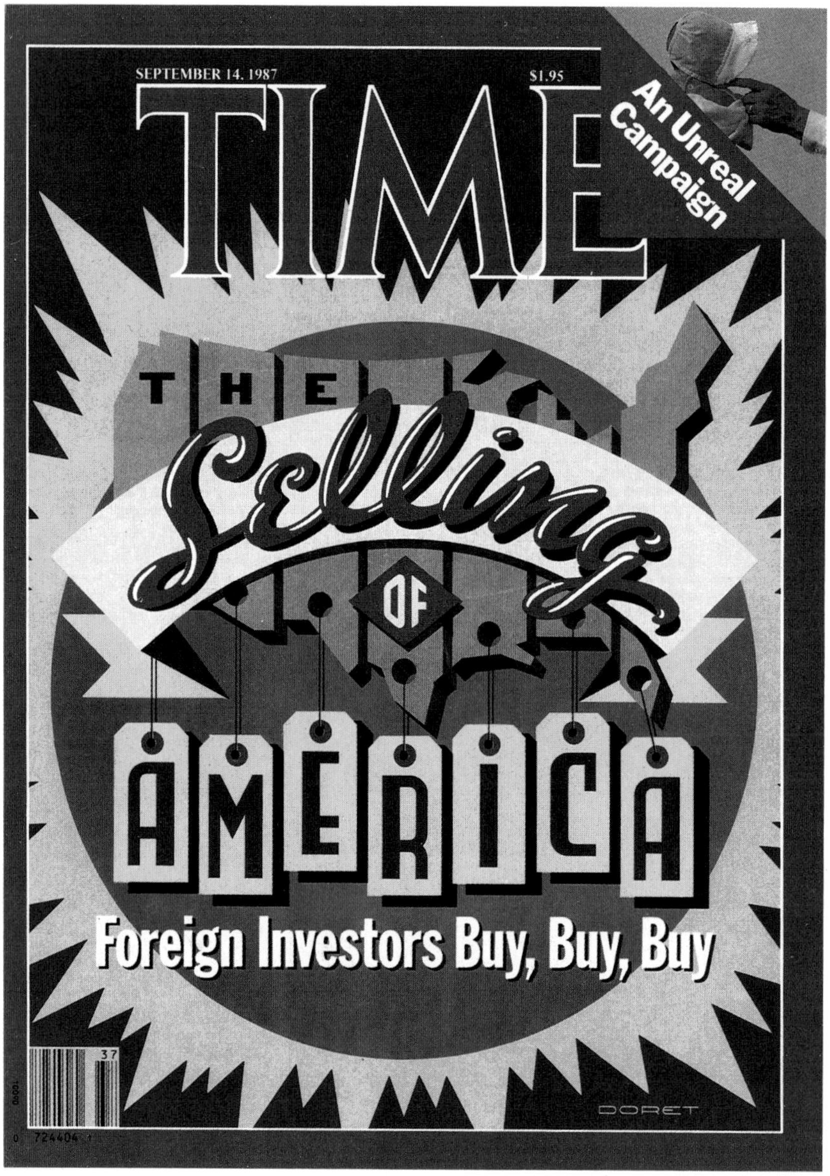
SEPTEMBER 14, 1987
$1.95
TIME
An Unreal Campaign
THE
Selling
OF
AMERICA
Foreign Investors Buy, Buy, Buy
DORET

THE SELLING OF AMERICA (1987), *Magazine cover*
TIME MAGAZINE, *Client*
MICHAEL DORET, *Designer*
MICHAEL DORET, *Illustrator*
RUDY HOGLUND, *Art Director*

TORONTO BLUE JAYS SCOREBOOK MAGAZINE (1987), *Series of covers*
CONTROLLED MEDIA COMMUNICATIONS, *Client*
MICHAEL DORET, *Designer*
MICHAEL DORET, *Illustrator*
SHARI SPIER, *Art Director*

lems for me, because if someone then wants to create an additional piece (something that stylistically matches the original I've done—say, a spine for a book jacket), I have to do more work.

To me, typefaces are not as important as the total configuration and feeling of a piece. That's why I don't really draw specific faces. I feel strongly about symmetry and geometry. Somehow they permeate my work whether I like it or not.

Concerning the need for less rigidity: I'd like my work to get looser, which for me is about as easy as swimming upstream. The old work is quite often done very crudely, but you never notice that unless you really look. Today people prefer a machined, perfect look, and a certain amount of soul can be missing from this work. I don't think it's important for something to look untouched by human hands. In fact I'd like my work to be a little cruder.

About the *Toronto Blue Jays Scorebook Magazine*: This was one of my favorite jobs because baseball imagery is so rich, and I was given free rein. Originally they wanted eight separately designed covers to use throughout the baseball season. Because this was a physical impossibility for me, I proposed doing four that could be repeated using the same mechanical with radically altered colors. Another plus was not being required to use the Blue Jays logo, which is awkwardly designed and not compatible with my style. I tried to do each color treatment differently; for example, I reversed the one with the dark vertical stripes on a light background to create a second version. It was a challenge to give the duplicates a different character.

For the imagery I did a lot of research of baseball memorabilia—not to copy exactly, but to see how elements were used. The crossed bats recurred over and over; the script lettering is, of course, traditionally baseballesque; pinstripes are taken from the uniforms. I then added my own touches, like the marbleized texture, which has nothing to do with baseball graphics but was needed to add dimension to the piece.

About *Trademarks of the '40s and '50s*: This was throwing in everything plus the kitchen sink from fifties imagery: the boomerang, rocket, and loopy letters. The color palette is very different for me—especially the chartreuse—but it was a welcome break from the usual.

On the prospect of doing free-standing work: People always ask me why I don't do work for myself. I can't. I like to solve problems. I'm not like a painter who can create from scratch. I need the problem, specifics, and limitations. If I didn't have those constraints my work would just flounder.

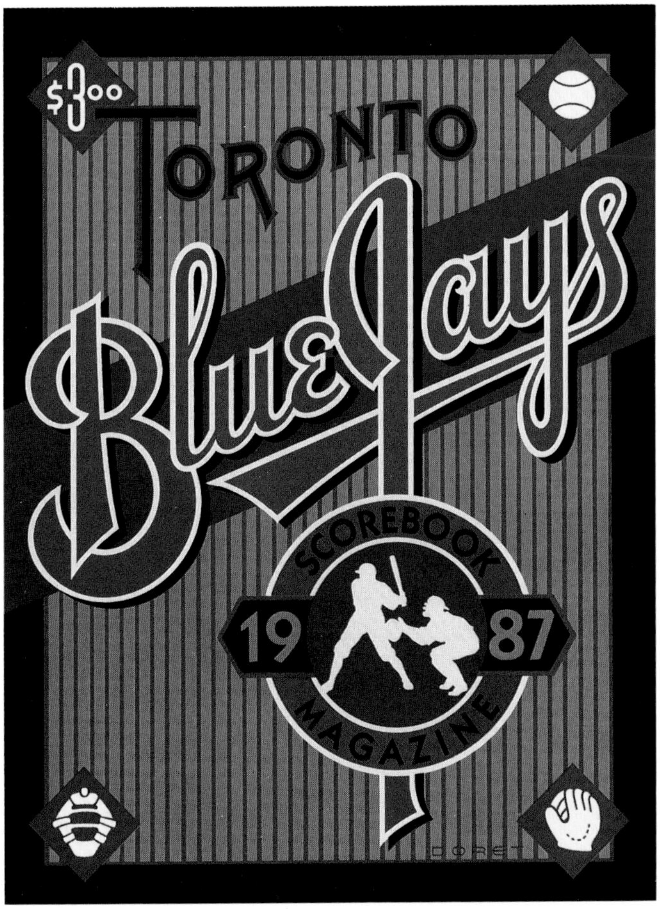
$3.00
TORONTO
Blue Jays
SCOREBOOK
19
87
MAGAZINE
DORET

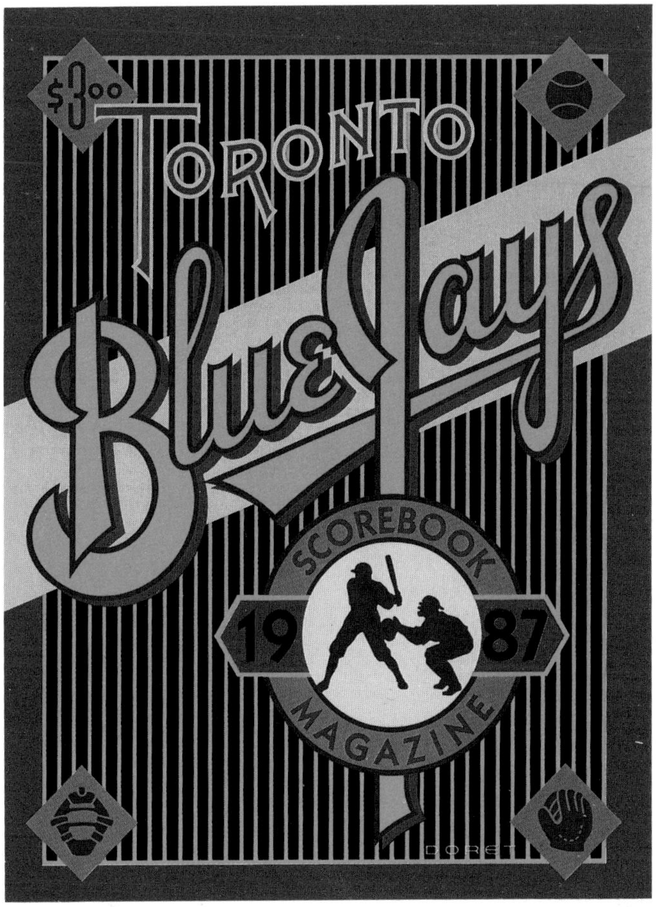
$3.00
TORONTO
Blue Jays
SCOREBOOK
19
87
MAGAZINE
DORET

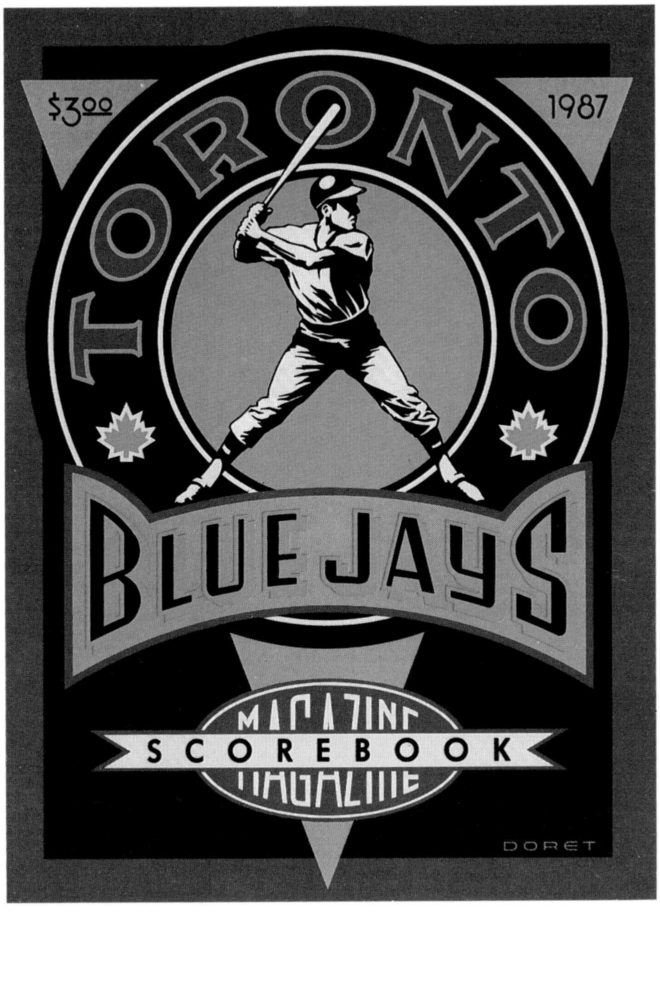
$3.00
1987
TORONTO
BLUE JAYS
MAGAZINE
SCOREBOOK
DORET

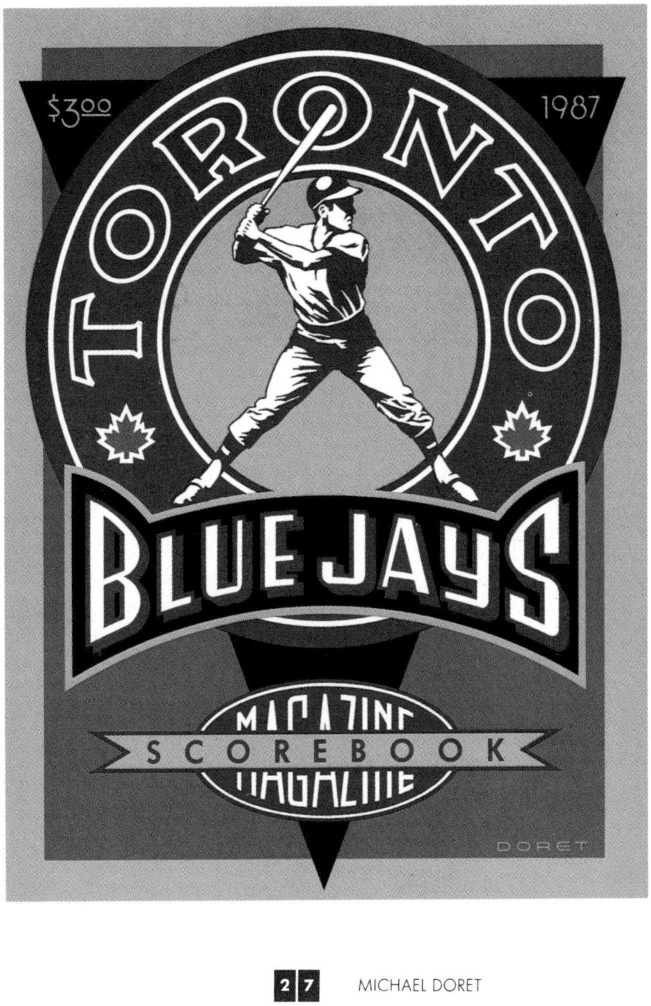
$3.00
1987
TORONTO
BLUE JAYS
MAGAZINE
SCOREBOOK
DORET

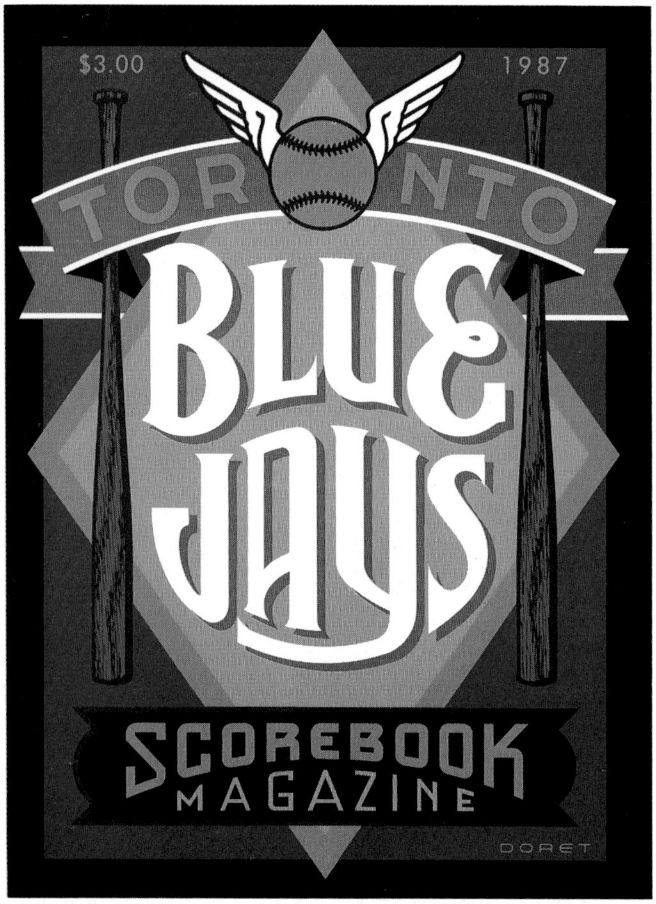
$3.00
1987
TORONTO
BLUE JAYS
SCOREBOOK
MAGAZINE
DORET

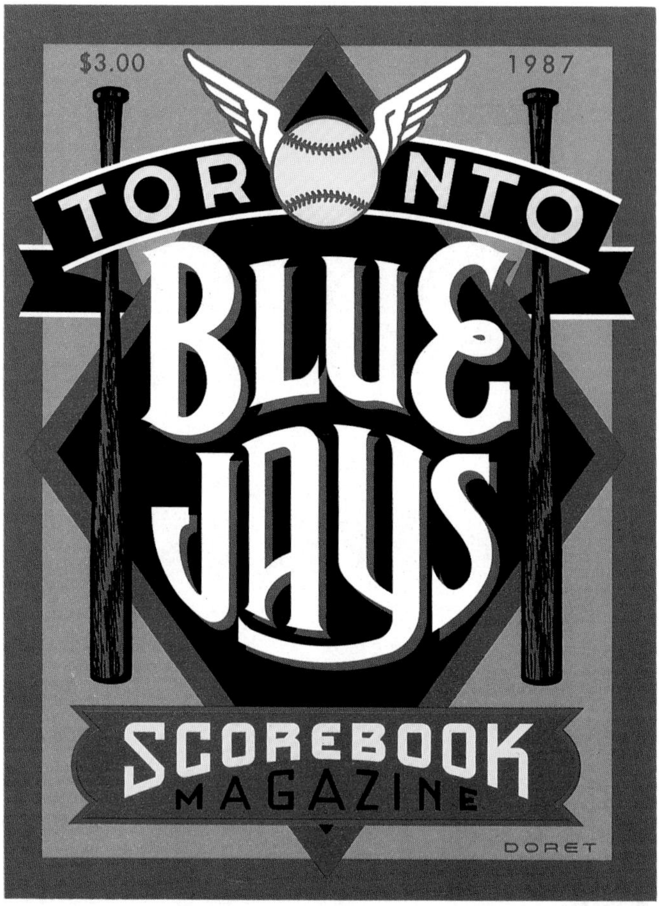
$3.00
1987
TORONTO
BLUE JAYS
SCOREBOOK
MAGAZINE
DORET

$3.00
Toronto
BLUE JAYS
1987
Scorebook Magazine
DORET

$3.00
Toronto
BLUE JAYS
1987
Scorebook Magazine
DORET

Trademarks
OF THE
'40s & '50s
Eric Baker
Tyler Blik
DORET
with an introduction by Steven Heller

TORONTO BLUE JAYS SCOREBOOK MAGAZINE (1987), *Series of covers*
CONTROLLED MEDIA COMMUNICATIONS, *Client*
MICHAEL DORET, *Designer*
MICHAEL DORET, *Illustrator*
SHARI SPIER, *Art Director*

TRADEMARKS OF THE '40S AND '50S (1988), *Book cover*
CHRONICLE BOOKS, *Client*
MICHAEL DORET, *Designer*
MICHAEL DORET, *Illustrator*
ERIC BAKER, *Art Director*

NICK GAETANO

An impressive client roster indicates Nick Gaetano's success at combining painting and design. He has done animation for Jell-O, Clairol, Excedrin, and General Electric, among others, and has also produced advertising imagery for such diverse clients as Sony, Meyer's Rum, the United States Postal Service, Federal Express, Dr. Pepper, and the Norwegian Caribbean Lines. His editorial illustration has appeared in *Time*, *The Atlantic*, *Fortune*, *TV Guide*, and *New York* magazine. His book jackets are the focus here; Gaetano explains the process of making what can be called mini-posters as dust jackets and paperback covers.

About conceiving the covers for a series of books by V. S. Naipaul: These covers were initiated because the art director, Judith Loeser, was enamored of a 1930s typeface designed by A. M. Cassandre. I am not really sure why she wanted that period look, since the books do not take place during that time. But I guess the type suited her tastes and didn't misrepresent the stories. She also wanted it to have a tropical feeling, since Naipaul often writes about the third world.

For typographic reference I pulled out a book on Deco design that showed a French store sign sculpted in metal. It had quite a few nice features to work with, such as the depth of the letters, which adapted well to an airbrush rendering. I had done some other possible treatments for my own satisfaction, but ultimately presented only the black-and-white pencil sketches for these. Incidentally, some clients require that I provide color sketches; others are quite content with a tight black-and-white sketch. Some art directors and editors are just blind to a pencil drawing, thinking, perhaps, that a rough is just too rough, or that a pencil sketch should show volume of mass the way an airbrush does.

There were ultimately ten Naipaul books, and I admit that I did not read any of them completely. My wife Thedia reads all the books and underlines sections that she likes and feels are pertinent. What I did read of these excerpts was enjoyable. Naipaul's prose is extremely poetic and full of striking images. I don't have any patience with texts that do not evoke imagery.

In *Finding the Center* I used a crocodile because it is a magical symbol—the African symbol for night. One can tell, of course, that it is not a real crocodile. And I am not interested in reality; pattern is singularly more important. The story is about Africans who live in abject poverty but have a power the white people cannot understand. Owing to their deep-seated relationship to the land and to animal spirits, they are able to transport themselves into different realms of reality, and so talk among themselves about the ability to fly from one town to the next during the night. Although Naipaul doesn't use the term, it is like astral projection.

With *The Overcrowded Barracoon* I thought of using a cult figure, but Judy preferred that people not appear on these covers. This story takes place on a tropical island overflowing with inhabitants. To the outside it looks like paradise, but on the inside it is a prison—a place without a future and with virtually no present. The people are dirt poor with no escape in sight. So my initial drawings showed a small island covered with large people. It looked somewhat like a New York City subway in the middle of the Caribbean. Judy did not want to do that either, so we got rid of the people and showed a solitary island form surrounded by water.

For *The Mystic Masseur* we decided on something that was more decorative yet symbolic. I did not want to render a simple little island with trees sticking out of it. The lushness of the vegetation is really important to the setting and necessary for me to establish the tropical ambience. I made the palm leaves bigger than the island itself, which is what I would have done with the people in my first idea for *Barracoon.*

Mr. Stone and the Knight's Companion is set in rural Ireland; I chose to situate it in a decrepit cottage, but Judy did not want the cottage to look too disheveled, so we cleaned it up to look like an English country house, which is what I finally did. The burning field in the background is based on a passage from the book.

For *In a Free State* I rendered the pattern of rain as the primary symbol. The color breakdown represents the passage from day to night as portrayed in the story. On the side of the "road" I flattened everything out by using an African pattern I had seen on a basket. I like making things seem both dimensional and flat at the same time, which refers to my interest in cubist painting.

In *A House for Mr. Biswas* Judy did not want me to use the strange pattern I had originally proposed. She wanted the house to be plain and simple, as it was finally done. The magical quality that still came through is what I do for myself without any explanation. It is a quality that I am always looking for but can only explain as intuitive, not intellectual. Often I feel blind to what I'm doing until my hand starts working; I sort of scribble things, then it starts filling in the face,

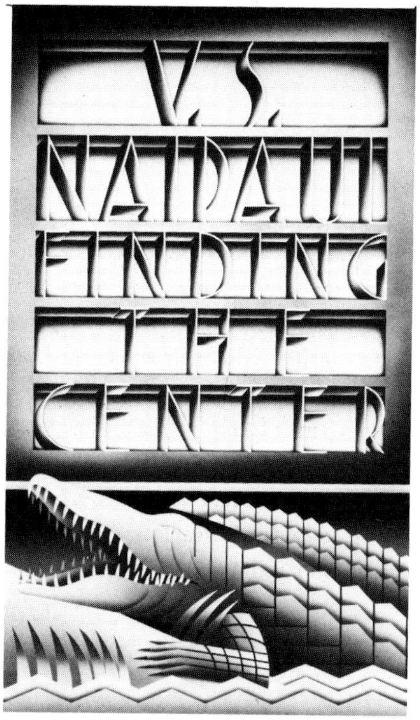
V.S.
NAIPAUL
FINDING
THE
CENTER

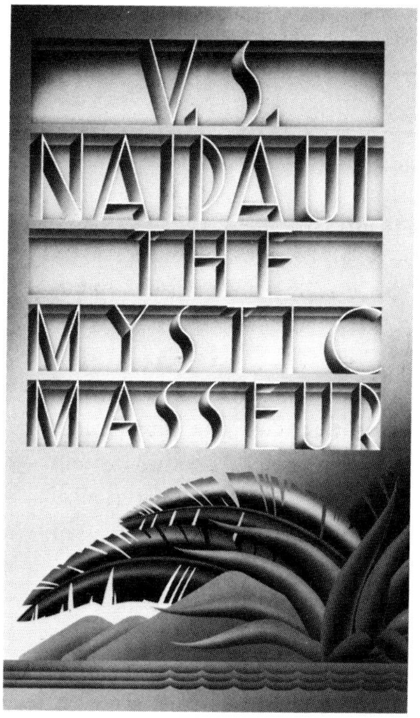
V.S.
NAIPAUL
THE
MYSTIC
MASSEUR

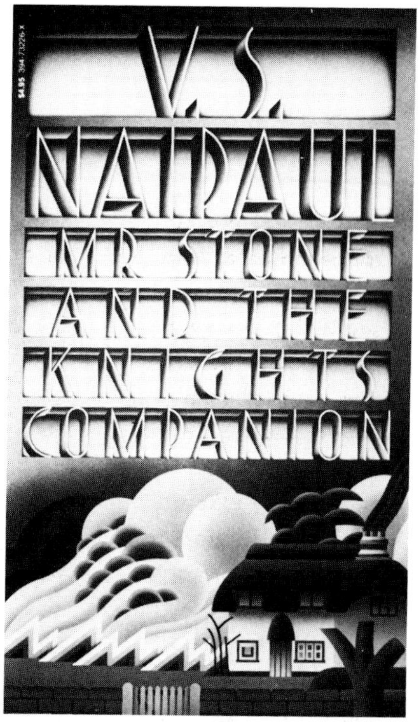
V.S.
NAIPAUL
MR STONE
AND THE
KNIGHTS
COMPANION

V.S.
NAIPAUL
IN A
FREE
STATE

V.S.
NAIPAUL
A
HOUSE FOR
MR. BISWAS

V.S.
NAIPAUL
THE
OVERCROWDED
BARRACOON

and only then do I know where I am going.

These covers were done in gouache with airbrush. However, I do not use gouache anymore because it is just too delicate and limiting. I use only acrylic these days.

About the architecture of the Naipaul series: I felt that if we were going to do a series of books, this architectural way of presenting the type would be consistent and give them strength as a unit. It did, too—at least initially. Toward the end of the series one of the editors got a little nervous that the covers were beginning to look too much alike; but it was an unfounded fear. I even received letters from readers who bought the books simply because they liked the covers.

The covers are like two-dimensional reliefs. The images are stylized because I did not want them to seem the least bit real. Moreover, since the lettering is so stylized and architecturally constructed, the imagery had to be subordinated to that idea. All the backgrounds—the clouds, wa-

FINDING THE CENTER, THE MYSTIC MASSEUR, MR. STONE AND THE KNIGHT'S COMPANION, IN A FREE STATE, A HOUSE FOR MR. BISWAS, THE OVERCROWDED BARRACOON (1983–85), *Book covers*
VINTAGE BOOKS, *Client*
NICK GAETANO, *Designer*
NICK GAETANO, *Illustrator*
JUDITH LOESER, *Art Director*

HENCE

HENCE (1988), *Book jacket*
ALFRED A. KNOPF, *Client*
NICK GAETANO, *Designer*
NICK GAETANO, *Illustrator*
CAROL CARSON, *Art Director*

ter, and so on—are also structured in the way I design in general. One does not always get the freedom to do things like this—especially with paperbacks, where the imagery has to aim low at a mass market. This became a very personal series of paintings. After the first book was completed, Judith came by just to check the pencils for the illustrated portion since we had already agreed on the typographic treatment.

About the jacket for *Hence*: This novel takes place in the twenty-first century, but it is written as if it were today's time. It is a book within a book that was supposedly written in 1995 about a chess game between a boy and a computer. The boy comes into his father's office and sees this chessboard glowing, set up with little seashells instead of chess pieces. It is a surrealistic scene—and I thought it was the most magical scene. The pieces are cut by a ray of light that both relates to the first recognition of the machine and was a means to dramatize the image.

Carol Carson, the art director, asked that I do the type because she likes the way I always try to invent my own letterforms. Even when I use an existing face, I work it over with the airbrush to give it a twist. But I find that it is more fun to invent faces—not the whole alphabet, just what I need. Since this story is locked in a strange time frame, I felt that the type should virtually disappear. After the idea was accepted, the type did not change much from the first sketches to the finish.

The type was the first element I decided upon; the chessboard, which I rendered in a sort of odd trapezoidal shape, came second. I just wanted to play with it at an odd perspective. I enjoy playing with light, having it come from wherever I want and turn things around so one sees backs and fronts and sides. I force perspective by making some things big and others small. In fact when I paint for myself I am always abstract. I attempt to make all the pieces work together. And that happens most successfully when the type and illustration have a similar structure. Color was another important consideration because the author, who had cover approval, was keen on bright hues.

About typography in general: Book covers and jackets sell the author and the title. The editors do not much care about the picture as long as it is appropriate to the story, so I usually begin a project by deciding on the type design. I am not really fond of script faces, roman faces, or serifs. Some people work well with flourishy stuff; I do not. I like my work to be geometric and as architectural as possible; and I try, when possible, to inject a cubist sensibility.

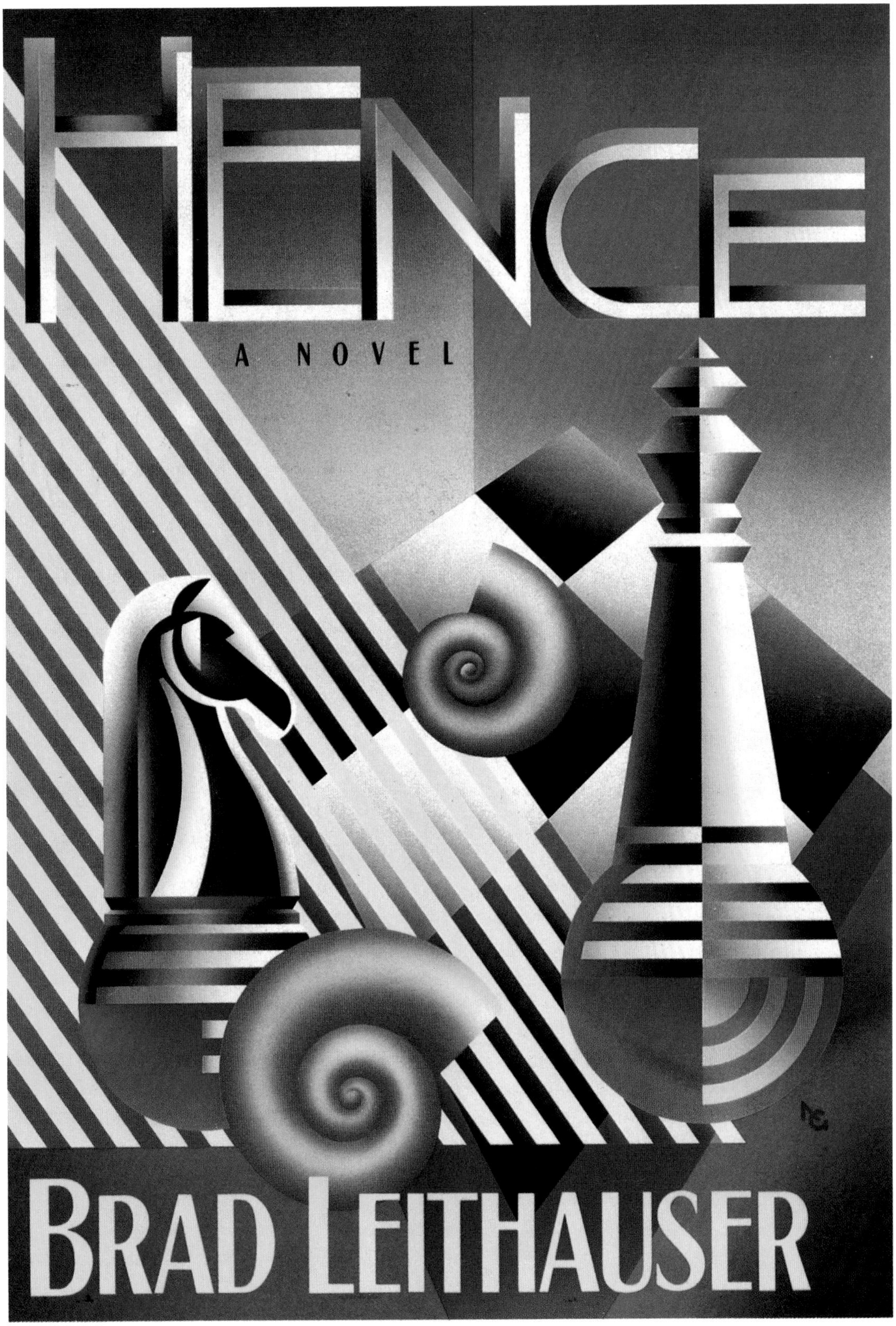
HENCE
A NOVEL
BRAD LEITHAUSER

DAVID LANCE GOINES

A beginning as an apprentice pressman in a small, politically active Berkeley, California, print shop introduced David Lance Goines to an art form that has consumed him for the past twenty-five years. In the process, he has become one of America's foremost creators of the limited-edition advertising poster. Indeed, he prefers "poster-maker" to "illustrator" as a description of what he does. As well as mastering his craft, he has become a self-educated authority on typography and letterforms. Here Goines discusses his philosophy of image making and comments on a few of his recent posters.

VD - DON'T GIVE THE GIFT
THAT GOES ON GIVING VD
Berkeley VD Clinic 830 University Avenue
Telephone: 845-0197
Drop-in hours: Monday: 1:30-5:30
Wednesday: 4-6
Friday: 8:30am-10:30am

Some early influences: My mother is a fine-artist and calligrapher, and much of my interest in the alphabet comes through her. She provided her children with a pleasant, pervasive artistic environment, doing things like beautifully lettering our names on our lunch bags. In my teens I copied letters from the Speedball lettering book. In my youth I was drawn to the more garish examples, but as I grew more accomplished I turned to classical forms. In the process, even my handwriting turned into lettering.

About imagination: I can't draw pictures at all well from imagination alone. I need a model before me. I write good technical prose and can clearly recount an actual event, but I'm no good at making up a story. Some artists and writers can conjure up art from thin air; others, like me, need a firmer grasp on reality. This is perhaps why letters hold such an appeal for me.

Everybody finds one part of the job more difficult. I have a dreadful time coming up with a basic idea for a poster. I start by making tiny sketches, accompanied by notes. Sooner or later, if I bang on the old idea box long enough, something always falls out. But it takes me as long to come up with the idea as to do the whole rest of the job.

On words versus images: I see no reason to separate the two. Indeed, as a poster artist I am *compelled* to combine them; the words and image reinforce one another. A poster is like a one-panel cartoon in which the picture alone might be vague; likewise, unillustrated words lack punch; but together they get the joke across. I think of posters as much the same. So, far from feeling burdened by the necessity of incorporating words into my images, I find it a pleasure.

About the poster for the Berkeley VD Clinic: I delight in making visual puns. A visual pun is just like a verbal pun, a play on words, except that it is a play on images. In this I owe much to the Surrealists, such as René Magritte. In his paintings he often blended one thing into another—feet into shoes—or made a point by the juxtaposition of images—a locomotive smoking away in a fireplace. A rose turning into a noose is much the same kind of thing; and, as is often the case with Surrealism, the image can strike the audience as unpleasant or disturbing. The line of type explains the purpose of the image, and the viewer bounces back and forth between them. I rarely use type, but in this early poster it seemed appropriate, although the words and image are not as integrated as I have come to prefer.

On hand lettering: In general, for poster work I prefer hand lettering to type. In printed advertising the type and art are often at some variance, as though the words were sort of tacked on as an annoying afterthought, spoiling an otherwise nice illustration. But with advertising, the words are just as important, and word and illustration must seamlessly reinforce one other. With hand lettering, the line will inevitably partake of the same quality as the drawing. The same feeling will permeate the entire image, and words and picture will be seen as a whole. Furthermore, with hand lettering, words can comfortably be made to fill greater or lesser spaces. If type were the only option, the words might look as if

CHEZ·PANISSE
CAFÉ & RESTAURANT
FIFTEENTH BIRTHDAY
1517 SHATTUCK AVENUE· BERKELEY·CALIFORNIA 94709 548-5525

CHEZ PANISSE FIFTEENTH BIRTHDAY (1986), *Poster*
CHEZ PANISSE CAFÉ AND RESTAURANT, *Client*
DAVID LANCE GOINES, *Designer*
DAVID LANCE GOINES, *Illustrator*

BERKELEY VD CLINIC (1971), *Poster*
PRO BONO PUBLICO FOR THE BERKELEY VENEREAL DISEASE CLINIC, *Client*
DAVID LANCE GOINES, *Designer*
DAVID LANCE GOINES, *Illustrator*

they had been forced into a space that was really unsuitable for them.

The slow, contemplative process of hand lettering also gives me time to mull over the details of the design, usually making all the difference between a really satisfactory job and one that is merely adequate. In addition, you can do it yourself: no need to try to explain to some mulish typographer, or wait over the weekend when you want it *now*.

The Chez Panisse fifteenth-birthday poster provides a good illustration: the art is a block-

RAVENSWOOD (1979), *Poster*
RAVENSWOOD WINERY, *Client*
DAVID LANCE GOINES, *Designer*
DAVID LANCE GOINES, *Illustrator*

CHILDREN'S HOSPITAL (1987), *Poster*
CHILDREN'S HOSPITAL, OAKLAND, *Client*
DAVID LANCE GOINES, *Designer*
DAVID LANCE GOINES, *Illustrator*

print, very rough and coarse. The lettering is rough as well. The large lettering was cut into the block, and the small lettering was drawn to reflect the same coarse line quality. After I'd finished, I didn't like the blockprint letters so I redrew them, taking care that the same feeling was preserved. My taste in line quality owes much to the influence of the German poster artists Ludwig Hohlwein, Koloman Moser, Hans Rudi Erdt, and Lucian Bernhard, whose work displays this same rough, "accidental" line.

Perhaps I admire good lettering more than a good image because it is rarer—and because I'm not as good at it as I would like. One disadvantage of doing *everything* is that you never get *really* good at anything.

On rough lines versus smooth lines: Rough lines are easier to see. The receptors in your eye are designed to signal to the brain only change, not a steady state. The visibility of an image increases proportionately to the amount of changing information in it. Given a choice between a rough line and a clean one, the former is to be preferred; since there is more of it, it is easier to see. A hard, sharp line is also a hard, sharp contrast—a sort of visual barrier where the eye might be inclined to stop rather than continue. A rough line eases the transition from one area to another.

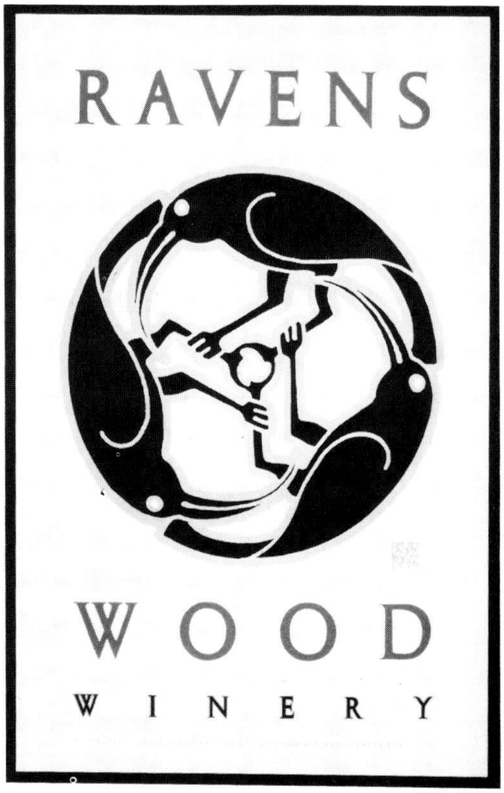
RAVENS
WOOD
WINERY

Although I'm less critical when selecting display faces and more so for text faces, some types are easier to read than others. The concept of rough and clean lines can be useful in evaluating legibility. For example, serif type is easier to read than sans serif. Extra information is provided by the serif, and its horizontal thrust improves legibility. With a face like Helvetica, much of the variety has been removed, resulting in a typeface that is not only boring, but, because of the lack of horizontal emphasis, monotonous weight, and great similarity between the letters, also hard to read. Typographers should keep in mind Einstein's dictum, "We should make things as simple as possible, but not simpler." Oversimplification is the great error of the Bauhaus.

On scale: The original sketch is usually very tiny, about the size of a large postage stamp. By working small, I am unable to overload the design with unnecessary detail; too much detail turns to mud at a distance, and this technique forces simplicity. Furthermore, working small is also working fast, and this diminishes the temptation to like a design just because the investment in drawing it was so large. Many little drawings can be made in a short time, and so one is slower to reach the "to hell with it, this is good enough" stage. Last, working small allows decisions about figure, ground, and proportion to be made without excessive eye or head motion, so the sketch will look a lot like what the viewer will see when the poster is finished. My camera-ready artwork is almost always about one-fourth the size of the finished poster. I like working small and enlarging the drawing—it makes the lines rougher and more interesting.

Lettering on posters: Words are part of the composition. In the case of a book or record jacket the words must be in the top third, or they will be invisible in a display rack. Although I

CHILDREN'S
HOSPITAL
OAKLAND

SWINERTON & WALBERG (1988), *Poster*
SWINERTON & WALBERG BUILDERS, *Client*
DAVID LANCE GOINES, *Designer*
DAVID LANCE GOINES, *Illustrator*

generally place the lettering below the image, with a poster the words don't have to be anyplace specific. With *Ravenswood,* "Ravens" is at the top and "Wood" at the bottom, and the image is captured between them. With the poster for Children's Hospital I wanted a greater integration of word and image. Again I surrounded the image by splitting the words, but I thrust the image more into the foreground by placing the top lettering behind it. This is also a reference to the old *Saturday Evening Post* way of integrating the words and the picture. I go through phases where I prefer the look of one style over another, but in general I try to match the feeling of the lettering to the subject.

On Japanese influences: Nineteenth-century advertising based on the idioms of fine art was weak and unsuited to quick, casual observation. It tended to be cluttered and difficult to understand. Some early advertising was no more than a message tacked onto the reproduction of a fine-art painting. Luckily, European artists became aware of the Japanese woodblock print at exactly the moment they were struggling to deal with the requirements of modern advertising. Advertising demanded simplicity of concept and execution, and woodcuts provided a model that solved almost all the problems at once. My artistic training was gotten by emulating Art Nouveau and Jugendstil designers, and it was only later that I became aware of the original sources.

On the Swinerton & Walberg poster: The initial drawing didn't get the "joke" across because I was trying too hard to incorporate realistic perspective. So I made the hole in the fence perfectly round, giving a plain view of the construction site. Now the viewer could see what the boy was looking at. As I often do, I then transferred the drawing to a linoleum block, because a blockprint makes an interesting line. Furthermore, the blockprint line is necessarily bold, resisting excessive detail. In this case, I did the lettering separately. When all the elements were combined, I Xeroxed it and made a color sketch. I like photocopies because they give a nice black line that repels thinned gouache, so I can slop the color on and everything still looks tidy. I try to keep the color simple: what I learned at my mother's knee was "two colors, black and white." I do a few sketches to explore color combinations and show the one I like best to the client. I rarely make substantial changes after this stage.

On printing: I was a jolly left-wing pressman for years before I ever turned my hand to art. My training has stood me in good stead, and sometimes I am scarcely able to believe my good fortune: I do what I really enjoy and make a living at it too. I work alone, and just like the little red hen do everything myself: art and lettering; camera work and stripping; plate making and presswork; cutting and wrapping; billing and customer relations. This makes me slow, but it saves much aggravation. I print solid color, mixed to match the sketch. This, too, takes time, but the constraints of PMS or TOYO would be intolerable.

SWINERTON
& WALBERG
BUILDERS
1888 - 1988
1988
ONE·HUNDRED·YEARS
580 CALIFORNIA STREET·SAN FRANCISCO·CA·94104·(415) 421-2980 CA.LIC.№92

STEVEN GUARNACCIA

From his first spot illustration in the *New York Times* in 1977 to his animated advertisements for banks, Steven Guarnaccia has been an exemplar of the witty—often satiric—line. In recent years this consummate illustrator-cartoonist has become more involved in the totality of an assignment, preferring whenever possible to be involved in the entire design process. Often he works out typographic solutions in concert with his wife, designer Susan Hochbaum, and has become increasingly more adept at producing the complete solution himself. The work discussed here includes a variety of projects, such as those art directed and designed by others plus a book jacket designed by Guarnaccia that typifies his distinctive pop-culture roots.

About his early impetus to become an illustrator: I sometimes feel like an illustrator who can't draw because I was one of those people who, in conventional drawing classes, always drew in unconventional ways. I was never very good at rendering nature: I always preferred to conjure images from my head. Though I had never been interested in drawing from life, in fact, I realized I had really been observing things all along and keeping them in a mental repository, because I do know how to draw those pieces of the environment that I never formally studied. The subjects that interested me most were not found in the natural environment but rather in popular culture: comic strips, animated cartoons, and children's books.

I also love to draw things with a lot of detail. If I don't know what a car or machine actually looks like, I fudge it. Part of the reason my style developed the way it did is that I was *always* able to render convincingly things that weren't necessarily true. It's a matter of intuitively knowing what to leave in and take out that makes a drawing believable.

On the development of personal style: I wasn't aware that I was developing a style in the early days. When I talk to students today about style I tell them they shouldn't worry about it, that it just seems to come and that it's not something one can force. Artists who have a personal style have a way of seeing and representing things that makes sense to them—it's their personal visual language. When I came to New York, I didn't think I had a distinct style, but I had always drawn in a personal way. By the time I received my first assignments I wanted to expand my vocabulary, so for a while I worked in many different styles and drew inspiration from the work of Saul Steinberg, Guy Billout, and Seymour Chwast.

An early interest in word and image: I am as interested in writing as drawing. My early goal, in fact, was to become a children's book writer and illustrator—which seemed to be the highest calling. Letterforms were my primary inspiration. I imagined them as characters with personalities. The lowercase *E*, for example, is one of my favorites because of its feisty, bad-boy quality.

About the MultiGroup campaign: I was approached by Altman and Manley, a Boston-based advertising/design firm, to work on a recruitment brochure for MultiGroup, a health-care organization. They did not want typical health-care material—which, of course, sounded encouraging. Bob Manley devised an idea for a toy-like object, complete with die cuts, and I came up with the orange/purple, pink/green color schemes. The die cut shown here of the family is actually a wrapper that holds a map and book together and becomes a free-standing piece that can sit on a desk or be worn like a crown by a child. After this we did a series of newspaper ads, posters, and brochures. I co-designed some of the ads, which were very large blowups of smaller drawings. I also did the design and storyboard for three animated television commercials. After the project was over Altman and Manley hired me as a freelance art director—not as an illustrator, but an idea person. Since I come up with my own ideas for illustration, it was a logical next step for me to do the same for larger projects that might use photography or another artist's work. I could come up with ideas that I could not draw.

The Boston Globe Magazine
SNAP DECISIONS
Winners of the 1985 Globe Photo Contest
ALSO:
Silence in outer space
The bizarre diary of Arthur Crew Inman

EXCUSE ME, COULD YOU TELL ME WHERE TO FIN[...]

On working with art directors: The best art directors allow illustrators to make their best work. Each has a different approach which forces illustrators to adapt accordingly. There was an art director at the *New York Times* who liked nothing better than to stroll by the place where the freelancers were drawing and see three or four of his illustrators hard at work. It was one of the few occasions where I've actually worked under the gaze of an art director, and it had its own benefits and brought out lots of good work. Ronn Campisi, the former art director for the *Boston Globe Magazine*, was a different story: his common prescription before I'd begin a job was, "Surprise me." He had the power, unusual for an art director, to dictate what would go on the cover of the magazine. This meant that he could receive a piece of art at the eleventh hour with no idea what it was going to look like. He was in effect saying, "I know you can do it, I trust you.

RECRUITMENT BROCHURE (1983)
MULTIGROUP, *Client*
BOB MANLEY, *Designer*
STEVEN GUARNACCIA, *Illustrator*
BOB MANLEY, *Art Director*

SNAP DECISIONS (1985), *Sunday magazine cover*
BOSTON GLOBE MAGAZINE, *Client*
LYNN STALEY, *Designer*
STEVEN GUARNACCIA, *Illustrator*
LYNN STALEY, *Art Director*

FREE AGENTS
by Max Apple

FREE AGENTS (1984), *Book jacket*
HARPER & ROW, *Client*
STEVEN GUARNACCIA, *Designer*
STEVEN GUARNACCIA, *Illustrator*
JOSEPH MONTEBELLO, *Art Director*

Whatever you do is going to be fine." That kind of trust makes me feel weightless, but it's also a bit unnerving.

Problems that arise when the illustrator does not do the overall design: Despite the great freedom afforded by some art directors, things can fall apart when the illustrator is not involved in some fashion with the overall design decision. Some art directors will just stick type where it doesn't belong. And that's one of the givens in this business. But sometimes the art director truly enhances a drawing, such as in the cover for *Ambassador* magazine where the art director decided to weave the drawing through the logo as opposed to just sticking it in a box with type on top.

The *Globe* cover for "Snap Decisions" is a terrific example of design collaboration. The art director gave me carte blanche in coming up with an image for the special photography issue. I left my rough watercolor edge on the artwork with the idea that it would be cropped off. Lynn Staley came back with the edge intact but overlaid it with a white photo border, which effectively conveyed the idea of a snapshot. The process is like playing tennis with somebody who's as good as or better than you are.

About the jacket for *Free Agents*: For years I had wanted to do book jackets, but I had heard criticism that my work was too editorial, which I suppose meant that it looked like magazine illustration—too narrative and not posterish. Many of my illustrations had decorative or humorous borders that commented on the editorial content, could be used as design elements, and sometimes were used for texture. *Free Agents* is basically a variation on the texture approach. Since all the elements are the same size, they work together as a pattern of interrelated symbols. The letters, which are the same size and weight as the images, were meant to look like decorative random forms.

In praise of decoration: In the beginning I was drawing almost exclusively in black-and-white. Concept, à la Steinberg, was most important to me: the way something was drawn and its idea were one and the same, and I wasn't very interested in decoration for its own sake. But that

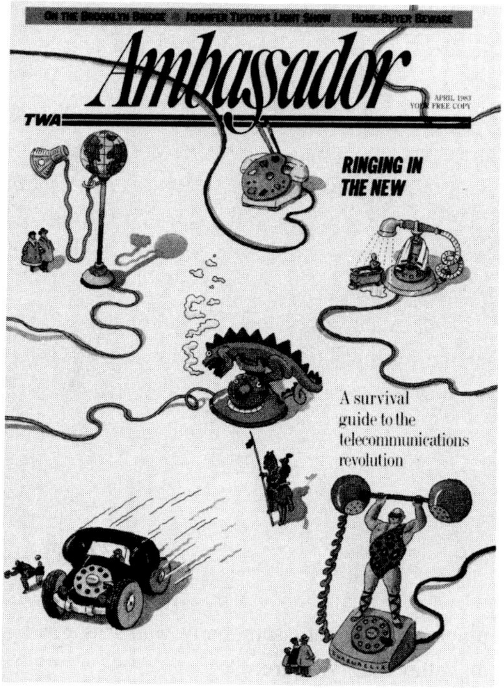
On the Brooklyn Bridge • Jennifer Tipton's Light Show • Home-Buyer Beware
Ambassador
TWA
RINGING IN THE NEW
A survival guide to the telecommunications revolution

approach got boring after a while, and I started looking for ways of approaching a drawing that would not be so conceptual. Sometimes I simply wanted to do things that looked pretty. The forms I use in *Free Agents* and other, subsequent projects derived from "illustrated" pajamas covered with tiny spaceships and cowboys that my brother and I used to wear as kids.

About the cover for *Madam I'm Adam*: I worked on this cover with my wife Susan Hochbaum, who is an associate at Pentagram in New York. (Parenthetically, we met while working on a job together.) She knows much more about type than I do, though I'm probably a bit more carefree about the type I choose—my tendency is to funk things up. Our differences made for a good complementary relationship. In this case, I basically came up with the image; we selected the type and background pattern together; and she decided upon the final design. We fought a bit, but all and all it was a terrific way to work.

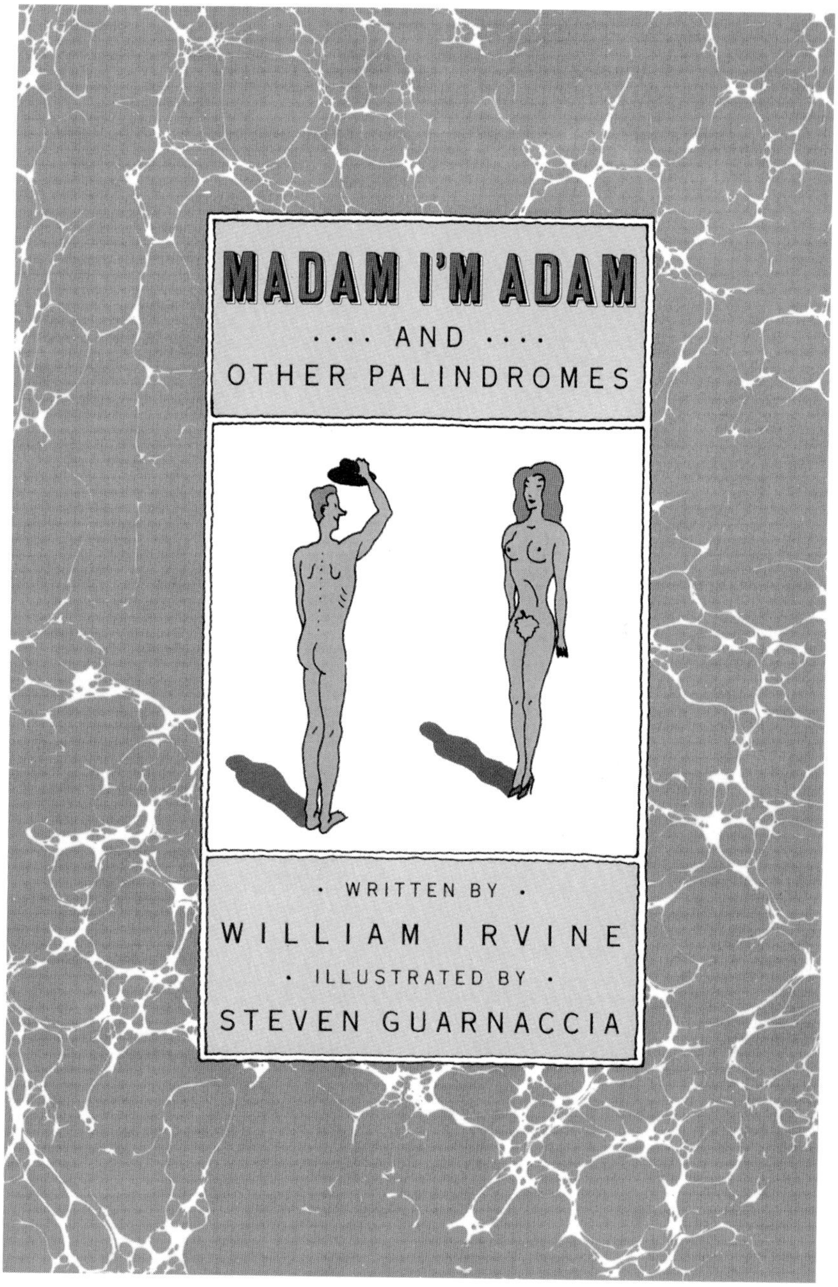
MADAM I'M ADAM
.... AND ....
OTHER PALINDROMES
· WRITTEN BY ·
WILLIAM IRVINE
· ILLUSTRATED BY ·
STEVEN GUARNACCIA

RINGING IN THE NEW (1983), *Airline magazine cover*
TWA *Ambassador*, *Client*
MARCIA WRIGHT, *Designer*
STEVEN GUARNACCIA, *Illustrator*
MARCIA WRIGHT, *Art Director*

MADAM I'M ADAM (1987), *Book cover*
SIMON & SCHUSTER, *Client*
SUSAN HOCHBAUM AND STEVEN GUARNACCIA, *Designers*
STEVEN GUARNACCIA, *Illustrator*
RUTH KOLBERT, *Art Director*

SETH JABEN

With a fine-art printmaking background, Seth Jaben started his career as an editorial illustrator. From 1983 to 1987, he conceived and directed the entire identity, promotion, and packaging program for E. G. Smith Inc., a fashion-conscious sock company whose owner, Eric Smith, is a lawyer--cum-businessman, and whose products are sold in fashionable department stores and boutiques. Here Jaben talks about his various responsibilities, ranging from bag and label design to point-of-sale displays.

About his style of illustration: Most of my work is surreal. Some of it may be from dreams but more often it comes from things I like to imagine happening or things I'd like to look at. For example, I wish that somebody would actually build my design for the E. G. Smith Color Institute Building, which looks like a gigantic sock. It would be the same principle as if the Life Savers building were a gigantic roll of Life Savers. The Miracle Screen catalog for spring 1986 is inspired by Chinese screens. I love those screens, and I am influenced by Indian art, so I decided to make a portable screen of my own. I always try to make my projects into something that I personally would want to own. The cloud bags just came from looking out my studio window and thinking about making a mural of the sky. I decided on it for the bag because clouds are an optimistic symbol—they form a composition that's always changing. I originally wanted to draw the clouds, but in the end I thought a photograph would be more compelling. I am also influenced by Chinese pharmaceuticals and the way Egyptians used lettering. My Rainbow catalog, which shows the variety of available colors, reminds me of an outdoor billboard.

On marketing: What I am trying to do is create a unique world, and my illustration style offers its distinctive character. Today, it's not enough to have a product; you have to say we're thoughtful people, we have an outlook, we have a world view. When people buy the socks they don't think they are just buying a product, but a whole point of view. Ten years ago products didn't have this.

On design: I knew nothing about type; I didn't even have a typebook when I first started. I had to call friends of mine who were designers because I didn't know how to spec type. I have learned what I have to know, though. It's like drawing: I do the picture first and then make the type work. I see type as illustration.

On the Rainbow campaigns: I didn't do any market research; E. G. Smith Inc. trusted me and I just did what I liked to do. The cloud bag was conceived as a holiday gift. If you bought two pairs of socks you got a bag. It was really fun seeing people around New York carrying it. I wrote a press release that said, "This is for city people who don't have a view of the sky." I wanted to make it sculptural, too, because it was used as a display. This was the first time that this very small company decided to structure itself like a big company. The cloud campaign included a full-page ad, a counter card on an easel back, and consumer promotion. I took what I call my fine-art style and made it advertising. I chose to identify the designer with the product—to humanize it. Calvin Klein, for example, just has a typeface solution, which I think is uninteresting. My idea to put a small picture of E. G. Smith on the label made him more accessible. I also had him write "love, eric" on all the products.

About the logo: This is based on looking at ancient seals and flags. I was wondering what kinds of images were important to people. One recurring theme suggests protection—people want to feel safe within their environment. The symmetry of this logo gives a feeling of security. Some

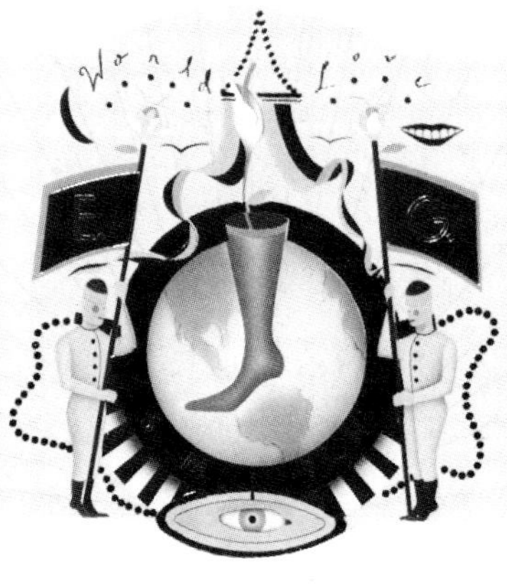

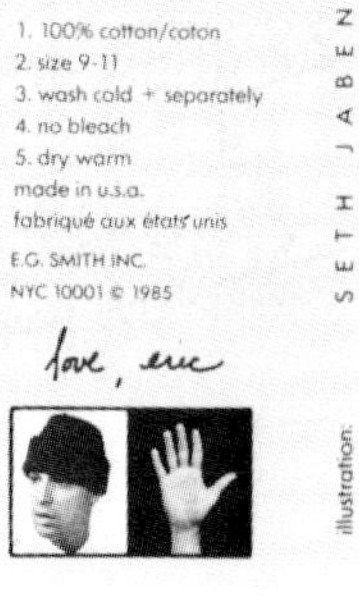
1. 100% cotton/coton
2. size 9-11
3. wash cold + separately
4. no bleach
5. dry warm
made in u.s.a.
fabriqué aux états unis
E.G. SMITH INC.
NYC 10001 © 1985
love, eric
SETH JABEN
illustration:

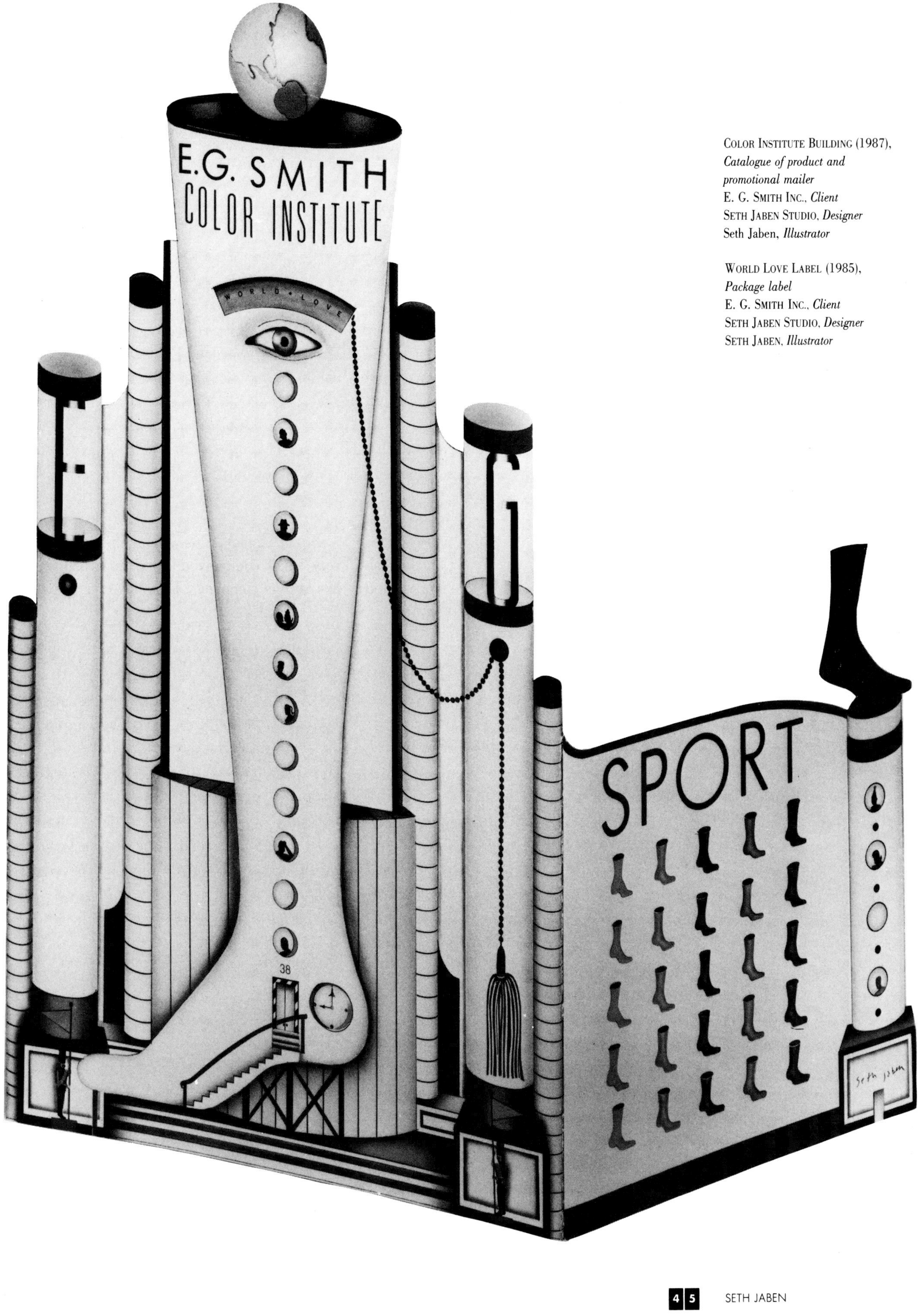
E.G. SMITH
COLOR INSTITUTE
WORLD • LOVE
E
G
SPORT
38

COLOR INSTITUTE BUILDING (1987),
Catalogue of product and promotional mailer
E. G. SMITH INC., *Client*
SETH JABEN STUDIO, *Designer*
Seth Jaben, *Illustrator*

WORLD LOVE LABEL (1985),
Package label
E. G. SMITH INC., *Client*
SETH JABEN STUDIO, *Designer*
SETH JABEN, *Illustrator*

MIRACLE SCREEN (1986), *Catalogue of product and promotional mailer*
E. G. SMITH INC., *Client*
SETH JABEN STUDIO, *Designer*
SETH JABEN, *Illustrator*

E.G. SMITH
seth jaben
BOOT SOCK
NUB-NUB SOCK
STRIPE BOOT
MEN'S CREW
SPRING 1986

would consider this corporate identity; I would call it a state seal.

On a preference for illustration over photography: Photography is reality; I'm giving the consumer fantasy. Today everyone has a T-shirt that has a piece of art on it. The more idiosyncratic you can be the more interesting you are. Everyone wants to make a statement.

On his involvement with other areas of the business: As a printmaker and then an illustrator I came into advertising through the back door. But I'm no longer going to define myself as an illustrator—that's only what I did for the first five years. Now I'm going to be a product designer, and this came about because the stores were saying, "Why don't you have the guy who's doing all your creative direction design your socks?" The Japanese licensing companies told E. G. Smith they could duplicate this sock product overnight. What they couldn't imitate was the personality and image I created.

MIRACLE
E.
G.
SMITH

CLOUD BAG (1986), *Shopping bag*
E. G. SMITH INC., *Client*
SETH JABEN, *Designer*
SETH JABEN, *Illustrator*
SETH JABEN, *Photographer*

MCRAY MAGLEBY

All colleges and universities use advertising and promotional materials. Some have on-campus art or "communications" departments; many do not. Mostly, the printed materials range between competent and mediocre; few are prize winners. The posters that announce interdepartmental events at Brigham Young University are decidedly among the latter. Under the direction of McRay Magleby, routine campus communications have been raised to a highly spirited, aesthetically superior art form. Magleby has, in effect, developed a nationally recognized "poster school." His ever changing yet always distinctive graphic style, combining image and letter with wit and grace, has resulted in posters that are effective for the momentary need yet transcend timely requirements. Here Magleby discusses a few of the hundreds of posters conceived and designed for a range of campus activities.

About being an autonomous design department within the university: We are essentially an on-campus commercial studio, started by the school because Provo, Utah, is too far from Salt Lake City to get things effectively designed and published. The administration had originally hired an art director from Los Angeles who whipped the otherwise sloppy printers into shape; but he was so hard-nosed and difficult to get along with that his tenure was shortened to a year. Then I was hired. I work directly for Brigham Young University, not the departments that call upon me to do the work. In fact, since the departments are coming to us as "clients," they don't even have to use our services if that's their choice. At one point our department was completely self-supporting, but the various chairpersons complained that the fees we charged them were much too high. Now a partial subsidy from the school helps to reduce the billing by half. Still, the departments must *buy* our posters.

About landing the job at BYU: I was working in Salt Lake City at an advertising agency when I applied for the job. I had taken a rather large portfolio to my first interview at BYU, but since it was with an English professor, the head of the scholarly press, he didn't even care to look at the work; he just asked questions, which at the time seemed to have little relevance to design quality. I apparently got the job because they were looking for someone who wouldn't be as hard-nosed as my predecessor, could get along peacefully with the printers, and wouldn't make them work too hard. Needless to say, I took the job, and after some time the whole operation developed terrifically. We have the best printer in Utah, an amazing typesetter, and an excellent design staff.

Why BYU has a more progressive design philosophy than most institutions: It started because the administration was having trouble with getting the students to register on time. They needed some obvious reminder and came to me wanting a poster that had just the relevant dates and locales, which I did but with little positive effect. I realized that registration is a curiously traumatic experience, and that the least we could do to make it easier for the student was to create posters that were more fun to look at and, hopefully, respond to. The first series included things that looked like common products—Campbell's soup, Cheer detergent, Kiwi shoe polish—and humorously altered the wording to relate to registration. It worked. The registration department was so inundated with registrants because of the posters that they dropped all other forms of advertising, including newspaper and radio. Now, actually, the posters have become somewhat unnecessary because of a new phone-registration system, and I'm dreading the day when the school says they don't need them any more. The fact that the students look forward to seeing the new ones each semester may, however, ensure their continuance.

Concerning the illustrative and typographic quality of his work: I was trained as an illustrator, and that was my first job. But I sensed that the designers at the studio where I worked were having more fun, so the job lasted only for a week. This was in part due to the fact that the kind of illustration I was given wasn't very stimulating. The studio was also fanatical about type; it rubbed off, and I became that way too. Since BYU is a conservative school, we tend to use more classical type designs—though not always—which emphasize sensitivity to spacing and size relationships. Today my preferred method of working is to both design and illustrate, to create a total work.

About the "Button Your Lips" and other library posters: The library people came to us because they were having a problem with excessive talking in the reading room and simply wanted a way to keep people quiet. They also wanted posters done in such a clever way that people would steal them to hang in their rooms as an added reminder. They came to us as a committee with such a bad idea that I've blocked it from memory. I actually had the idea we used, but told them to give us a day or so to think it over because I didn't want to spill the beans so quickly that they thought it was a cinch. The

Campus
FALL SEMESTER
Cream of
Deadline
SOUP
UP
YOUR SCHEDULE

CAMPUS SOUP (1979), *Student registration reminder*
REGISTRATION, BRIGHAM YOUNG UNIVERSITY, *Client*
MCRAY MAGLEBY, *Designer*
MCRAY MAGLEBY, *Illustrator*
MCRAY MAGLEBY, *Art Director*

committee did ultimately allow us to come up with the concept, which included the writing and art. As a rule, for the whole process we bill the departments around $700 for 100 posters, but we always run over budget by nearly $500 at our expense. That's why we usually print extras:

Button Your Lips (1988), *Poster for library quiet campaign*
Lee Library, Brigham Young University, *Client*
Garin Ipsen, *Designer*
Garin Ipsen, *Illustrator*
McRay Magleby, *Art Director*

PLEASE
BUTTON
Your
L·I·P·S
MAKE THE LIBRARY YOUR SILENT PARTNER FOR ACADEMIC EXCELLENCE

PLEASE
P·I·P·E
D·O·W·N
MAKE THE LIBRARY YOUR SILENT PARTNER FOR ACADEMIC EXCELLENCE

PIPE DOWN (1988), *Poster for library quiet campaign*
LEE LIBRARY, BRIGHAM YOUNG UNIVERSITY, *Client*
MCRAY MAGLEBY, *Designer*
MCRAY MAGLEBY AND SHARI HALL, *Illustrators*
MCRAY MAGLEBY, *Art Director*

to sell later to recoup the loss. And we eventually *make* some money.

We did a series of four posters on this theme of silence. In order for the writer and I to find the best way to influence the students to be quiet, we went through the thesaurus and found all the slang expressions for silence. We selected four that would be fun to illustrate, including "pipe down," "button your lip," "not a peep," and "shut your trap." The library people were a little worried that the patrons would be offended—and indeed it did take them by surprise when they read it—but the idea was funny enough not to really bother people. We also extended the campaign to bookmarks and little cards. The first idea I had was for "Pipe Down," using a smoking pipe; but that looked too much like a No Smoking sign, so I decided upon the musical variety. For "Shut Your Trap" I took some liberties with a real animal trap because I didn't have to be overly detailed to communicate the idea—I put wolves in the corners to emphasize the point.

Concerning the production process: I initiated the series, doing two of them completely. Then one of our interns collaborated with me on the last two (I did some loose sketches, and he designed the final). I had seen the stamps for the promotional book for Dickson's Inc., which The Duffy Group had designed [see p. 129], and it inspired me to make images that resembled stamps. After roughing out the first set, I had one of our designers render the border, and I rendered the type from an old book (each piece has a slightly different face). I always start in pencil, then make photocopies and color them with markers and colored pencil. For silk-screen printing, which is our preferred reproduction medium, we always try to figure out the color breaks in advance that will limit the number of passes throughout the press. Fortunately, we have an excellent serigrapher who can successfully execute even the impossible.

About the vegetable series for student registration: I've done so many different themes, including series of fruits, that I just decided this was the right time to do vegetables. I told the writer to think in those terms. In this case, he wrote the copy and I tried to make it fit. For my part, I researched some real vegetables before starting. I bought a bunch of radishes, for instance, and before they wilted, photocopied the leaves for reference. I did not do any real drawing. Instead, I cut all the patterns out of amberlith. The ultimate test, therefore, was in the printing.

You will notice that I leave a lot of space around these and all my posters, because the ones we decide to sell must be large—people pay more for large pieces. The registration office, however, doesn't like to have large posters because they take up too much room on a bulletin board. Therefore I allow for extra space so they can be trimmed for school use.

On a left-brain approach: I tend to think scientifically. First I do what feels right emotionally, then I start to apply scientific and mathematical formulae to refine a composition, to lock it in and basically make it comprehensible for people with left-brain orientation.

About typography: Type is to be read first; then, and only then, should it act as a design element. I usually want to relate the texture of the piece to the type itself. The weight of the line and an outline of a border will be the weight of, say, the thin stroke on the serif. But sometimes I design type to be removed, and those are the hard ones to integrate.

About imagery: The picture draws the viewer to the message. Sometimes the type serves that function, but I usually rely on the image as the first signal. A poster works on several levels: I don't like to give away the idea at the outset. Rather I prefer to fool viewers so that what they think they are seeing is actually not what they see. Then, of course, the type explains the poster's intention. Often the subtle twist occurs to the viewer in a split second. Playing with the different levels of consciousness allows people to remember all the more, because if they make the discovery, they are involved in the creative process.

T U R N I P

TURNIP (1988), *Student registration reminder poster*
REGISTRATION, BRIGHAM YOUNG UNIVERSITY, *Client*
MCRAY MAGLEBY, *Designer*
MCRAY MAGLEBY, *Illustrator*
NORMAN A. DARAIS, *Copywriter*
MCRAY MAGLEBY, *Art Director*

RICHARD MANTEL

As an art director and designer for Columbia Records and *New York* magazine during the 1960s, Richard Mantel primarily assigned illustration to others, but at the same time he had the urge to solve more purely pictorial problems on his own. Designing book jackets was the first step in a total process. Over a period of time he developed his painting skills and focused more intently upon a career as a freelance illustrator. In the late 1970s, as an associate of Push Pin Studios, he found the opportunity to use all his skills. Today he is a generalist in the best sense of the term: his design and illustration styles, though distinctive, are also eclectic. Mantel continues to be the art director for *New York* magazine's "advertorials" and accepts only the most compelling illustration assignments. Discussed here is a range of projects, from book jackets to posters to menu design, that required the marriage of typographical and pictorial skills.

On the difference between the illustrator-designer and the designer-illustrator: Because I was unfulfilled performing solely as an art director–designer, overseeing other's illustration, I developed painting skills and ultimately became an illustrator. Doing freelance book covers and jackets, I came to appreciate the creative freedom inherent in being both a designer and illustrator. Indeed I found that working for certain publishing houses one can function as one's own art director. They don't usually impose the image or approach, but rather give the title, author, and oftimes the manuscript; in turn I present them with a solution. The larger my visual vocabulary, the more varied my solutions can be. It was during one publishing season that I decided to further develop my illustration skills, and can remember spending a grueling month working on one painting that now would probably take me only a week.

As an art director I learned to solve conceptual problems for others before I could solve pictorial problems for myself. One of the earliest problems I encountered in combining the two disciplines was that, owing to my design background, I often tried to stretch myself as an illustrator to do something that as an art director I would demand of someone else. The results were often poor because I had expectations I myself couldn't fulfill. It took me a long time to find my own pictorial voice, but now I can make the distinctions; now I know how far I can take something. And I'm able to draw upon different disciplines as I need them for different assignments, such as those totally typographic or collaged or a union of typography and illustration.

About the bus shelter poster for *Brat Farrar*: This is a murder mystery elegantly set on a large estate in England. The story involves identical-looking men, one who inherits the family fortune and the other who poses as his long-lost twin (believed dead for ten years) and tries to usurp the inheritance. When I first saw a tape of the program, I had the idea to do a painting of the "brothers" standing close to each other, because seeing identical twins is so visually jarring. I also wanted to subtly convey a sense of violation—as if a ghost were coming back to haunt. I selected the typeface for its clarity and elegance—and so it would not distract from the central image. Other considerations were more prosaic: for example, the name Brat Farrar is fairly long and, for the sake of clarity, could not be broken into two lines because it is also fairly strange. The typeface I chose, Torino, has the added advantage of being slightly condensed, so the title was large, even in one line.

About the book covers and jackets for *The Artistic Animal* and *Eyes of Eternity*: I did *Eyes of Eternity* for Harris Lewine, who was art director for Harcourt Brace in the early seventies. He was great to work for. He wasn't a designer, really. He couldn't talk about typography or what specific imagery he wanted, but he had remarkable energy in the manner in which he conveyed the content of the book. He had a pure, visceral instinct about which person should do which job. He was willing to take chances, to present work to editors that he knew would be unexpected; and he was fearless in fighting for work he believed in. With someone as trusting as Harris, I did everything possible not to let him down.

The chimpanzee head used in *The Artistic Animal* is an old engraving. I came upon it while browsing through the picture collection at the New York Public Library, and its shape suggested a blob of paint to me. In fact the author talks specifically about the artistic creativity of apes and chimpanzees, so it was one of those rare times when a specific piece of reference I happened upon suggested the idea I needed but hadn't really thought of. Though this idea is strong, it's hard to say whether it works as design. Yet I do like shaking up perceptions—what one expects to see—by playing with the viewer's sense of scale, color, or reason. I like sneaking up from behind, and the monkey as paint blob is certainly a surprise. From the price on the cover one can see that the book is rather old; and frankly, were I to do the cover today I would never have used the Baskerville typeface. Although it suits the purpose, it looks a bit musty.

Being a collage, *Eyes of Eternity* is an alto-

MYSTERY! PRESENTS
JOSEPHINE TEY'S
BRAT FARRAR
NO ONE KNEW
HE WAS AN IMPOSTOR-
EXCEPT HIS MURDERER
A THREE-PART SERIES
BEGINS SATURDAY, NOVEMBER 15
9PM CHANNEL 13 PBS
CC CLOSED-CAPTIONED FOR HEARING IMPAIRED VIEWERS
Mobil
Mantel

BRAT FARRAR (1987),
Bus shelter poster
MOBIL CORPORATION, *Client*
RICHARD MANTEL, *Designer*
RICHARD MANTEL, *Illustrator*
SANDRA RUCH, *Art Director*

ALEXANDER ALLAND, JR.
$3.95
THE ARTISTIC ANIMAL
AN INQUIRY INTO THE BIOLOGICAL ROOTS OF ART

EYES OF ETERNITY
A SPIRITUAL AUTOBIOGRAPHY
BY VESNA KRMPOTIĆ

THE ARTISTIC ANIMAL (1972),
Book jacket
DOUBLEDAY, *Client*
RICHARD MANTEL, *Designer*
RICHARD MANTEL, *Illustrator*
DIANA KLEMIN, *Art Director*

EYES OF ETERNITY (1977), *Book jacket*
HARCOURT BRACE JOVANOVICH, *Client*
RICHARD MANTEL, *Designer*
RICHARD MANTEL, *Illustrator*
HARRIS LEWINE, *Art Director*

gether different kind of pictorial solution. But as I've said, I will use any medium when appropriate. The manuscript was about the author's search for self and the spiritual transitions she had undergone while traveling. The Sphinx and pyramids were mentioned, and I grabbed that image immediately; but to add a level of emotion and drama, I decided to do a sequential mood shift at the bottom, where the color changes from panel to panel. The type is positioned to line up with the angle of the pyramids, and the lines simply accentuate that relationship. Hence, in addition to provoking the imagination, the enigmatic title, *Eyes of Eternity*, becomes a design element; on one level it functions as information and on another it becomes part of the motion and rhythm of the picture.

About the business identity for Benjy Levy, a "close-up" magician and mentalist: The inspiration came from an A. M. Cassandre poster—the way, for example he would cut into space in a cubist manner, making two or three planes from one. The mark itself looks like Levy, part of whose act is to be introduced to three hundred guests at a party and remember all their names four hours later. The card is an obvious allusion to his trade, and the printing technique (which cannot be seen in reproduction here) makes further reference to it: his face is blind-embossed, making him seem to appear and disappear. It was the most fun I'd had with a job in a long time.

On doing the identity for the New York restaurant Manhattan Island: A friend owns this restaurant, and by coincidence it hap-

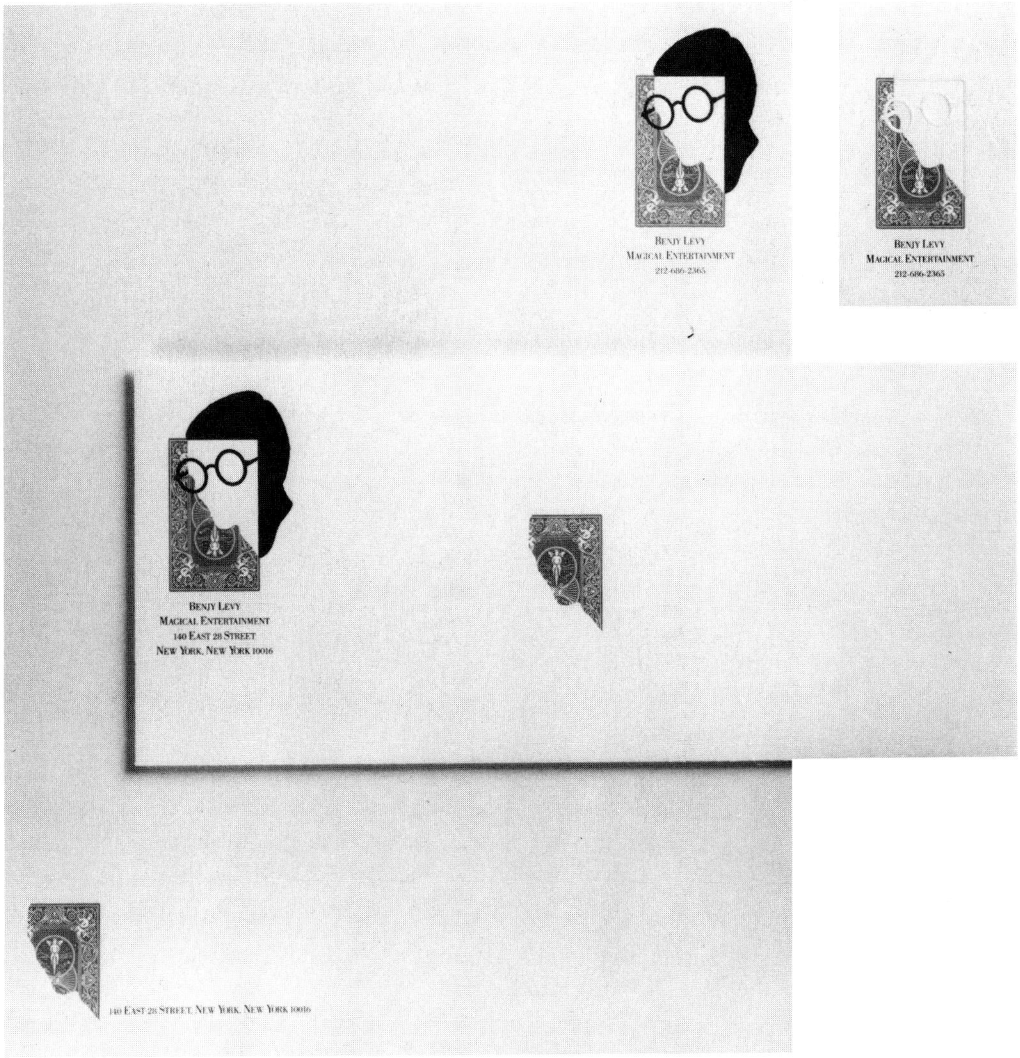
BENJY LEVY
MAGICAL ENTERTAINMENT
212-686-2365
BENJY LEVY
MAGICAL ENTERTAINMENT
140 EAST 28 STREET
NEW YORK, NEW YORK 10016

BENJY LEVY: MAGICAL ENTERTAINMENT (1988), *Identity (letterhead, business card, envelope)*
BENJY LEVY, *Client*
RICHARD MANTEL, *Designer*
RICHARD MANTEL, *Illustrator*
RICHARD MANTEL, *Art Director*

pens to be located in the building where I live. I decided that I wanted to play with the name ironically, and so combined the idea of the tropics with Manhattan Island. I looked through my reference books and found an old black-and-white cityscape from the thirties. I did some hand work to abstract it a bit more than the original. For the palm tree, I saw an illustration that someone else, Cathleen Toelke, had done, and realized that her silhouetted configuration was just what I needed. I called her agent and negotiated the right to place the basic shape of the palm tree over my cityscape. The box in which it sits suggests a city window, while the colors are what one expects of the tropics.

It's quite difficult to design something that is to be sized both 1 inch and 2 feet high. It had to function equally well on a matchbook and on a large poster, so the shapes could not be too fussy. Of course the type had to be readable, but I wanted it to be more exotic and eccentric than the classical type forms I usually use. Unlike a book jacket or even a poster, working on a menu means that people do not have to look at it from 40 feet away; nor does it have to compete on a rack with other menus. A designer can have the luxury of restraint.

On the relationship of graphic symbols to content in the book jacket for *Apaches:* This title conjures up a number of responses; one thinks of pastoral America one hundred years ago, and innocent native Americans roaming the land. But one also thinks of hardship, violence, scalping, and other brittle kinds of imagery. I felt this title was so evocative that it didn't need to be visually overdramatized or embellished to elicit a strong emotional response. This is a case where something totally unexpected has a remarkable symbolic strength. The image is from an old lithograph that reminded me so much of an Indian headdress I couldn't ignore it. While it had symbolic meaning, however, it was also rather dull, so I had to liven it up. I dropped an Indian pattern into the type and also used it in the border to tie it together and make it more visually interesting. I think that the power of the book's title, coupled with the "quietness" of the picture, creates an interesting tension.

About being an art director who assigns illustration: I regularly assign illustration as design director of *New York* magazine's special advertising sections. I do the format and design and oversee them all the way through production. I also direct the illustration, which provides me with a wonderful opportunity to work with other illustrators. These artists often come up with wonderful solutions that I wouldn't think of. And I have the freedom to conceive of visual solutions I could never execute myself.

MANHATTAN ISLAND

MANHATTAN ISLAND (1988), *Restaurant identity (logo, menu cover)*
MANHATTAN ISLAND, *Client*
RICHARD MANTEL, *Designer*
RICHARD MANTEL AND CATHLEEN TOELKE, *Illustrators*
RICHARD MANTEL, *Art Director*

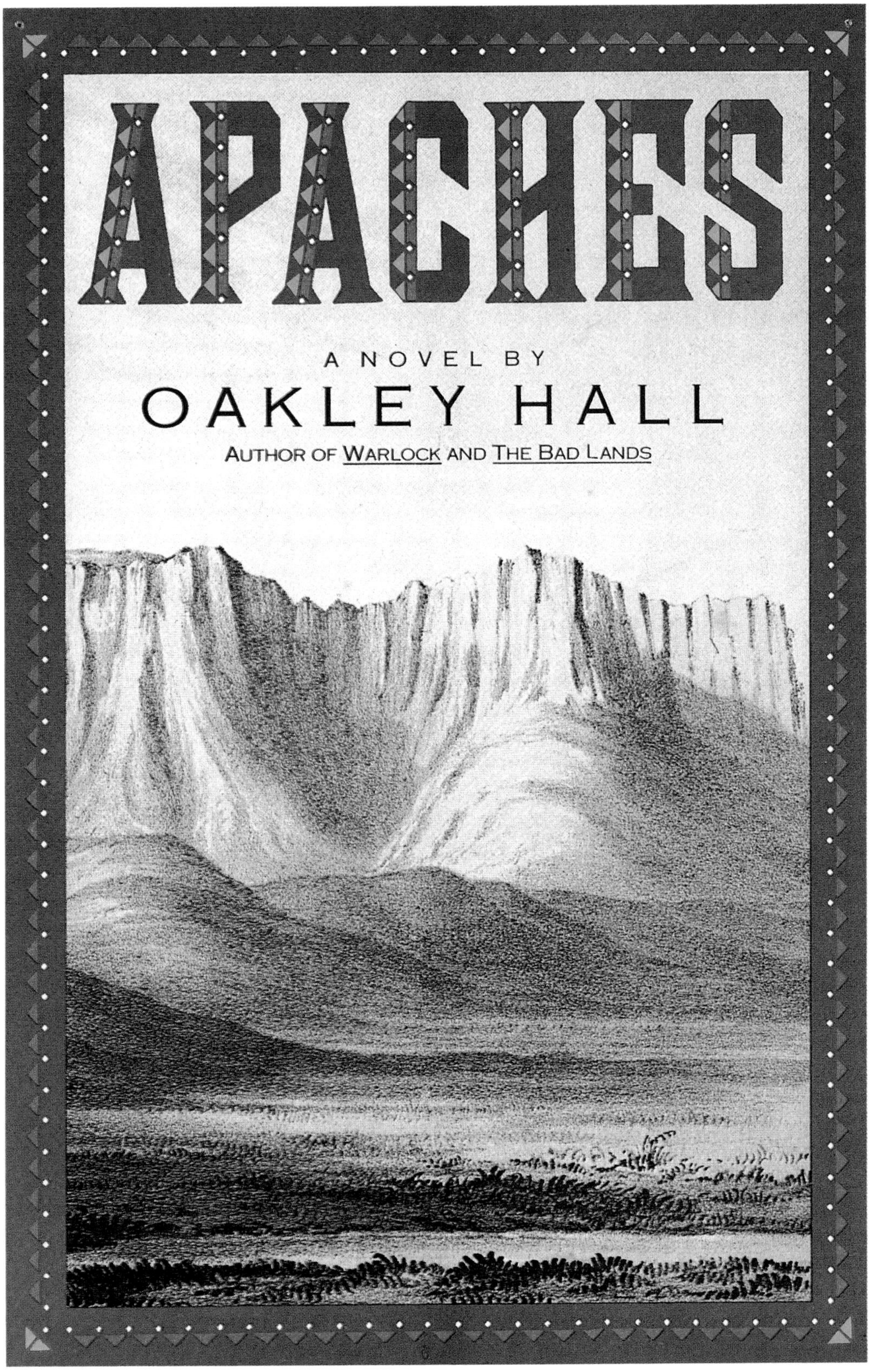
APACHES
A NOVEL BY
OAKLEY HALL
AUTHOR OF WARLOCK AND THE BAD LANDS

APACHES (1986), *Book jacket*
SIMON & SCHUSTER, *Client*
RICHARD MANTEL, *Designer*
FRANK METZ, *Art Director*

FRED MARCELLINO

Being typecast as a designer within a specific discipline can be a major constraint unless one is passionate about the subject; then it can be called a niche. Fred Marcellino has created a very secure niche within the publishing industry, but not at the expense of creativity and versatility. Marcellino produces an average of thirty jackets and covers every year; and though most are given his characteristic illustrative and typographic imprint, in virtually every publishing season he transcends his elegant tried-and-true style with a work of innovation and distinction. Marcellino balances a penchant for mysterious imagery with classical tastes in type in a way that captures the essence of a book. Here he details the thinking behind a few of his many jackets in which type and image are used in the manner of the master posterists of the 1930s.

On deciding not to be a "pure" illustrator: I didn't start out to become an illustrator or a designer. Instead I studied fine arts at Cooper Union in New York City, where as fate would have it, all the students were required to take three years of lettering and calligraphy. In my freshman year I had to learn about the roman and italic letter and then, at the end of the year, produce a ten-page book. After three years I was well versed in the application of letterforms. So, having few of the prejudices that might come with a strict design training, when I decided to become a graphic designer I began by combining letters and pictures. There was nobody to tell me that I couldn't handle both.

From the very beginning I looked for work that demanded more than just illustration. In fact, when an art director calls me with an assignment that has already been conceptualized or designed on a page, I make a mess of it. I cannot function well when someone has come up with the idea, because then I feel that I must fulfill his or her expectations as opposed to simply using my own head.

About the publishing industry: I am involved in publishing because what works best for me is getting a manuscript and being told to "do something wonderful." And that is not as much of an exaggeration as it might seem. I'm very fortunate to be given a lot of freedom. From experience I know what things I cannot or would not do, and the manuscript imposes its own boundaries since a jacket must be true to the book. So here I can be the illustrator, typographer, designer, and art director; and while there is usually an art director in every publishing house, never has an idea been dictated to me and rarely is one even suggested.

A general note about process: I think of mine as a collage sensibility—even when I am painting or drawing. Though it isn't always evident in my work, I am always pasting disparate images and ideas together. My process begins with reading the manuscript; then I do thumbnail sketches—very tiny hieroglyphics—which are really part of the thinking stage; finally I end up with a very tight sketch, which is a requirement in publishing, since sketches are reproduced in catalogs. Editors and marketing people simply insist on them.

A difference between "literary" and "commercial" books: The demands on me as a designer depend on the positioning of a book in the marketplace. If I am dealing with a decidedly commercial project, everyone from the agent to the author is going to say that I must make the name scream across the room. With less commercial enterprises the author's ego is not so involved; indeed, as a rule they are happier with a jacket that serves the book well than with one that blasts their name. In the end, of course, a well-designed jacket is more visible than one with gimmicks like giant type in fluorescent pink and gold foil stamping.

Yet no matter what kind of book is involved, a jacket cannot cheat. It has to be arresting, but it must honor the text as well. It drives me crazy when I read a book and find the jacket has little relation to the text. On the other hand, some designers who are not as involved with books as I am see fidelity to a book as almost a handicap to the design process.

About the *Fantomas* jacket: This book was written in the 1920s and was one of the first thrillers ever published. The character Fantomas, an elusive and famous criminal, was adored in France, where many sequels to the book were produced and a movie was made. This image of Fantomas comes from a very old poster I found in a tiny reproduction. I simply redid the poster, eliminating everything except the central figure and lower cityscape, and designed my own type to fall across the image. In fact, the simple addition of the type totally transformed what was essentially a found-image.

I was fascinated by the face on the original poster. Fantomas is a masked man with a secret identity. Somewhere along the line it struck me that I could substitute the letter *O* for the eye, and then magically it came together. I drew the typeface based on the elliptical *O*. And I wanted the *M* to look like a wink, which determined the

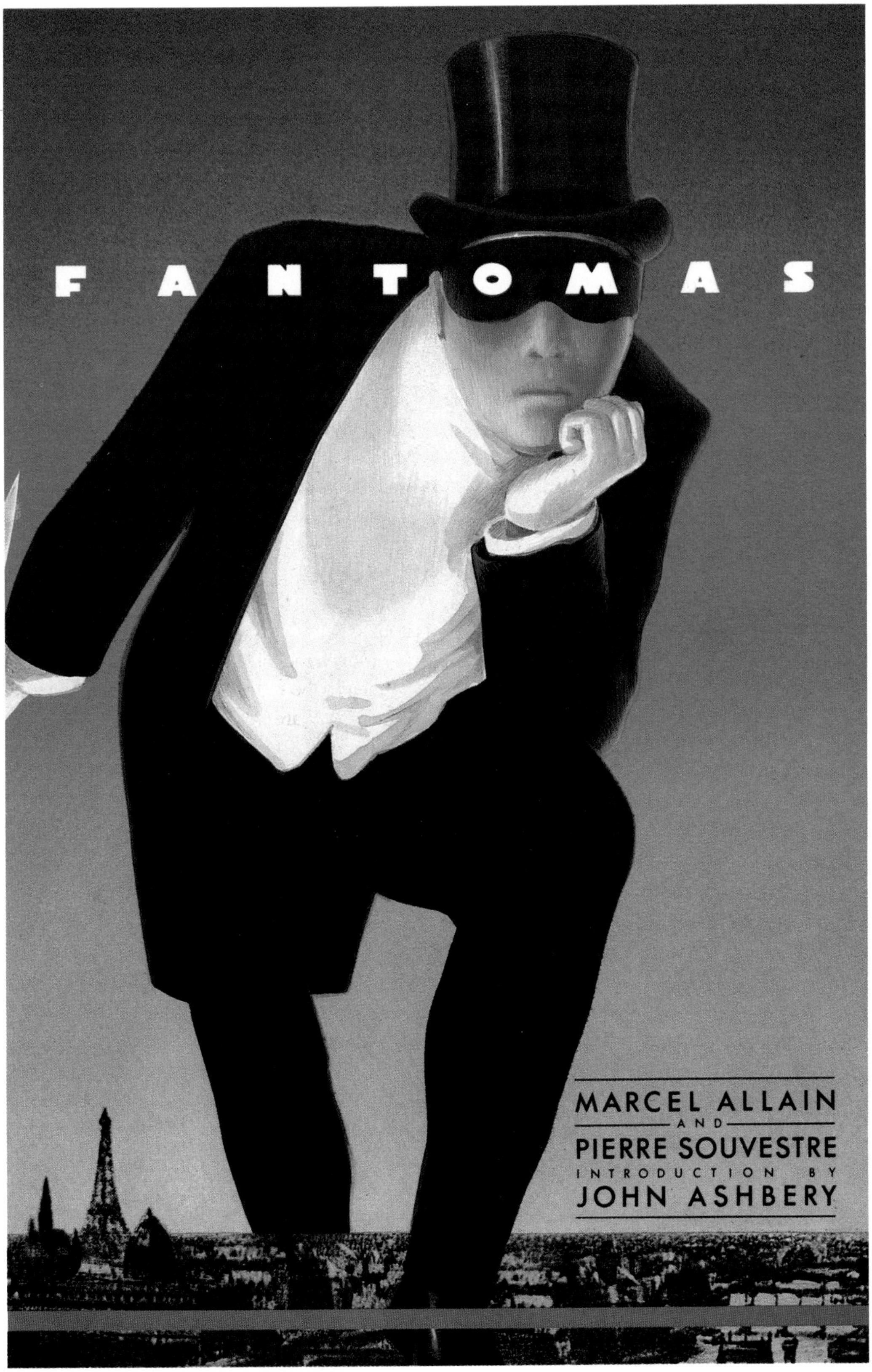
FANTOMAS
MARCEL ALLAIN
AND
PIERRE SOUVESTRE
INTRODUCTION BY
JOHN ASHBERY

FANTOMAS (1986), *Book jacket*
WILLIAM MORROW, *Client*
FRED MARCELLINO, *Designer*
FRED MARCELLINO, *Illustrator*
CHERYL ASHERMAN, *Art Director*

THE ENGINEER OF HUMAN SOULS (1984), *Book jacket*
ALFRED A. KNOPF, *Client*
FRED MARCELLINO, *Designer*
FRED MARCELLINO, *Illustrator*
SARA EISENMAN, *Art Director*

rest of the letters. I also wanted it to have a twenties character. Indeed the cover's success is dependent upon the typographic treatment. A paperback company wanted to reprint it, but did not want to use my type because they believed the reader would not understand it. I persuaded them to use it, but their compromise was to reproduce the title again outside the illustration area. Now it says *Fantomas Fantomas.* Not exactly subtle.

On *The Engineer of Human Souls* jacket: Josef Skvorecky is an emigrant author, and the book is autobiographical fiction. I wanted to get across the idea of the writer as a commanding force inextricably tied to his craft. He and his words are the landscape..This everday object (the typewriter) takes on a monumental scale due to subtleties of placement and cropping.

The type is based on a typewriter face, but I decided to construct the lettering in perspective. It is not the most refined face. Photolettering could have done a much slicker job, but I decided crudeness was an asset in this case. For the author's line I used something found in a Speedball lettering book. I find lots of type with unique character in offbeat books like that; and once cleaned up they work very well.

About the *World's End* jacket: T. Coraghessan Boyle's book is a serious novel concerning the many generations of a family that has lived along the Hudson River since the days of the first Dutch settlers. It is not linear, however; it doesn't start in the 1600s and end up in the 1980s, but rather goes back and forth. I thought the cover should do that too. I wanted a layered feeling, a landscape that is also a room with a window revealing another landscape. All together it suggests movement in time, but within the confines of a very specific place.

I found a photograph of a river, Xeroxed it both large and small, and then painted on top of the whole thing. As is true of a lot of my illustration, the finished work incorporates a Xerox. Even the little ship is a Xerox from another source. I use a lightweight Strathmore paper, sometimes a colored stock, and then work with airbrush or acrylic paints. The shadowed typography seems to have a three-dimensional presence in the room.

Concerning illusion: I do not like jackets where the illustration simply repeats the title. To have a book called *The Red Room* and then put a red room on the cover seems redundant. Sometimes it's more interesting to work in counterpoint to the title. I think it's provocative to have an expansive title like *World's End* confined in a tight room. For *The Engineer of Human Souls,* making the type and illustration one and the same reinforced and gave weight to the name of the book. The key is to sometimes put a twist on the title without confusing the issue.

About *The Drowned and the Saved* jacket: This is one of Primo Levi's books about his experiences in the concentration camps, and was published after he committed suicide in 1987. The idea is very simple; all the drama is focused on the shadow cast by the type. Intuitively it seems right for the book. At once there's a sense of lightness and weight. The monolithic structure suggests oppression. Is it a factory? A smokestack? I don't know. I basically decided that I wanted an immovable force—some kind of power—and then wanted the title to cast this ethereal, soft shadow. The cloud is there to give the composition scale; without it the sky would not be an effective frame.

The type is based on Futura, but I handlettered it in order to control the angles of the *E* and *T.* Although the typeface for the author and title are the same, one casts a shadow while the other does not—there's no logic; you just accept it.

On the repetition of forms and a personal vocabulary: I like to find images and put them together in new ways. I don't just draw out of my head. Even as a child I did not draw fantastic images, but rather borrowed pictures from life and rearranged them. I use everyday symbols in order to communicate directly—windows, skies, beds, pens—images that introduce a familiar context. From there I can juxtapose, contradict, elaborate, or surprise.

THE
ENGINEER
OF
HUMAN
SOULS
Josef Skvorecky

WORLD'S END (1988), *Book jacket*
VIKING, *Client*
FRED MARCELLINO, *Designer*
FRED MARCELLINO, *Illustrator*
NEAL STUART, *Art Director*

WORLD'S END
A NOVEL BY
T. CORAGHESSAN BOYLE

THE DROWNED
AND THE SAVED
PRIMO
LEVI

THE DROWNED AND THE SAVED
(1988), *Book jacket*
SIMON AND SCHUSTER, *Client*
FRED MARCELLINO, *Designer*
FRED MARCELLINO, *Illustrator*
FRANK METZ, *Art Director*

JAMES MCMULLAN

From his early days at Push Pin Studios in the mid-1960s, James McMullan has practiced the pictorial magic that results from a brew of image and letter. His record albums, book covers, and posters attest to his skill and passion. Moreover, he has become an evangelical force in reconstituting drawing as a major requisite in the teaching of design. Over the past decade McMullan has designed numerous theater posters, succeeding, where many have failed, in producing memorable icons and innovative artworks in a genre that traditionally has tight creative constraints. As the posterist for New York's Lincoln Center Theater, he has developed strong images that are unique yet have distinct "family" ties to one another. Here McMullan discusses the process of designing these theater posters, as well as covers—what one should call mini-posters—for a series of books by Jorge Luis Borges.

About his theater posters for Lincoln Center: By the time I had done the *Anything Goes* poster I had already done posters for *The House of Blue Leaves*, *The Front Page*, and *Death and the King's Horseman.* And there was some pressure on me to make each one different enough to distinguish the different plays. Yet there is going to be a family resemblance, though not necessarily in terms of style; each is concerned with body language more than, say, emphasis on the portraits alone.

On deciding upon an image: I always read the play. Indeed reading is the minimum requirement. If there is a chance to watch rehearsals I will. With *The Front Page,* which is an old play that was made into a movie, I got a videotape to afford myself additional insight. For *Death and the King's Horseman* I watched a rehearsal and talked to the author. With *House of Blue Leaves* I asked the leading actor, John Mahoney, to play the piano for me while I took some photographs on which I based the painting. In the case of *The Front Page* I used a character actor who had the perfect physiognomy to represent both the play and newspapermen in general. In the case of *Anything Goes* I asked a friend to model for me while I took pictures of her on the Staten Island Ferry. I usually have a vision of what I want before I take the photographs, but certain qualities surfaced in the way this model posed that I had not anticipated.

I really start to play when I get the photographs and then move things around. Rarely is it just *boom-boom* on the first sketch, though occasionally I have lucked out. Usually the photo just gives me the energy of the pose. In the photographs for *Anything Goes* the model is wearing a little hat and a long dress with long sleeves. In the poster it's quite different. I always try to leave myself a little space before the "final-performance" artwork. Indeed, all the Lincoln Center posters changed from the first sketch to the finish.

On lettering: With hand lettering you can have exactly what you want—the rhythm, density, and color—and it can be fine-tuned and adjusted. I

FRONT PAGE

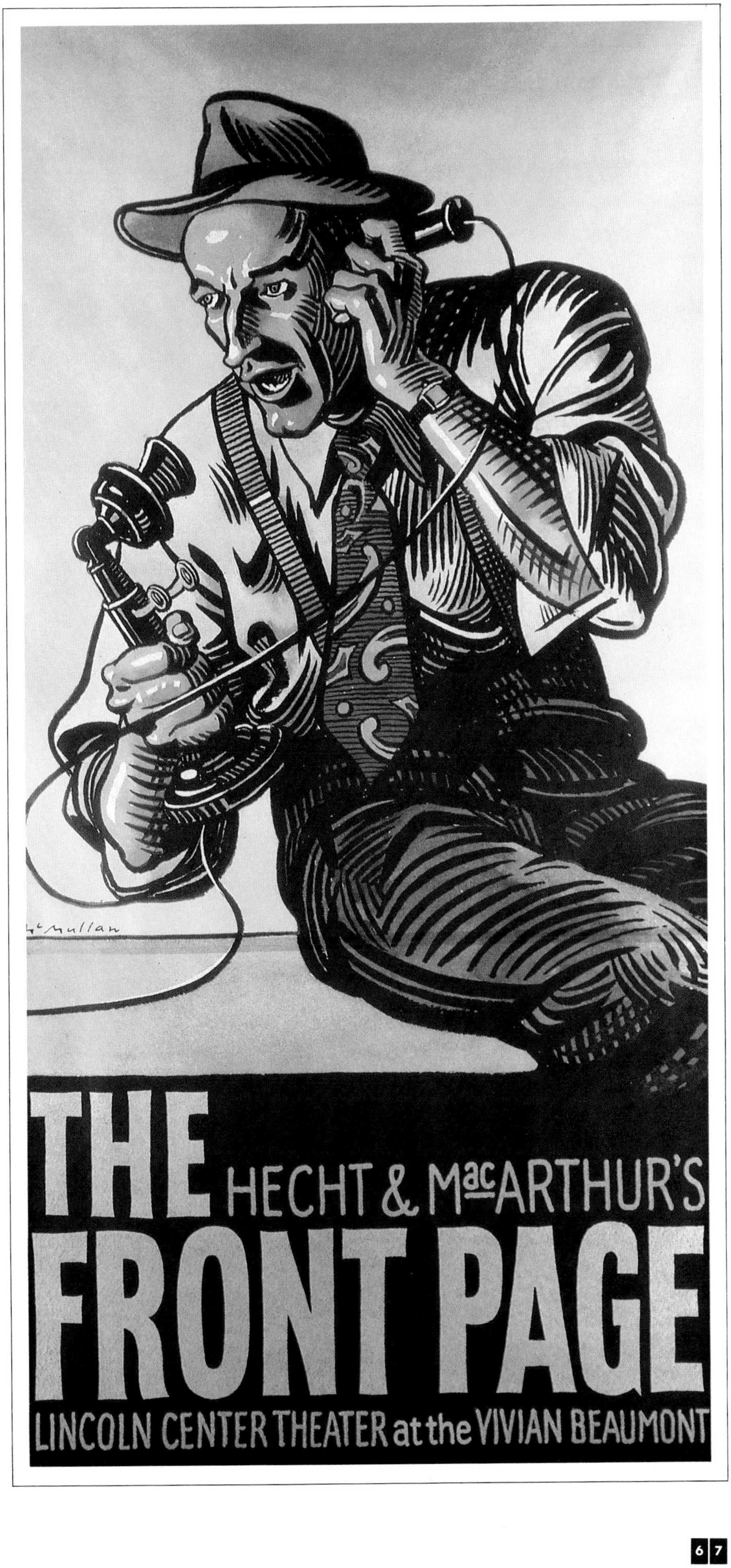
McMullan
THE
HECHT & MacARTHUR'S
FRONT PAGE
LINCOLN CENTER THEATER at the VIVIAN BEAUMONT

THE FRONT PAGE (1986), *Poster*
LINCOLN CENTER THEATER, *Client*
JAMES MCMULLAN, *Designer*
JAMES MCMULLAN, *Illustrator*
JIM RUSSEK, *Art Director*

Death
and the King's
Horseman
by
Wole
Soyinka
Lincoln Center Theater at the Vivian Beaumont

THE HOUSE
OF BLUE
LEAVES
BY JOHN GUARE

play around with hand lettering because it is an overlooked category of endeavor. Of course, I am not the only one doing it, but maybe the impulse to letter and the impulse to paint seldom coexist in the same person. Some people who specialize in lettering, like Michael Doret, do a kind of illustration, but it really is more rooted in lettering. Maybe they are coming to it with primarily lettering instincts while I come to it with painterly instincts.

About painterly versus design instincts: I am caught between a very painterly approach to poster making represented by Toulouse-Lautrec and the more structured (or designed) poster represented by Ludwig Hohlwein, or for that matter Push Pin, where there is the implication of a grid. Most often some sense of a grid is operative in my work, but I seem to be quite willing to violate its architectural purity if the result works.

I am not, however, an artist who can make something by refining it through layers. I've never been good at doing anything by putting it under tracing paper to make it better. The only way I seem to be able to make something better is to attack it from a white surface again—in other words, do it over. A lot of what interests me in my work really derives out of an immediate sense of drawing rather than the refinement of shapes.

The Toulouse-Lautrec side of me tends to make my compositions fairly active. I am usually not interested in one central, stabilized kind of object; the subjects are, however, in some way *balanced,* if not stable. Even in *The Front Page* I did not let the guy sit foresquare. I needed to twist him around and destabilize him. In much of my work things are off center.

Combining type and lettering in the Borges covers: I like the fact that the type sets up a basic architecture which the informal handwriting can play off. I designed it so that the Borges name would run across the top, and a little colored rule would relate to some of the colors below. A spectrum of color was also planned to go on somewhere in each of the compositions. This is sort of a dumb idea, but often dumb ideas are good ones because they are simple enough to allow more things to happen. If the idea becomes too strong, then one is always serving the idea. It wasn't hard to incorporate a little spectrum in each painting, though. It was more important with some than with others.

The interesting thing for me is that all of the lettering was done right into the art—a risky proposition. It is brush lettering because I rarely use a pen.

About composition: I never start a picture without knowing where the edges are; I always start by drawing a rectangle. I notice among the students I teach that they can almost be divided up between those who think about the subject and radiate their compositions out from it, and those who contain the subject and come back in from the edges of the rectangle. I don't think that one always has to work in a rectangle; people compose where the rectangle is implicitly rather than explicitly stated. But I am always thinking about what the shape of the background is doing to the main subject. Somewhere there is an implicit rectangle that holds it together. And, of course, a printed page is a rectangle.

About the poster for *Anything Goes*: The producers had the vision of a Twiggy-like woman from the 1960s as the main character in this poster. If the woman represented anyone, it was Reno Sweeney, who was anything but svelte. Ever since Ethel Merman played the role people have always thought of this character in zaftig terms. But the producers wanted her to be more elegant and felt that in my sketch her shoulders in particular were too aggressive. In fact, I did a black-and-white version of it in which I modified the shoulders to make her look more streamlined, but it didn't work without enough shoulder to look over; the looking-back gesture wasn't interesting. Finally I came to my senses and did it the way I had originally conceived it; and once printed, everybody was happy.

On dealing with authors: Sometimes the producers' concern over a famous or difficult playwright will cause problems. They rejected my sketches for *Death and the King's Horseman* because they said Wole Soyinka, the playwright, simply did not like them. No other reason was given, and I had the feeling that no one was particularly anxious to defend my design to the author. They arranged a meeting between Soyinka and me so he could articulate his reservations. Although he was not very clear and only said that my sketch was "not metaphorical enough," he

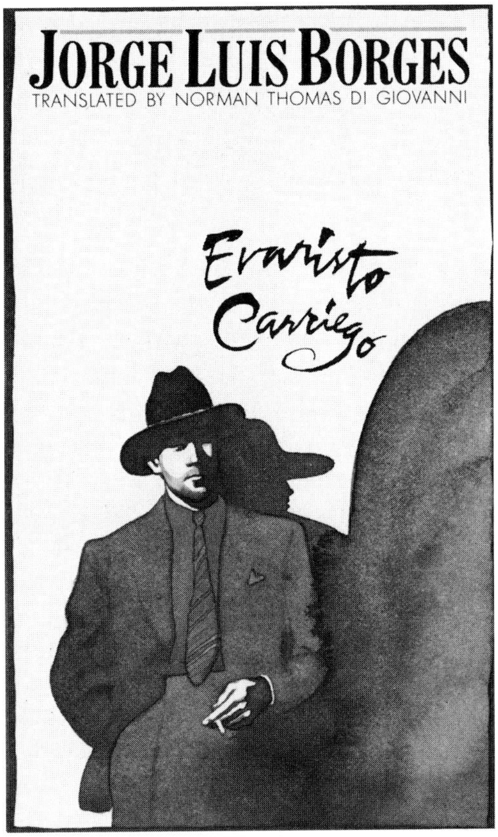

JORGE LUIS BORGES
TRANSLATED BY NORMAN THOMAS DI GIOVANNI
Evaristo Carriego

EVARISTO CARRIEGO (1983), *Book cover*
E. P. DUTTON, *Client*
JAMES MCMULLAN, *Designer*
JAMES MCMULLAN, *Illustrator*
NANCY ETHEREDGE, *Art Director*

DEATH AND THE KING'S HORSEMAN (1987), *Poster*
LINCOLN CENTER THEATER, *Client*
JAMES MCMULLAN, *Designer*
JAMES MCMULLAN, *Illustrator*
JIM RUSSEK, *Art Director*

THE HOUSE OF BLUE LEAVES (1986), *Poster*
LINCOLN CENTER THEATER, *Client*
JAMES MCMULLAN, *Designer*
JAMES MCMULLAN, *Illustrator*
JIM RUSSEK, *Art Director*

In older days a glimpse of stocking
was looked on as something
shocking. but now,
God knows,
ANYTHING
GOES

ANYTHING GOES (1987), *Bus poster*
LINCOLN CENTER THEATER, *Client*
JAMES MCMULLAN, *Designer*
JAMES MCMULLAN, *Illustrator*
JIM RUSSEK, *Art Director*

agreed to let me watch a rehearsal, and from that experience I came up with the design that was used. It is hard when authors are involved, because they have an internal vision of what they are doing that is very complex; it is difficult for them to accept that a poster, since it is an enormous simplification, is always going to be kind of a lie.

Concerning realism and abstraction: I grew up at a time when the *Saturday Evening Post* was the big magazine for illustration. And there was a sense in the pictures by Rockwell and others that even though they were realistic, they were solidly composed and complex too. That helped me to believe that out of realism can come a very interesting abstract connection. My whole art education is based on the notion that everything is implicitly abstract. In terms of intuition, that is the way I build a picture—the way I draw. I suppose because I am so interested in the abstract rhythms and shapes that underlie (or can underlie) realistic subject matter, I have not been as motivated as some artists to abandon realism. There is a lot of flattening in my work, but there is also the illusion of the three-dimensional and the flat playing back and forth.

About drawing: To be able to draw is to be able to think coherently about something and to express that thinking. For me it has always been inextricably linked with feeling out the rhythm of shapes and expressing the idea of energy and animation.

When I teach drawing I try to help students experience it as something inherently clarifying and enjoyable. It is difficult both to teach drawing and do it, but I seem to be invested in making teaching a success these days, so a surprising number of students are getting much better. It appears to me that with drawing, students can't focus their efforts on disguising their lack of hand skills by playing around with the painting surface. There is a kind of "buck stops here" feeling in struggling to draw—I feel it reconnects me to the world and regenerates me on some level. Drawing is a harnessing of energy. Without it one is at the mercy of reflexes, which is why so much modern art is boring: what one sees is the repetition of essentially unharnessed reflexes. Drawing gives those reflexes a kind of purpose and an organization—it makes the process more interesting because there is a kind of yin-yang going on. The subconscious is pushing from one side, and rational thought and the discipline of one's craft are pushing from the other.

About design: Design is all intuition and reflex too. It seems strange that in a vocation that is so fundamentally visual more emphasis isn't put on drawing. Many designers seem to be working out of response to texture and color alone, with some help from the grid systems. I'd think we'd see more interesting spatial solutions, more Matisse-like thinking, if designers drew more.

There was a time when people who dealt with posters and advertisements and stage design believed they were artists and were using different aspects of their sensibilities to solve different kinds of problems; they did not have to feel so specialized. This fragmented design field makes it easier for mediocre talent and for corporations to deal with them (they're so fragmented themselves), but I'm surprised more people don't want to do it all.

ANYTHING GOES
LINCOLN CENTER THEATER AT THE VIVIAN BEAUMONT
McMullan

TOM NIKOSEY

After being graduated in 1972 from Pratt Institute in New York City, Tom Nikosey wanted to design record album covers. Moving to Los Angeles he set out to find a job in the music industry. He designed logos for bands to use on their drum heads, but then Nikosey's big break came when he got a freelance job with Ed Caraeff, a photographer and designer who worked on covers and promotion directly with the recording artists themselves. Nikosey's debut album design was a collaboration with Caraeff on Eric Clapton's *No Reason to Cry*. For this he designed a Western-style title and rendered all the tune titles on the back side. It was Nikosey's first "total package": many records, posters, and book covers later he continues to practice "total design." Here he describes the union of graphic and typographic elements on a series of covers he has designed for *RSVP*, the annual directory of creative talent.

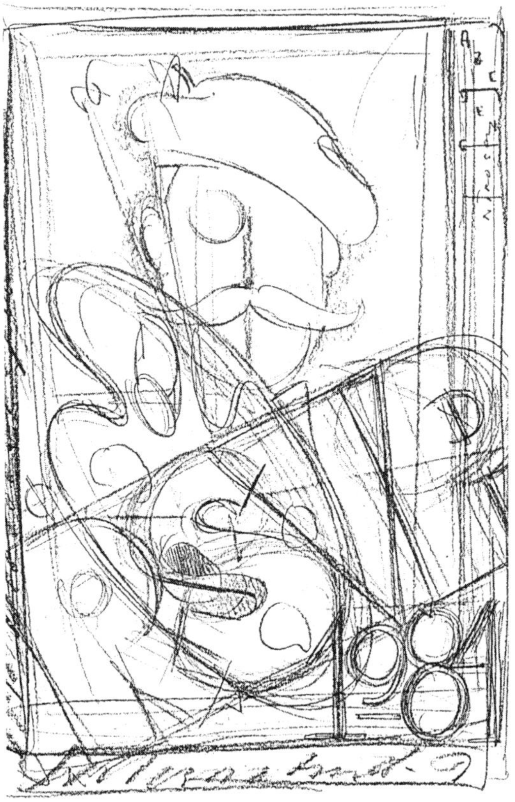

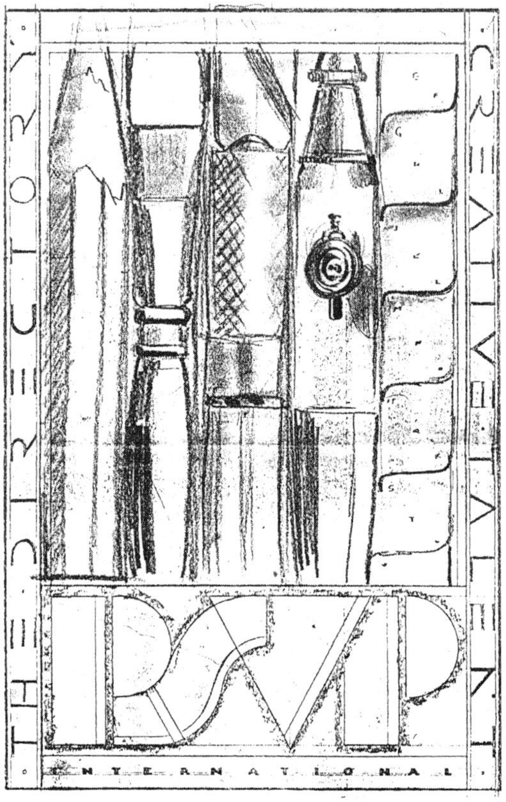
THE DIRECTORY
CREATIVE TALENT
RSVP

On developing a distinctive style: Around the time that Ed Caraeff and I split in 1975 I started using the airbrush. The first time was for the logo for a Commodores album. It was not only illustration—it was design. I don't paint with the airbrush, it's a design tool for me. Actually I do not consider myself an illustrator but rather use drawing, color, and other techniques to execute the design idea. The Commodores job gave way to the *Sergeant Pepper's Lonely Hearts Club Band* logo, used for the movie version and soundtrack album. After proving myself in the typographical arena I was given more album covers to do. Then came movie graphics, such as the image for *Hooper*, where I was combining logos with illustration. There are a few people who do that now, but when I started the field was virtually empty.

On designing album covers: The process can be difficult because I work with musicians who often have ideas of their own. But that can also be a challenging situation, and fruitful once you've earned their trust. More exciting, just a few weeks after an album is released it can potentially be seen all over the world. And if it's a big enough promotion the designer usually gets to do a Sunset Boulevard billboard. It was a great experience for me to have an image blown up to such mammoth proportions; but when I realized what kind of visibility I had, I began to think seriously about exactly what it was I was doing. Consequently I felt a tremendous responsibility to the public not to put out mediocre work.

About the covers for *RSVP*: This is a book that advertises the talents of illustrators, photographers, and designers. After advertising in it myself for the first few issues I offered do the cover. I realized that it had to have a year-long shelf life. It had to grab the art director's attention. Yet it was also an opportunity to develop new styles. The first one I did was number 5, which was very successful. And with number 6 a style emerged that got me excited: it was the beginning of my tile style, done in acrylic with airbrush and ruling pen. (I was interested in building a three-dimensional object on a two-

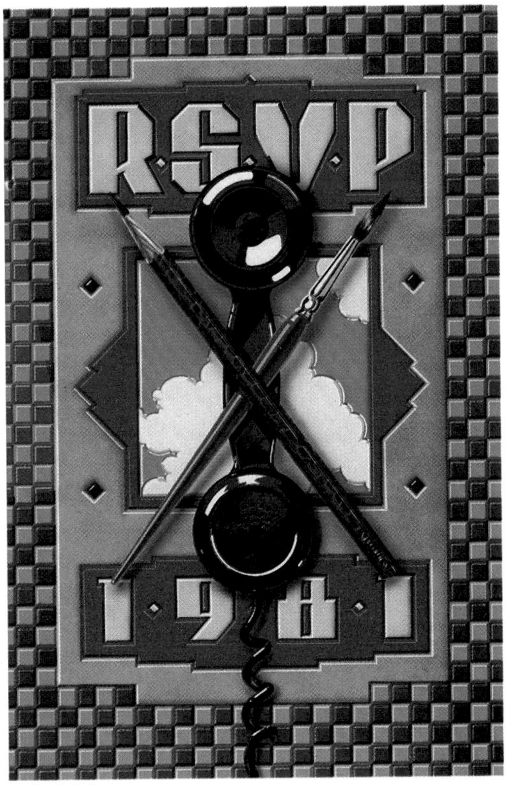
RSVP
1981

RSVP
THE DIRECTORY
7
OF CREATIVE
TALENT

RSVP #6 (1981), RSVP #7 (1982),
RSVP #8 (1983), RSVP #9 (1984),
Magazine covers
RSVP INC., *Client*
TOM NIKOSEY, *Designer*
TOM NIKOSEY, *Illustrator*
RICH LEBENSON AND KATHY
CREIGHTON, *Art Directors*

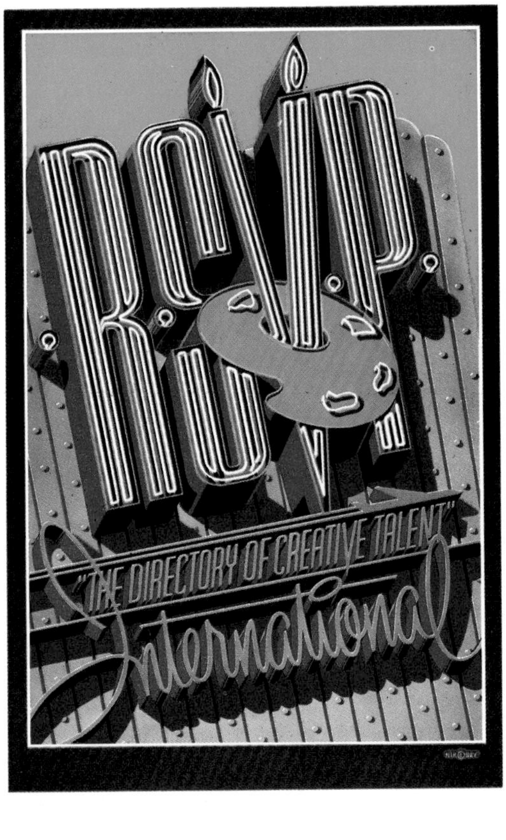
RSVP
"THE DIRECTORY OF CREATIVE TALENT"
International

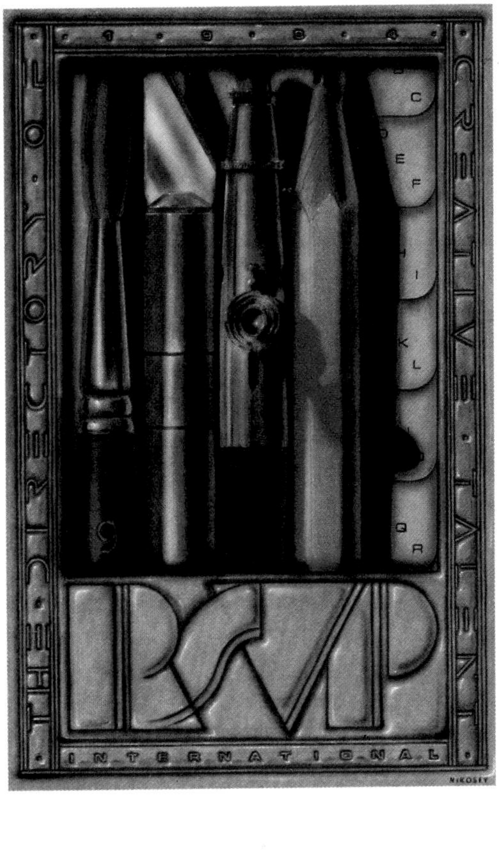
1984
THE DIRECTORY OF CREATIVE TALENT
RSVP
INTERNATIONAL
NIKOSEY

RSVP #10 (1985), RSVP #11 (1986),
RSVP #12, (1987), RSVP #13, (1988),
Magazine Covers
RSVP Inc., *Client*
Tom Nikosey, *Designer*
Tom Nikosey, *Illustrator*
Rich Lebenson and Kathy Creighton, *Art Directors*

TENTH
ANNIVERSARY
RSVP
THE DIRECTORY OF CREATIVE TALENT INTERNATIONAL
1985

INTERNATIONAL
RSVP
THE DIRECTORY OF CREATIVE TALENT
11

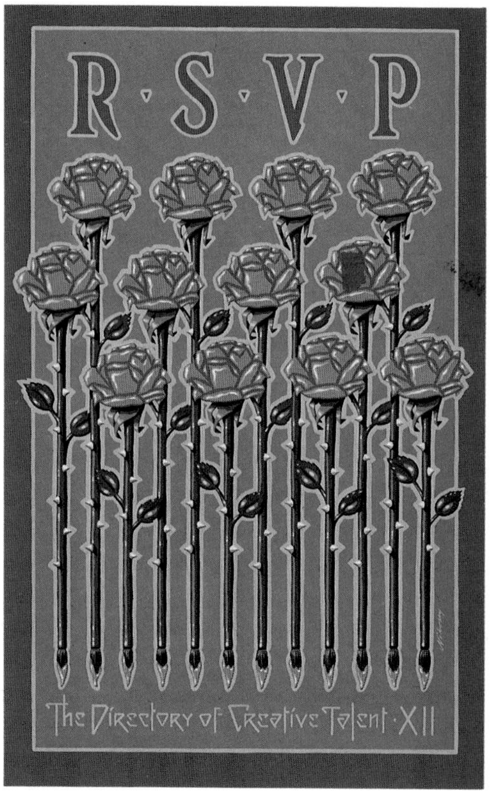
R · S · V · P
The Directory of Creative Talent · XII

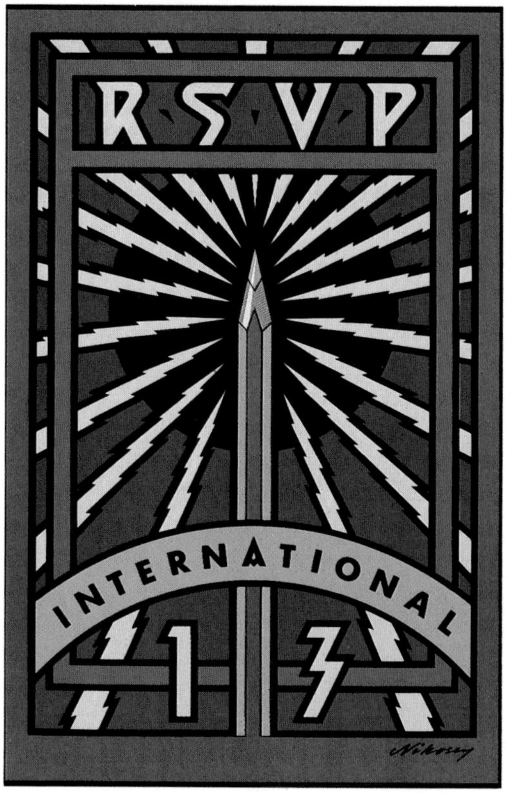
RSVP
INTERNATIONAL
13
Nikosey

dimensional surface.) It was also about designing the whole page, which is my preference. I always take the shape of the publication into consideration, and with few exceptions everything is planned specifically to fit that shape. I also came up with the idea to print it on front and back covers, so that the image is always visible.

With number 7 I wanted to do something more graphic, and developed the postage-stamp concept rendered in line. For number 8 the publisher was interested in highlighting the typography because it was the first international edition. I had to rethink the graphic problem entirely, and based my solution on the work of Robert Cottingham, a photorealist painter who focuses on the details of old neon signs. While he works with photographs, I had no real-life reference, so this comes completely from my imagination.

The following year I wanted to try pastels, which nobody expected given my previous media. But since I do have comparatively free rein, I could experiment. I wanted to create a mood with number 9. Mood, I believe, is obtainable with pastels. I was so excited by the results that I couldn't wait to hear the response from the publisher. I literally waited by the phone; but he didn't call. The next day I called him and asked, "What do you think?" "It's nice," he replied unenthusiastically. I had such high expectations that his indifferent response was shattering. I suggested that he live with it for a couple of days. And, sure enough, he called me back a day later and said that everybody loved it.

With number 10, the tenth-anniversary special, I wanted to do something that was literally going to be engraved in stone or metal or something that seemed long lasting. The original idea was influenced by an Italian coin. It was a brass material inset into a nickel-plated circle that was machined together. I saved it knowing that I would use it somehow for something. The *RSVP* cover is very similar; the outside material is like brushed steel, and the inside is made to approximate brass. Because of budget and deadline constraints I actually had to hand-paint the inside a brass color.

COMMODORES (1977), *Record album cover*
COMMODORES/MOTOWN RECORDS, *Client*
TOM NIKOSEY, *Designer*
TOM NIKOSEY, *Illustrator*
CARL OVERR, *Art Director*

On the conceptual link between type and image: I do not believe that this relationship has to be overstated. As a matter of fact, as much as I am energized by Ludwig Hohlwein, I draw inspiration from the Bauhaus and Swiss design too. When those designers chose type it was deliberate and functional. For me lettering must not be cosmetic alone, but conceptual. Taken to the next step, it should be integrated.

About readability: Some of my *RSVP* covers are more legible than others; the one I am working on currently has a somewhat obscured title. Since *RSVP* is distributed internationally the title is not as important to people who cannot read English. I want the cover to be immediately recognizable as an artist's directory, so I tend to focus on the image of the pencil or brush. Legibility is secondary to the impact of those icons in this particular project. However, I guess I'm from the old school of lettering artists in that I feel logotypes and lettering should be legible *and* drawn well.

MELANIE MARDER PARKS

A freelance illustrator, Melanie Marder Parks works in a variety of styles with a number of different media, including pen and ink, gouache, and paper cutout. She trained as a painter and calligrapher at The Cooper Union, and there her love for paintings and the decorative arts was formed. Her style varies as job requirements demand, with influences ranging from the twentieth-century Paris school to Russian Constructivist austerity to the English Arts and Crafts movement. This versatility is put to good use not only in the variety of work she does but in the expanded freedom—and interest—it offers her. Here she talks about several intricate book jacket assignments and a distinctive shopping bag she designed for Bloomingdale's.

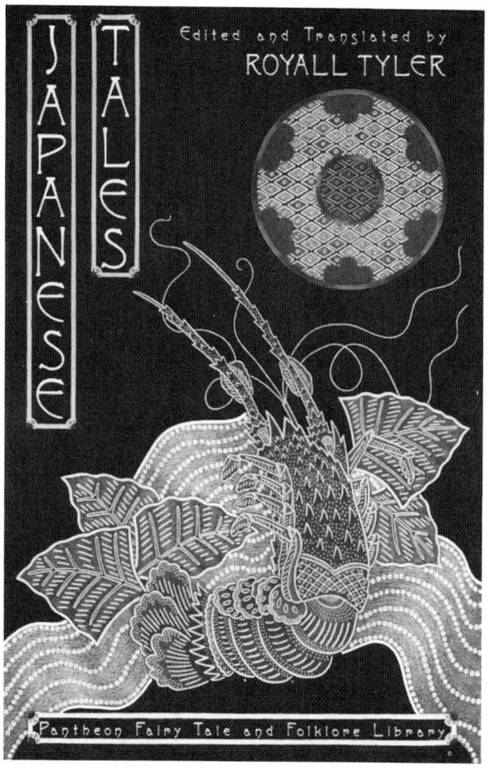
JAPANESE
TALES
Edited and Translated by
ROYALL TYLER
Pantheon Fairy Tale and Folklore Library

About the book jacket for *Japanese Tales:* When Louise Fili, art director of Pantheon Books, gave me an assignment to illustrate this book of folktales, she said: "Use your judgment. Do what you feel is right. Do something beautiful." Still Louise knew what image she wanted: a crayfish found on a kimono, which I then translated into pattern and line. She gave me a book on kimonos which inspired the patterns I produced. She also told me she wanted to run the type vertically to simulate Japanese characters. The media and style were left up to me, and I had to try quite a few things to finally reach the look I wanted. In this case the art director had quite a clear idea of what was required. Although that saved me a great deal of time and trouble, I often find research is one of the most stimulating and rewarding parts of a project.

I worked same size on a piece of black French paper with Prisma colors, gouache, and a little pastel pencil. The jacket has good luminosity, though the gouache was just straight Winsor & Newton. No tricks. No ruling pen. Just a double- and triple-zero brush. For the very fine lines I used an old English calligraphy pen.

About the jacket for *Yiddish Folktales:* When Louise gave me this assignment, she said, "Now, be honest. We need an intricate papercut for this in the style of old Yiddish cuts. Do you think you can do it?" I thought I could, though I had never done anything in quite this way. I had worked in cut paper before for a record cover, but in the manner of Matisse: painting pieces of paper, cutting them out, and gluing them down. This was a particular challenge, because instead of cutting out individual pieces of paper, I had to cut from a single piece, giving it the appearance of lace. I based the image on Jewish folk art decorations that are used for various festivals and religious occasions. The basic design of the cover was left to me, but we agreed that Louise would do the type because time was of the essence on this job. I knew that she would select just the right typeface. With this kind of title there is always the danger of the type looking like fake Hebrew lettering.

About the jacket for *Arab Folktales:* For reference Louise gave me a pile of the author's rare antique Arabic weavings, which she made me

YIDDISH
FOLKTALES
EDITED BY
BEATRICE SILVERMAN WEINREICH
TRANSLATED BY LEONARD WOLF
PANTHEON FAIRY TALE AND FOLKLORE LIBRARY

ARAB FOLKTALES
TRANSLATED & EDITED BY
INEA BUSHNAQ
PANTHEON FAIRY TALE & FOLKLORE LIBRARY

ARAB FOLKTALES (1986), *Book jacket*
PANTHEON BOOKS, *Client*
MELANIE MARDER PARKS, *Designer*
MELANIE MARDER PARKS, *Illustrator*
LOUISE FILI, *Art Director*

JAPANESE TALES (1987), *Book jacket*
PANTHEON BOOKS, *Client*
LOUISE FILI, *Designer*
MELANIE MARDER PARKS, *Illustrator*
LOUISE FILI, *Art Director*

YIDDISH FOLKTALES (1988), *Book jacket*
PANTHEON BOOKS, *Client*
LOUISE FILI, *Designer*
MELANIE MARDER PARKS, *Illustrator*
LOUISE FILI, *Art Director*

PALAIS-ROYAL (1987), *Book jacket*
ALFRED A. KNOPF, *Client*
MELANIE MARDER PARKS, *Designer*
MELANIE MARDER PARKS, *Illustrator*
SARA EISENMAN, *Art Director*

MODERN ITALIAN COOKING (1987), *Book jacket*
SIMON & SCHUSTER, *Client*
LOUISE FILI, *Designer*
MELANIE MARDER PARKS, *Illustrator*
LOUISE FILI, *Art Director*

PALAIS-ROYAL
A NOVEL BY
RICHARD SENNETT

MODERN
ITALIAN
COOKING
Exquisite food for every day—
Recipes from the contemporary culinary style
Fresh interpretations of traditional dishes
BIBA CAGGIANO

promise to guard with my life. I suspect she knew of my interest in textiles and remarked that the stitches on the weaving reminded her of some of my work. She also knows that my work is quite varied, that I do not like doing the same thing over and over. I selected patterns with slight irregularities and unique color combinations—not the clichéd tapestries. Then I reinvented the patterns, emphasizing the stitching look. I put quite a few coats of gouache on the finish to build up the surface and make the colors rich. I also made a few attempts at hand lettering the title. At first they were unsuccessful because I tried to make the letters true to original embroidery and the results were overcomplicated. However, the finished lettering does have the spirit of weaving and is at the same time legible.

On calligraphy, typography, and illustration: Calligraphy means the art of beautiful writing. If it is not done beautifully with the pen or brush or quill the first time, it's not really calligraphy; everything else is hand lettering (letters that are drawn, built up, painted). Calligraphy is the foundation of typography. Chancery cursive, for example, became the italic in roman typeforms.

Some people devote their lives to the nuances of type and lettering but I love letterforms when I can incorporate them into my illustration. Of course, with book jackets lettering and illustration must be balanced. I tend to favor making the illustration more important than the type. It is a personal preference: I think a jacket is much more attractive when there is an image on which to focus—though I have seen much handsome work done with type alone. As long as a jacket has beauty and harmony it will be a success.

About the jacket for *Palais-Royal:* Sara Eisenman, the former art director of Knopf, had seen a decorative map of India I had done incorporating calligraphy and delicate patterns and she wanted the same feeling for this book. She gave me quite a lot of good source material, including a wonderful black-and-white photograph of the Galerie d'Orleans, which I had to redraw because I wanted a head-on perspective. It had to be accurate and at the same time have an old-world

feeling of an engraving. The main character was the architect for this particular *galerie* in the Palais-Royal in Paris, among the earliest glass-and-steel structures, built in the mid-nineteenth century. My lettering was based on the Mayflower Windowboxes sample and done in brush.

On the jacket for *Modern Italian Cooking*: Again I worked on this with Louise Fili, who designed and art directed it. I also did the interior drawings for the book, which are in my other style—my hard-edged graphic style. I started learning how to work with French curves and such tools when I was at Columbia Records for a year after college, and I really resisted it because it seemed so mechanical. But ten years later I began to enjoy the process. I actually had started working in a "constructivist" style for an article on Russia in *Harper's* magazine, designing nearly a whole alphabet and borders. From that work came my 1983 Bloomingdale's shopping bag. That was a thrill, seeing my art carried around the streets of New York. I also incorporated this style for newspaper illustration; the bold graphic shapes suit newsprint well. None of the images were ever actually swiped, but they are in the spirit of the avant-garde Russian work.

This was one of the more difficult assignments. The people at Simon & Schuster, the publisher, were not exactly sure what they wanted. Louise and I thought that since they liked the style for the interior drawings, perhaps that was the way to go. They wanted something modern and elegant, but our first couple of modern and elegant attempts were unsuccessful. We even tried, without satisfaction, to come up with an icon that would symbolize Italian cooking. Finally, after a few meetings with the S & S art director and the cookbook editor, we decided to do a more Postmodern interpretation of antipasto, a huge replica of which now hangs in the author's Sacramento restaurant. Everyone was very happy with this!

Bloomingdale's Shopping Bag (1983),
New Year promotion
Bloomingdale's, New York, *Client*
Melanie Marder Parks, *Designer*
Richard Hsu, *Art Director*

DANIEL PELAVIN

A graduate of Michigan State, where he majored in advertising, Daniel Pelavin began his career doing phototypesetting and layouts as an apprentice for a Detroit design firm. He developed his skills as an illustrator through drafting and industrial drawing and still uses a drafting machine. However, rather than languish as an assistant in a backwater commercial art studio, he developed a graphic personality that borrows liberally from past styles and blends elements of the thirties, forties, and fifties into a contemporary visual language. Upon arriving in New York, in 1979, he received editorial assignments and soon afterward began designing book covers. Here Pelavin describes the creative and technical process.

On early influences: I first became interested in lettering as a child when my aunt Rose showed me how to write my name. Then I was given a rubber stamp set (a thirties alphabet with outline-shaded lettering), which I played with for hours at a stretch. It was totally absorbing and probably left an indelible memory.

About drawing: I knew how to draw because I knew how to look and see. Drawing isn't something one has talent for; it's something that one must be willing to become good at. It's not so much a matter of eye-hand coordination, or of the ability to visualize in two dimensions, but rather of forcing oneself not to give up the first or two hundred fiftieth time one makes a poor drawing.

I have a particular kind of visual pathology, limited binocular vision. I do not see depth but perceive it in other ways. Basically I see everything as flat, which is is not a problem with my eyes but with the configuration of the pathways to the brain. I entertain the theory that it has affected the way I draw.

About the union of design and illustration: The positive aspects of this are not widely shared. I would say that the closest most designers come to the process is picking a color for a headline from the illustration. This is because illustration is commonly regarded as the reproduction of a painting. If you gave sodium pentathol to any editor at any magazine they still would not be able to tell you why they *need* art. Photography, yes, because it is "documentation," but art is irrelevant.

Bad effects in the jacket for *Sound Effects*: This did not turn out well for me because the color selection was the art director's, not mine. I had never used these colors before, and never will again. The book is set in the sixties, and though I did not deliberately pick a period style, I wanted to show a jukebox because it is the Pandora's box of rock and roll. The lettering is the emblem, so I wanted believable jukebox colors like orange and yellow. It is my design interpreted by someone with a different color sense—me dressed up in different clothes. It has been part of the growing

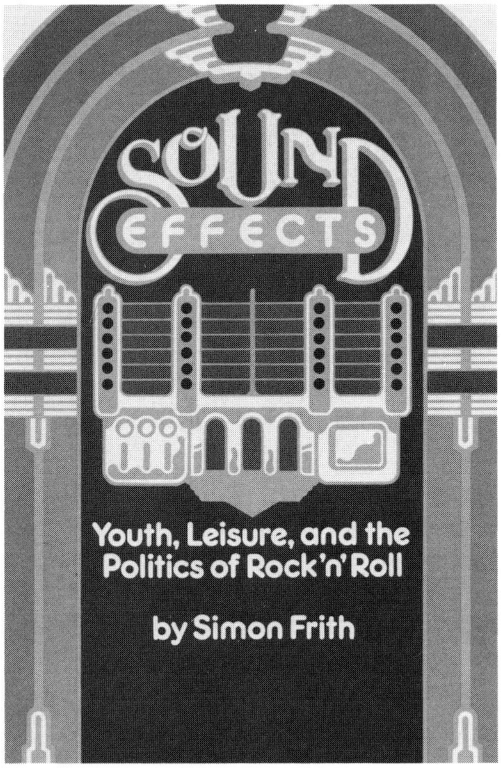
SOUND
EFFECTS
Youth, Leisure, and the
Politics of Rock'n'Roll
by Simon Frith

process to learn that when people force changes on my work I am usually troubled forever. Now my policy is to vigorously avoid allowing art directors to tamper with the colors I choose.

On the typography for *People Will Talk*: This is a gossip book written by John Kobal, a movie buff who had interviewed famous people from the thirties and forties. The editors insisted that all the names appear on the cover. I did a sketch which I thought looked very elegant. But I was made to change the *C* in "Conversation" because they felt the subhead did not relate well enough to the names. The type is all hand-lettered. I often design typefaces to complement the forms within the illustration.

About the "Bad Type" poster: The idea for this die-cut poster done for a typographer comes from old matchbook advertising. The purpose was to make customers aware of the variations that can be achieved using the right typefaces. I attempted to show that the type can relate to the image; for instance, if the drawing is hard-edged, so is the type.

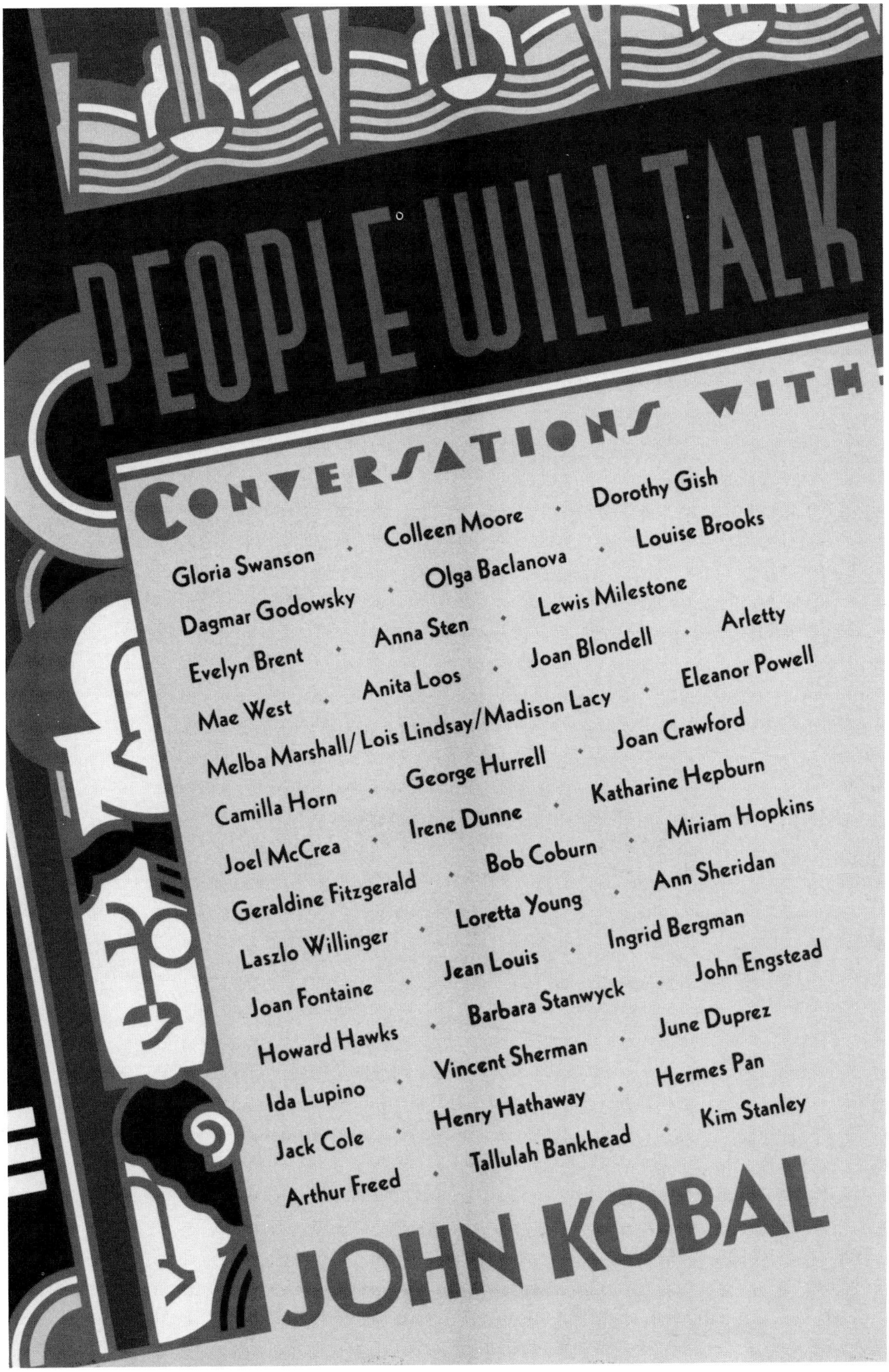
PEOPLE WILL TALK
CONVERSATIONS WITH:
Gloria Swanson · Colleen Moore · Dorothy Gish
Dagmar Godowsky · Olga Baclanova · Louise Brooks
Evelyn Brent · Anna Sten · Lewis Milestone
Mae West · Anita Loos · Joan Blondell · Arletty
Melba Marshall/ Lois Lindsay/Madison Lacy · Eleanor Powell
Camilla Horn · George Hurrell · Joan Crawford
Joel McCrea · Irene Dunne · Katharine Hepburn
Geraldine Fitzgerald · Bob Coburn · Miriam Hopkins
Laszlo Willinger · Loretta Young · Ann Sheridan
Joan Fontaine · Jean Louis · Ingrid Bergman
Howard Hawks · Barbara Stanwyck · John Engstead
Ida Lupino · Vincent Sherman · June Duprez
Jack Cole · Henry Hathaway · Hermes Pan
Arthur Freed · Tallulah Bankhead · Kim Stanley
JOHN KOBAL

PEOPLE WILL TALK (1986), *Book jacket*
ALFRED A. KNOPF, *Client*
DANIEL PELAVIN, *Designer*
DANIEL PELAVIN, *Illustrator*
SARA EISENMAN, *Art Director*

SOUND EFFECTS (1982), *Book jacket*
PANTHEON BOOKS, *Client*
DANIEL PELAVIN, *Designer*
DANIEL PELAVIN, *Illustrator*
LOUISE FILI, *Art Director*

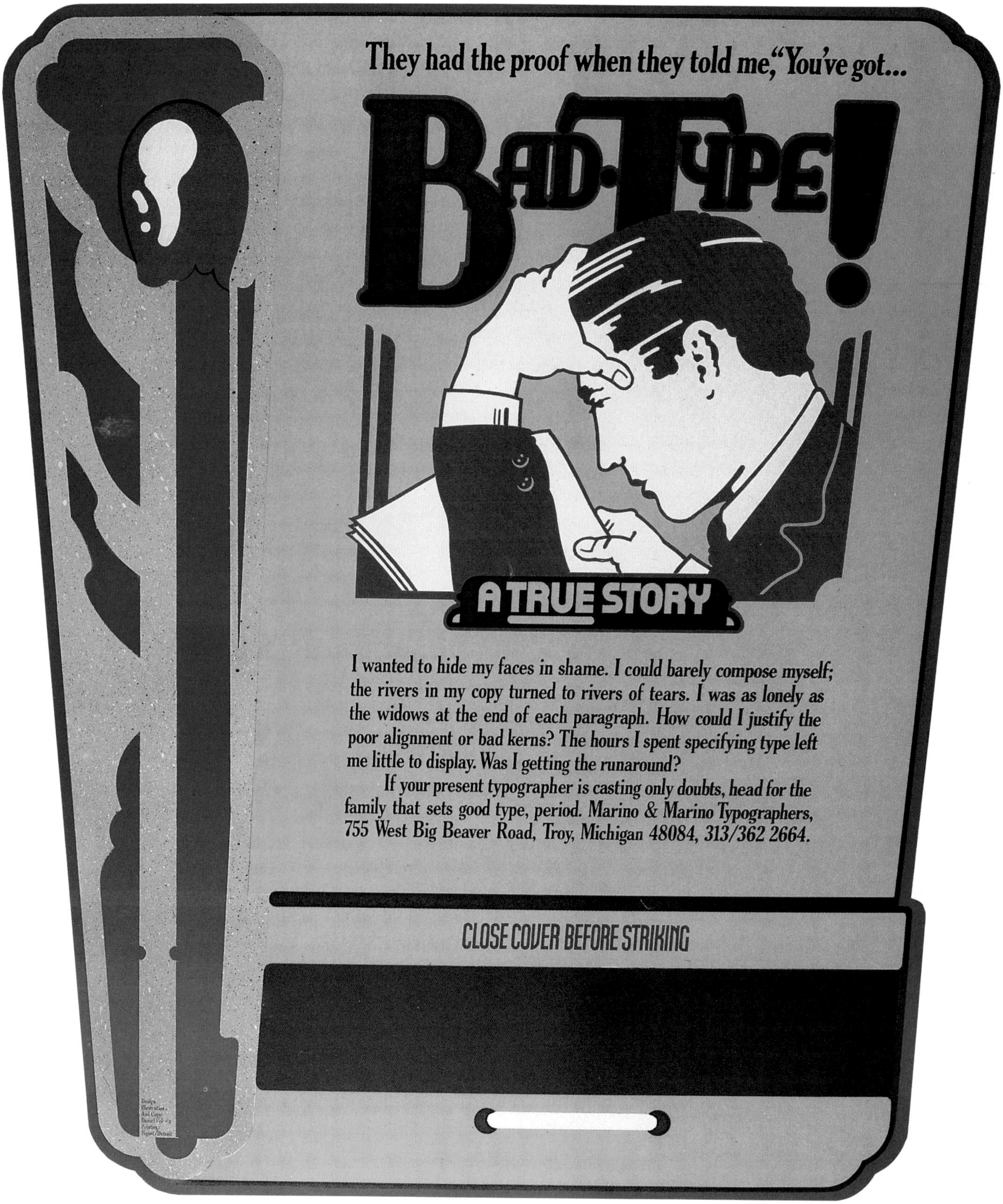
They had the proof when they told me, "You've got...
BAD TYPE!
A TRUE STORY
I wanted to hide my faces in shame. I could barely compose myself; the rivers in my copy turned to rivers of tears. I was as lonely as the widows at the end of each paragraph. How could I justify the poor alignment or bad kerns? The hours I spent specifying type left me little to display. Was I getting the runaround?
If your present typographer is casting only doubts, head for the family that sets good type, period. Marino & Marino Typographers, 755 West Big Beaver Road, Troy, Michigan 48084, 313/362 2664.
CLOSE COVER BEFORE STRIKING

THE CONDO LUX
VACATIONER'S
GUIDE TO
CONDOMINIUM
RENTALS
IN THE
SOUTHWEST
AND HAWAII
GET MORE FOR YOUR MONEY

THE CONDO LUX VACATIONER'S GUIDE TO CONDOMINIUM RENTALS IN THE SOUTHWEST AND HAWAII (1985),
Book cover (not used)
VINTAGE BOOKS, *Client*
DANIEL PELAVIN, *Designer*
DANIEL PELAVIN, *Illustrator*
JUDITH LOESER, *Art Director*

BAD TYPE (1979), *Poster*
MARINO & MARINO TYPOGRAPHERS, *Client*
DANIEL PELAVIN, *Designer*
DANIEL PELAVIN, *Illustrator*
JAY MARINO, *Art Director*

About the cover for *The Condo Lux Vacationer's Guide to Condominium Rentals in the Southwest and Hawaii:* The type for this is intentionally a period style conforming to old vacation guidebooks and travel brochures. I always draw upon different time periods for inspiration, going back and forth between them because in certain contexts it attracts attention more profoundly than doing an anonymous contemporary design. I am not locked into a particular period, but I can solve a 1980s problem with a 1940s solution if I use the correct symbolism. The historical reference taps into a sense of nostalgia or real memories that are tucked away. In fact, whenever an art director asks for something "current" or "today," I say everything I do is current. With this cover, the nostalgic look was more inviting than a recent photograph. But sometimes I show ideas like this to people who are conceptually blind. They've been trained to understand that rational or linear thinking is the only way to solve problems. They have no idea of lateral or visual thinking. They do not understand that images can be used as solutions.

On making visual noise: There's no secret to the way I work. It is like conducting an orchestra: if the music is loud it will be annoying; if it is too soft, people will go to sleep. Modulation keeps the audience interested. Visual communication is the same idea: while there are technical aspects of my work that remain constant, my line, shape, and color will change periodically to keep the viewer interested.

JAVIER ROMERO

A former law student turned successful advertising designer and art director in Spain, Javier Romero started his own ad agency and honed his drawing skills on the job. In Europe the total design is a venerable tradition. And though not in the forefront of the great European graphic design movements such as Art Nouveau and Art Deco, Spanish design certainly has been influenced by them—and so, in turn, has Romero. With a generous grant from the Spanish government, he left his homeland in 1980 to seek out greater challenges. Settling in New York City he opened a small studio and developed his now characteristic hard-edged Deco mannerisms, which he has given a contemporary twist and applied to a variety of assignments, from book jackets to *Time* magazine covers. Here he discusses a few of his recent assignments and, more important, his method of teaching design and illustration as one integrated discipline.

W O W
B R I N G O N T H E M E N
O O
W O W

On his first work experiences in New York: I came with a lot of energy, and was dying to do work . . . any work. My partner was a former record company art director, and he got me a lot of small record company jobs—which was fine, because I learned that when the budget is low the creative freedom is usually high.

On erasing the distinction between design and illustration: Here one is either a designer or an illustrator, and American students are never urged to major in both. My classes at Parsons School of Design and the School of Visual Arts are intended to join the two disciplines into one. An illustrator can be a designer and vice versa; and each can benefit from the other because greater knowledge allows room to expand one's ideas.

In Europe there is a different perception of design, illustration, and advertising as one related act. An art director is more versatile and does everything—the lettering, the illustration, and so on. There are those who are exclusively illustrators, of course; but they are fewer in number and are neatly pigeonholed.

Most of my students have a certain amount of professional experience, but still I have designers who are afraid to illustrate and illustrators who refuse to design. When I talk to designers and art directors, most apologize because they do not know how to draw. I say, "Don't excuse yourself, it's okay. But by the way, you can draw if you want." I believe that one should not be afraid of drawing, because so many more things are possible than one might think.

About the fallacies attached to drawing: Those who are afraid of drawing think of it as an exact rendering akin to photography with a pencil. That is not the right way to experience the process, because in this era of on-the-spot media, drawing is now a very personal vision. In fact, the closer one gets to reality, the less interesting it becomes. We went through that realistic process centuries ago, when great painters virtually photographed people and landscapes with their pens and brushes. It has been done, and we should move ahead. If someone wants to draw a chair, it needn't be a fancy, detailed rendering; it can be simply the impression or outline of a chair.

I tell my students to "try to be you. . . ," and as they get closer to expressing what they really *feel,* they become freer to play with color and experiment with shapes—to look at things with a fresh eye.

About having a distinctive style: A style is only a tool for the moment, and I am sure that in a couple of years I am going to be doing something else. In fact, one of the projects I am working on at the moment is computer-aided animation.

I've heard some people say that in a few years the illustrator, as we know him or her, will dis-

THE FLIRTS
HELPLESS
MAXI-SINGLE

M-11
BEATBOXBOYS
MEMO
12" SINGLE
A. give me my money!
einstein
yum yum-eat em up

GIVE ME MY MONEY (1984), *Record album cover for the Beatbox Boys*
MEMO RECORDS, *Client*
JAVIER ROMERO, *Designer*
JAVIER ROMERO, *Illustrator*
JAVIER ROMERO, *Art Director*

(opposite, top)
BRING ON THE MEN (1983), *Record album cover for Wow*
MEMO RECORDS, *Client*
JAVIER ROMERO, *Designer*
JAVIER ROMERO, *Illustrator*
JAVIER ROMERO, *Art Director*

(opposite, bottom)
HELPLESS (1985), *Record album cover for The Flirts*
"O" RECORDS, *Client*
JAVIER ROMERO, *Designer*
JAVIER ROMERO, *Illustrator*
JAVIER ROMERO, *Art Director*

appear. That use of the traditional materials will be outmoded by digital technology. I use a Macintosh computer to generate 90 percent of my work. Most of the time I even provide the separations on the disk. In the not-too-distant future an illustrator will be able to send all art through the telephone rather than waiting for an overnight courier. And if the client wants something changed, it can be discussed on the phone and done immediately. It allows one the time to spend on the creative side rather than hours and hours with a Rapidograph.

On typography: Communicating with type is something I learned in the United States; in Spain there is very little teaching on this subject. Here there is just so much more information that comes in newsletters, trade magazines, and in the environment.

About the shopping bag for Bloomingdale's: I had been working with John Jay, the creative director for Bloomingdale's, for a while before working on the shopping bag. We did some labels, packaging, and posters for the store. He is an excellent creative director because he does not impose too much direction on me. The worst art directors are those who direct you so much that all the life is taken out of a project. The best are those who call on you for what you *can* do, and just talk about the problem without imposing tight sketches of what you *should* do.

SUMMER BAG (1987), *Shopping bag*
BLOOMINGDALE'S, *Client*
JAVIER ROMERO, *Designer*
JAVIER ROMERO, *Illustrator*
JOHN JAY, *Art Director*

That was the case with the bag; it just seemed to happen naturally.

About the book jacket for *The Death of Rhythm & Blues:* Louise Fili at Pantheon Books is another art director like that. We will talk about a book jacket and then I'll feel free to come up with something. With this I originally worked on the type, but she decided to make the final rendering. We discussed it from the beginning, however, so that even though I did not do the lettering it was still a well-integrated piece.

I always have to show a sketch with her, but it is very loose. Indeed, Fili will choose from my portfolio the approach that is appropriate, and I follow my instincts from there.

More about instinct: The union of all the rational (e.g., typographical and informational) with the emotional or pictorial elements can be very effective in expressing feelings. But sometimes I get so many ideas that I cannot render them fast enough. Often it is frustrating because it takes too much time to put the idea in some reproducible form. What kills me is that my ideas go faster than my hands.

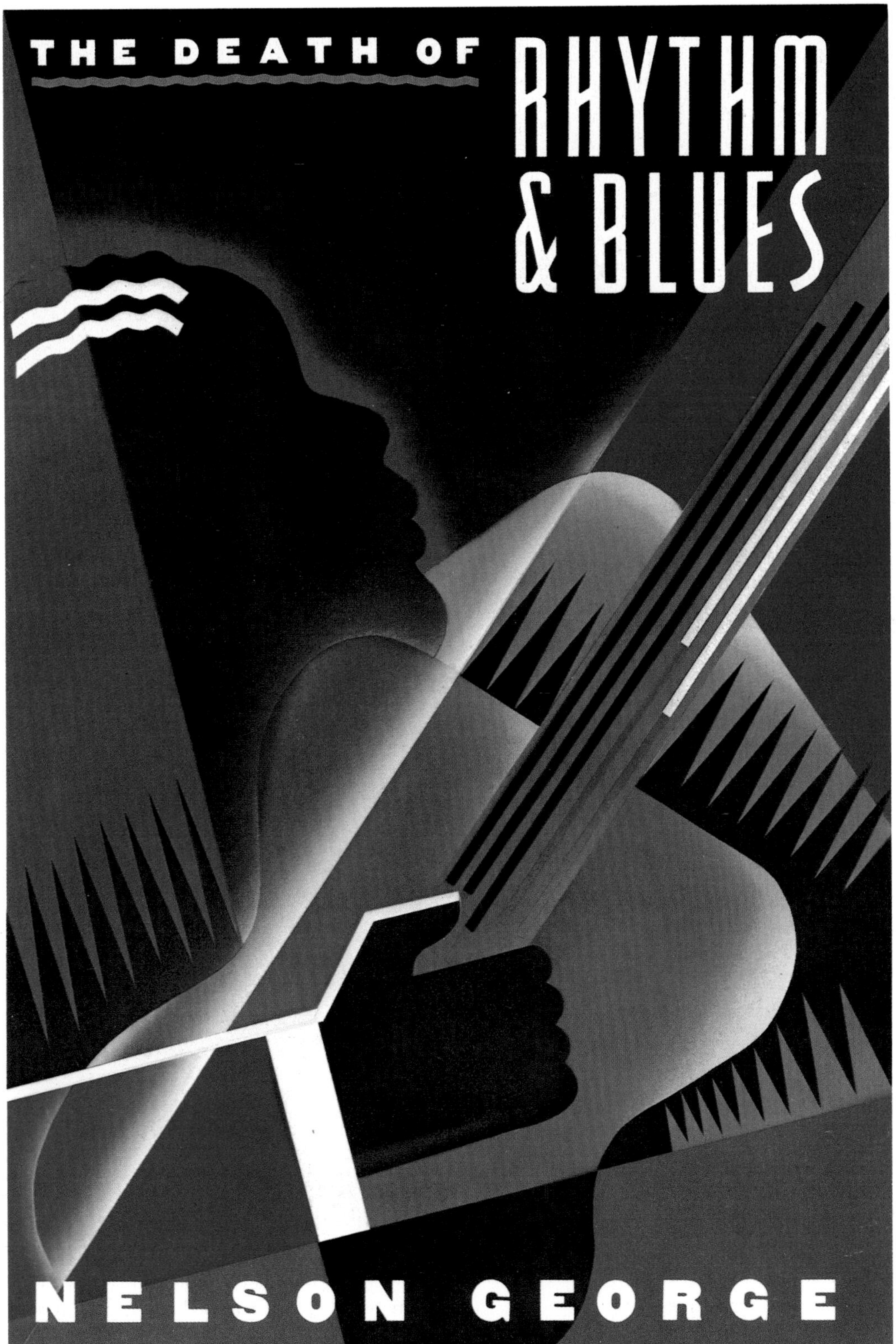
THE DEATH OF
RHYTHM
& BLUES
NELSON GEORGE

THE DEATH OF RHYTHM & BLUES (1988), *Book jacket*
PANTHEON BOOKS, *Client*
LOUISE FILI, *Designer*
JAVIER ROMERO, *Illustrator*
LOUISE FILI, *Art Director*

LAURIE ROSENWALD

A graduate of the Rhode Island School of Design, Laurie Rosenwald has become a truly international designer. Her work has taken her to Tokyo, Paris, Milan, and London, among other cities. In Paris she designed a line of products based on the Metro ticket and advertising for several retail stores. In Tokyo she designed and illustrated for magazines and fashion clients. Rosenwald is an eclecticist with a modernist bias. Her work is rooted in the traditions of the mid-twentieth-century posterists, and though she does "purely" decorative illustration for magazines, her preference is for the total integration of type and image. Here she discusses a few disparate assignments that show her versatility with forms and media and her consistent employment of drawing as the primary métier.

On design and illustration: This process is all just commercial art. As designers we do posters, T-shirts, book covers . . . there's nothing very esoteric or rarefied about it. It's a down-to-earth art: we use it and see it everyday, and it's disposable. When I was at Rhode Island School of Design the focus was theoretical; many of the teachers had gone to Basel, or were otherwise descendents of the Bauhaus and Swiss schools, and rigidly believed in simplicity. Conversely, I studied everything from painting and illustration to type. I was influenced by poster artists such as Toulouse-Lautrec, A. M. Cassandre, and Paul Colin, but I appreciated Herbert Bayer too.

What I do is not really "illustration," but rather "drawing." Illustration—at least the way it is taught today—is very concept-oriented. This is fine, it's just not what I do. It's not that I don't have concepts, just that I focus on the formal aspects of the craft such as the line quality, the way the thing *looks*—its clarity and straightforwardness. Someone like David Suter is a brilliant artist, strong because his concepts are intelligent and his drawing is superb. But every time he sits down to do a drawing I'm certain he doesn't begin by asking himself whether he should use gouache or crayons. He employs a rather consistent line quality and relies on problem solving. I, on the other hand, take either a simple or complex problem and simply try to make it *grab your eyeball.* I go for the response that "that looks different from anything I've ever seen!"

There are, however, certain concepts I am proud of. Once for a newspaper ad I had to promote a super-red lipstick and nail polish. Well, how does one do that in black-and-white? Instead of drawing the lipstick itself, I drew a man and then kissed the drawing on the cheek so it looked like a big smooch. Around his neck was a hand with long nails to signify the nail polish.

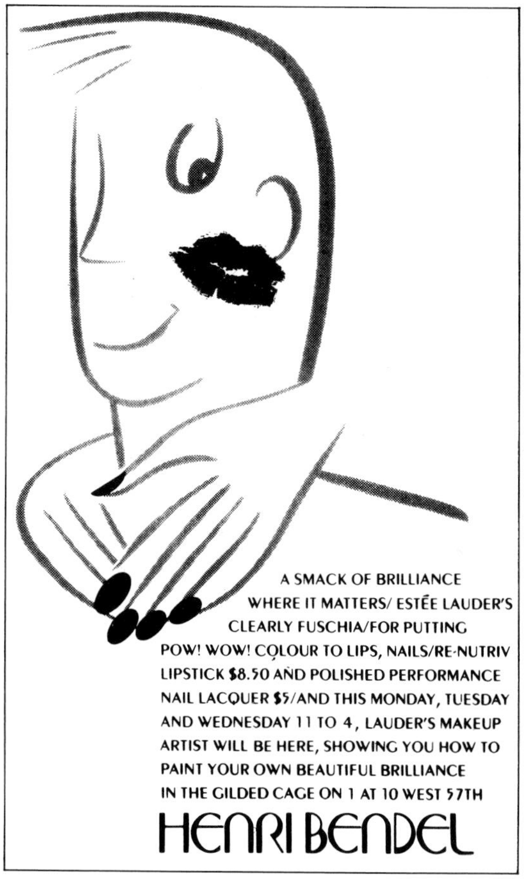
A SMACK OF BRILLIANCE
WHERE IT MATTERS/ ESTÉE LAUDER'S
CLEARLY FUSCHIA/FOR PUTTING
POW! WOW! COLOUR TO LIPS, NAILS/RE-NUTRIV
LIPSTICK $8.50 AND POLISHED PERFORMANCE
NAIL LACQUER $5/AND THIS MONDAY, TUESDAY
AND WEDNESDAY 11 TO 4, LAUDER'S MAKEUP
ARTIST WILL BE HERE, SHOWING YOU HOW TO
PAINT YOUR OWN BEAUTIFUL BRILLIANCE
IN THE GILDED CAGE ON 1 AT 10 WEST 57TH
HENRI BENDEL

About experimentation: Though I do not want to sound like I indulge my imagination with every assignment, I usually play out different things I am interested in at the time. It sounds scary, but I experiment with my clients a lot. When I get an assignment I never immediately know what I am going to do, because it is always going to be different from the last thing. For almost every project, I have a different approach or media. Sometimes I work only in black-and-white; other times in oil paint. I've worked with photographs, and I've done things that are 3D. I sometimes supply completely pre-separated art and other times not. Currently, I am doing something with Xerox copies. This is one area where I agree with the saying "form follows function." I usually allow the problem to determine the solution. Moreover, and perhaps most important, I work incredibly fast.

On the integration of type and image: I always think in terms of a one-shot image—it is the most natural way, especially when the idea and the execution come from one mind. Too often illustrators merely fill a space provided by an art director. I do not mind doing this on occasion, but I much prefer to design and draw the whole thing. Collaboration can be great, but specialization can sap a work of its energy.

TEAM
WilliWear
Willi Smith
Willi
Wear

T-SHIRT CELEBRATING BOUTIQUE OPENING (1988)
WILLIWEAR/WILLI SMITH, *Client*
LAURIE ROSENWALD, *Illustrator*
MARK BOZEK, *Creative Director*

ADVERTISEMENT FOR LIPSTICK (1983)
HENRI BENDEL, *Client*
LAURIE ROSENWALD, *Designer*
LAURIE ROSENWALD, *Illustrator*
PAT PETERSON, *Art Director*

Defining a successful piece of work: Does it sell the client's wares or ideas? Does it look wonderful? Does it make people think about an idea in a new way, yet is still accessible? I am not interested in making something that forces people to question the *meaning!* I often think designers go out of their way to make things incomprehensible and remove themselves from people. Sometimes I get too arty, as well; however, I'd rather fight to be right on the line than give in to "lowest common denominator" thinking from the beginning. You don't set out just to please the client or yourself in a vacuum. The trick is to succeed at both.

About the shirts for Williwear: Willi Smith, the late founder of Williwear, used to live in my building and we were good friends. I did the T-shirt design when the New York shop was opened. It says "London-Paris-New York" be-

Fall Preview (1984), *Magazine cover*
New York magazine, *Client*
Laurie Rosenwald, *Designer*
Laurie Rosenwald, *Illustrator*
Robert Best, *Art Director*

cause that is where the flagship shops are located. They wanted to communicate an international feeling, so I made it into a grand cartoon—not only using the famous landmarks but the cultural quirks of these cities too. It is not fall-on-the-floor comedy, nor is it a high concept, but it is charming.

Obviously I could not have made a sketch for this—it *is* a sketch. In fact, I prefer not to make sketches on the understanding that if one idea is rejected I can do others. I work as a sort of cook. I get a lot of ingredients together and then combine them in various ways. Though I sometimes sketch reference points for myself, I rarely map out an entire composition. I take pains to make things look exciting and at the same time be sneakily organized, clear, and direct. I want to be *crazy* and still communicate.

Doing the "Fall Preview" issue of *New York* magazine: Here is an example of process: this job included the cover, title page, and around forty inside pieces. I should not have done them as pre-separated art because it ended up being phenomenally complex, but I wanted the colors to approach the look of a silk-screen print even though it was a four-color process printing. I got the look by indicating percentages of color rather than by separating a painting. I did them all with black crayon. Some have as many as ten or twelve overlays. That times forty equals a nightmare, but it looks great.

About the *Passion* cover: Sometimes I never see the color until the piece is printed. With this cover of a Parisian magazine, I could have used any combination; it came down to knowing what worked well together in terms of dark and light, hot and cold, and so on. I basically select bright, attractive colors. I think some people get awfully scared about color being too gaudy, but I look at Matisse, or the Fauves, or David Hockney: they all use the brightest colors—green, purple, yellow, orange, blue—and they look great together. There is nothing to be afraid of!

About working in France: Unlike the United States, where my advertising clientele has been limited, I have done big posters advertising department stores, which appear in the Paris Metro. The French have a tradition of using abstract art. Here we have a Norman Rockwell tradition: the closer a drawing resembles a photograph, the better it is. This "American" aesthetic is surfacing more in Europe, however; but they are still open to Modern art. Take the Monoprix store—the French Woolworths: I've done very abstract designs for their mainstream products.

. . . And working in Japan: The Japanese have such a fascination with things American that I have done many section headings for a Japanese magazine that incorporate Americanisms in seeming nonsequiturs: "Commuter in Tokyo," "Department Store Deli," "Bread Club," and the grammatically incorrect "Best Restaurant and After Five." I made them correct certain mistakes but they refused to change others because to their ear it sounded funny. In fact there is a conscious misuse of English—whatever sounds good is right. There is a lot about Japanese culture that I'll never understand. I don't even want to try, because it makes the jobs more interesting.

About the windows for Bergdorf Goodman in New York: I had painted a mural in a New York disco that came to the attention of the Bergdorf art director, who asked me to do a window for their Jean-Paul Gaultier collection. Gaultier gets his inspiration from the street (even though he charges wild prices for his shirts), so they asked me to do something that had a street flavor. I'm good at doing things that are real New Yorky. I drew the Korean nail salons, Gray's Papaya restaurant stands, and "Live at Five" TV news show. I made masks for all the mannequins so that they would blend into the background drawing. I also did caricatures of Mayor Koch, Bess Myerson (before the scandal broke), and some of the models in the Gaultier fashion show.

On art and life: Owing to my way of working, I usually only get jobs that are right for me. Hence I try to make challenges for myself so my work will be an interesting way to spend the day.

gala special issue
$1.75 • SEPTEMBER 17, 1984
NEW YORK
Fall
84
Preview
JESSICA LANGE
Movies • Theater • Art • Music
TV • Books • Dance • Photography
Sports • Architecture • Nightlife
Fashion • Restaurants • Shopping

My life and my work are the same thing. My painting is no different from my design. I don't go to work from nine to five, I live and work in a big sort of *mush.*

It gives me great pleasure to see people walking around New York with my shopping bags. In a way, I am just as happy to see them in the trash bin or gutter too, because what I do should not be precious. Indeed design has become a snob thing, which is very much contrary to the

FALL PREVIEW (1985), *Magazine cover*
PASSION MAGAZINE, *Client*
LAURIE ROSENWALD, *Designer*
LAURIE ROSENWALD, *Illustrator*

Portraits by G. Gastaud • Les Halles Report • Fiction by E. Limonov • NY & London Disp
THE MAGAZINE OF PARIS
PASSION
PARIS
FALL
PREVIEW
1985
DANCE·CINEMA·SPORTS·BOOKS·ART·FASH
THEATER·POLITICS·SAINTS
RESTAURANTS

Nail Sculpting

Window Display Featuring Jean-Paul Gaultier Fashion (1984)
Bergdorf Goodman, New York, *Client*
Laurie Rosenwald, *Designer*
Laurie Rosenwald, *Illustrator*
Richard Currier and Angela Patterson, *Creative Directors*

Bauhaus. Is that how far design has come—to be more elitist than fine art ever was? Most of my clients, being in the fashion or entertainment business, support that notion. But I don't want to be perceived as contributing to that. I am a Modernist in that I want things to be attractive and clean, not difficult and uncomfortable.

On Postmodernism: This era is about combining old things in a new way—and that is good because we cannot pretend that we live in a vacuum. Not only have I been inundated with TV, but my parents used to take me to museums all over the world. That confluence of cultures has to be reflected in my work.

MICHAEL SCHWAB

Raised in Oklahoma and educated at East Texas State University, the School of Visual Arts in New York, and the Art Center College of Design in Pasedena, Michael Schwab now has a studio in San Francisco. Known for his illustrative posters, he combines 1930s nostalgia with modernist simplicity; his work is characterized by its large, flat areas of color, dramatic perspectives, and bold, graphic images of archetypal people. He works from photographs to achieve a certain realism that he cannot achieve from a figure drawing, and then stylizes his subjects so that the image has a universal quality. His work for Wilkes Bashford, a major retailer in San Francisco, has given him the freedom to create a distinctive visual identity. Here he discusses that process and his jobs for other fashion clients.

About his early relationship with word and picture: I started out as a freelance lettering artist. Indeed it was because of my skill at lettering that I could get enough work to pay rent in those early days. My sketchbook was full of type and images that were simple, graphic, and powerful. I am quite good at working out positive and negative space and dealing with color. I was always fascinated by the simple image, one that's been pared down to the most striking color, shape, and, ultimately, statement. Lettering or illustration is the same thing to me—it's the manipulation of shapes to sculpt them to their simplest forms; it's working with space in a dramatic way—black and white, positive and negative. But lettering usually takes a bigger part in the "theatrics" of my projects. As you can see, at times I give lettering a major role.

About the impact of lettering on a drawing: One of the primary influences on my work is probably the German poster artist Ludwig Hohlwein. He was a master at integrating type and image, and he produced the most powerful graphic advertisements of his era [1920s–1930s] without resorting to useless decoration. His posters are complete entities; the painted image and brushed letterforms cannot be successfully divorced. Likewise, when I'm drawing a person's face or a landscape, I do it in a stylistic and expressive manner similar to the way I do lettering, as you can see in the Wilkes Bashford work. I use hand lettering almost exclusively so that I can create the appropriate emotion. This means that all the graphic elements in my posters must be done in concert to achieve an overall emotional statement.

On the Wilkes Bashford posters and postcards: These were used to promote storewide sales and personal appearances by famous designers in the store. They seem simple, yet I put much time into them to create the right contours and curves. You'll see that I'll do anything to stay away from drawing eyes—I'll put sunglasses, goggles, even binoculars on them, or put them in the shade of a cap. Eyes add too much personality to my subjects, and I prefer to keep them distant and intriguing.

Typographically, the word *SALE*, which here is set in Glaser Stencil, looks like a quickly printed hangtag—something rubber-stamped or stenciled—which is exactly the feeling I wanted to convey. The choice of color, I believe, brought a certain elegance to this otherwise neutral version of stencil.

On the "Man with a Hoe": I did this linoleum blockprint as the cover for a typesetter's calendar here in San Francisco, and intentionally designed it to look like an old print. Kit Hinrichs was the art director, and various illustrators and designers in the city were each asked to do a different month. I was given the quote: "Surely, nothing is more alive than a word." It was a rather simple assignment: since it was for a typesetter, I felt that it was appropriate for him to be

SALE
Wilkes Bashford

SALE

SALE

growing letters. Kit liked the idea.

Kit's a great art director because he allows freedom and at the same time offers exciting ideas of his own. He also has his own design style, which has worked well with the illustrators he uses.

About the series of Esprit T-shirts: When he presented me with this assignment, Doug Tompkins, who owns Esprit, said, "I love type and simple images," so I knew that this was just perfect for me. He gave me a list of words that he wanted illustrated—that he felt were iconographic American images and would be saleable on casual clothing. Subsequent to that, however, he decided to narrow the project to one theme, and I had to do a series of ten illustrations using the same word. My specific theme was the word *relax.* These rough color sketches are not necessarily what I would show the client, but were enough for me to know how to proceed. I've incorporated some of the ideas—a quiet cup of coffee, a pleasant sunset, a cool drink—into the theme.

IMAGES FOR WILKES BASHFORD (1983), *Postcards/announcements*
WILKES BASHFORD, *Client*
MICHAEL SCHWAB, *Designer*
MICHAEL SCHWAB, *Illustrator*
MICHAEL SCHWAB, *Art Director*

MAN WITH A HOE (1988), *Cover art for a calendar*
REARDON & KREBS TYPOGRAPHY, *Client*
LENNY BARTZ, *Designer*
MICHAEL SCHWAB, *Illustrator*
LENNY BARTZ, *Art Director*

IMAGES FOR T-SHIRTS (1988)
ESPRIT, *Client*
MICHAEL SCHWAB, *Designer*
MICHAEL SCHWAB, *Illustrator*
WAYNE KOGAN, *Art Director*

IDENTITY/PROMOTION (1984)
SUSAN CRUTCHER, *Client*
MICHAEL SCHWAB, *Designer*
MICHAEL SCHWAB, *Illustrator*

Concerning the design of a film editor's letterhead: I wanted to be eclectic because Susan is a colorful, exciting woman who gets involved in lots of different things. But her primary job as film editor means bringing together lots of different images and rearranging them. That's why I use so many different typefaces in each word. The tour de force is her phone number: I just used every typeface I had available.

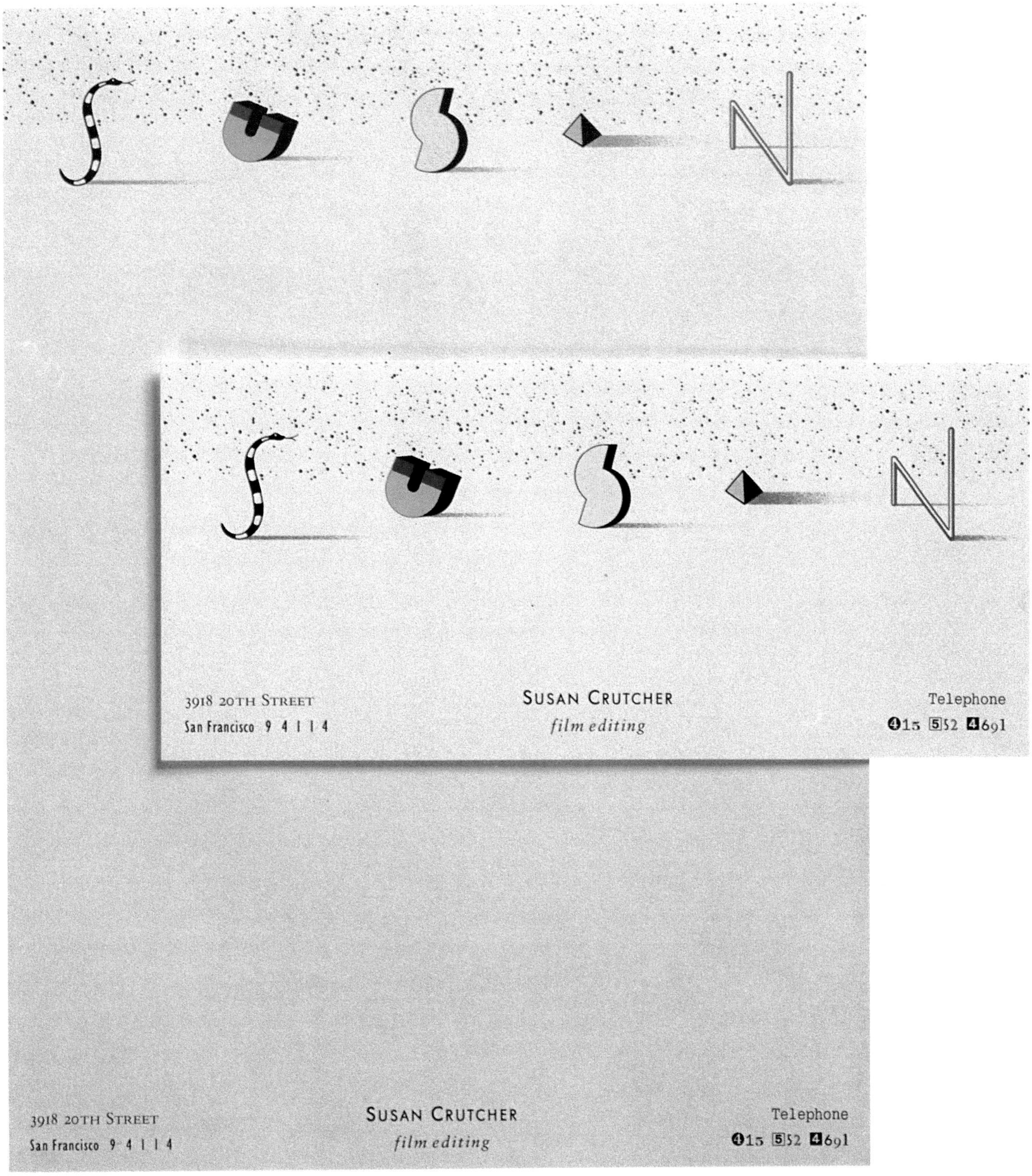
3918 20TH STREET
San Francisco 9 4 1 1 4
SUSAN CRUTCHER
film editing
Telephone
415 552 4691
3918 20TH STREET
San Francisco 9 4 1 1 4
SUSAN CRUTCHER
film editing
Telephone
415 552 4691

DUGALD STERMER

In late 1964 Dugald Stermer joined *Ramparts* magazine, a counterculture journal concerned with social issues, as its art director. He employed a group of influential American illustrators, not in the traditional role as slaves to texts, but as commentators on the current scene. In 1970 he embarked on his own path as an illustrator and enjoyed some success with a flat poster style that was rooted more in design than drawing. Dissatisfied with this lifeless approach he returned to magazine design but started to teach himself how to draw realistically. As design director for *Oceans* magazine he assigned himself a story on sea birds to illustrate. The resulting images were so well received that he soon devoted himself almost exclusively to illustrating. Though he enjoys the process of picture making without regard for type or layout, he often applies a designer's skill and sensibility to illustration projects, such as the magazine cover and book jackets discussed here.

TIME
TV's First Black Superstar
Comedian
Flip
Wilson

About being a designer: I was intimidated by the drawing and painting classes I took as a student at UCLA. I knew how to draw by the standards of our mothers, cousins, aunts, and uncles. Everybody thought that I was a great draftsman—everybody but the people who knew the difference, that is. And I soon learned that difference. Rather than fool myself, I discovered design as an alternative. My understanding was that designers translated manuscripts in a visual way, and that appealed to me. I hesitate using the word *communicate* because most people in this business really don't do that—they decorate. Communication starts with the written word; even music starts with a written notation. Hence, I thought designing was a way to make marks on paper that, while it wasn't actually drawing, did have some communicative function.

On leaving the comfort of designing for the challenge of illustrating: Though I really did not know how to draw when I decided to make the change, I'm always getting more competent. Knowing how to draw is like knowing how to play the violin. You sort of never actually know how to play, you just keep practicing. At first I wasn't confident as an illustrator, but I did it anyway. Sometimes I lucked out and my poster style was bought by *Time* magazine, but this approach was really a crutch. It was very flat and designey, bearing scant relation to real drawing. Yet *Time* liked it for portrait covers—which are like posters anyway. The funny thing about this business is that it will often reward you for the wrong things. It will praise you for something trendy at the moment, but will punish you the following year for doing the exact same thing. Though I was getting into shows, the style didn't bring me a lot more work because it wasn't very flexible.

I had a teacher in college who said about art, "Do something that makes sense for you, that's yours." I never quite knew what that meant in terms of illustration, but with design I gravitated toward a bookish, old-world rather than Bauhaus design that was, and is, a reflection of my tastes. Yet not until much later did my drawing evolve into the sense of craft and concern for detail that now characterizes what I do.

About the "LSD" cover for *West* magazine: I prefer a job when the solution to the problem is contained within the problem itself; rather, that is, than having to force a solution upon it. This was the case with the "LSD" cover. I received a call from the magazine that went: "We got a weird story that we don't know what to do with." And that's what happens more often than not: the illustrator is called upon to define and solve the problem. In this case, as with most assignments, I thought about the relationship of the words and pictures together. I was concerned that the lead of the article (which you can read on the cover) was not going to be changed, and queried the editor on its status. Since this was a curious question for an illustrator to ask, the editor wanted to know what I had in mind. I said that I wanted to play with it. I wanted to set it up so that the person reading it responded as if he or she was in the acid-head's mind. I wanted the reader to say, "What? LSD? In the era of cocaine and heroin? All this and you're writing about LSD?" Then I wanted all the brain synapses to snap, and I wanted the reader to act as if he'd just taken a couple of tabs of LSD and

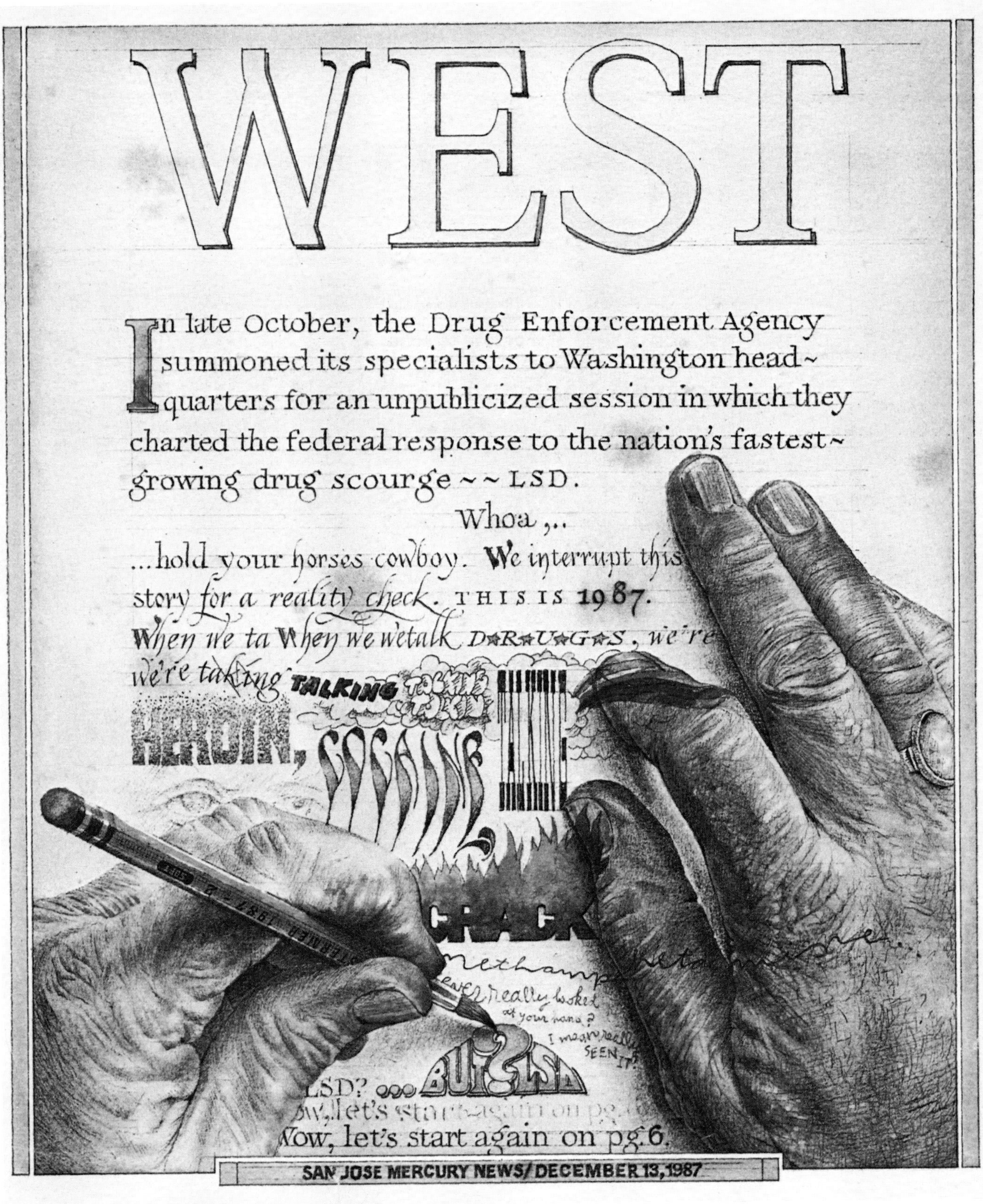
WEST
In late October, the Drug Enforcement Agency summoned its specialists to Washington head~quarters for an unpublicized session in which they charted the federal response to the nation's fastest~growing drug scourge ~~ LSD.
Whoa,..
...hold your horses cowboy. We interrupt this story for a reality check. THIS IS 1987.
When we ta When we wetalk D★R★U★G★S, we're
we're taking
TALKING
HEROIN,
COCAINE
LSD?
Now, let's start again on pg.6.
SAN JOSE MERCURY NEWS/ DECEMBER 13,1987

FLIP WILSON (1972), *Magazine cover*
TIME MAGAZINE, *Client*
DUGALD STERMER, *Designer*
DUGALD STERMER, *Illustrator*
LOUIS GLESSMAN, *Art Director*

LSD (1987), *Magazine cover*
WEST MAGAZINE, *Client*
DUGALD STERMER, *Designer*
DUGALD STERMER, *Illustrator*
BAMBI NICKLIN, *Art Director*

ONCE IN EUROPA
JOHN BERGER

had gone berserk. The editor was enthusiastic, and said "Terrific, will it come off?" and I replied that I didn't know until I tried it. The jobs where I'm not so sure what the outcome will be are usually the best.

I executed this cover realistically from the top down (I even drew the *West* logo). I stopped drawing at the middle and had a photographer take a picture of my hands drawing. I used that photograph as reference for the bottom half, where I started getting goofy with it—as you can see.

On being an interpretive realist: I try to draw things as accurately as I can. Whatever is inaccurate, or is considered "style," is probably due to my *inability* to make it more polished. When art directors tell me that a drawing is not

ONCE IN EUROPA
JOHN BERGER
PANTHEON

ONCE IN EUROPA (1988), *Book jacket*
PANTHEON BOOKS, *Client*
DUGALD STERMER, *Designer*
DUGALD STERMER, *Illustrator*
LOUISE FILI, *Art Director*

quite as finished as they had hoped, I tell them to get a hyperrealist, because as realistic as I am, I am incapable of being precise. My eyes and control are not that good. Nor do I have the patience.

I believe that the world of arts is made up of people who are either light to dark or dark to light. Marshall Arisman is dark to light (so is Rembrandt, Brad Holland, and Beethoven). This means he can endure seeing a bad painting in front of him maybe for six months—until he puts enough white in it so that the figures start to emerge from the darkness. I can't stand seeing my pictures ever looking bad. You've got to have a lot of courage, confidence, ego, or all three to have that canvas or paper look terrible for a time. It takes a different kind of courage, however, to make only the marks you need to make and leave

TEFUGA (1987), *Book jacket*
PANTHEON BOOKS, *Client*
DUGALD STERMER, *Designer*
DUGALD STERMER, *Illustrator*
LOUISE FILI, *Art Director*

everything else out. That's what I try to do: shorten the distance between my wrist and my brain, and make whatever I want to get across as simply as I can without sacrificing accuracy.

Stemming from my time as an art director, however, I do not like linear interpretation, or what I call the "*Redbook* style," where, for example, a story says a girl gets kissed on a beach and that's the scene that is duplicated in paint. I used to try to art direct a magazine so that the illustration said one thing, the story said something else, and the interpretation of the reader was the third point in the triangle. That makes the experience unique to each reader, because no two interpretations can be the same.

About John Berger's *Once in Europa*: This is not the sort of fiction you read before going to bed at night. It's difficult going, being a series of short stories by an author who is better known as a Marxist art critic. He also happens to be an old hero of mine. The art director, Louise Fili, did not know this when she assigned me the jacket. Moreover, Louise did not offer any ideas, so I was left on my own. What Berger is getting at in these stories is how the historical peasant class of France came to terms with the industrial and technological age—how technocracy encroached on the landscape, and cultural and political change occurred. Somewhere at the end of one of the stories he mentions a robin carrying a strip of paper with a legend, which I used literally as the centerpiece of my composition. I used graduated color to suggest the symbols of technocracy and the landscape, which are black and white at the bottom of the picture. The symbol for the peasantry (which couldn't be stifled for long) emerges into bright colors as it moves toward the top (even the lettering at the top becomes colorful), representing Berger's optimistic prognostication. The bird is, more or less, a symbol of life.

When I sent in a Xerox of the rough sketch to Louise, she didn't respond for a week or so. I've learned that if she loves something she calls right away. I knew this time it meant she was not all that convinced it was the right solution. Since I respect her judgment, it forced me to question the idea as well, but I was ultimately so convinced the sketch would work that I told her I would do the finish on spec. If I didn't like it, I wouldn't send it in; if she didn't, I would do another. She liked it. And even John Berger sent a letter saying that the illustration was absolutely perfect for the book. That's the best response of all.

About the book jacket for *Tefuga:* I'm tired of being typecast as a Classicist. Sometimes I like to go contrary to the centered, elegant, formal arrangement of type I seem to be known for. I did that with the Berger, and to a certain extent with *Tefuga.* This jacket is like a play within a play—a picture of a picture—which is appropriate because the story is told in flashback. The protagonist is drawing, but the drawing is a metaphor for what she's going through in real life. I also wanted it to look as though the reader were holding the sketch pad and drawing in it.

I've heard critiques that my use of lettering here is illegible. I suppose that if a book jacket is meant to be a poster, and a poster is meant to be read quickly, the placement of type may be less than successful. But if a book jacket is supposed to draw you into the drama, and you don't care whether the words are read first or last but are attracted by the whole composition, then it is successful. The lettering was intended to echo the drawing composition, but the fact that it goes both ways on the surface of the drawing pad and back on the cover is merely an accident or subconscious. After you've been in this business so long, things often happen that you are simply not aware of until after the work is printed.

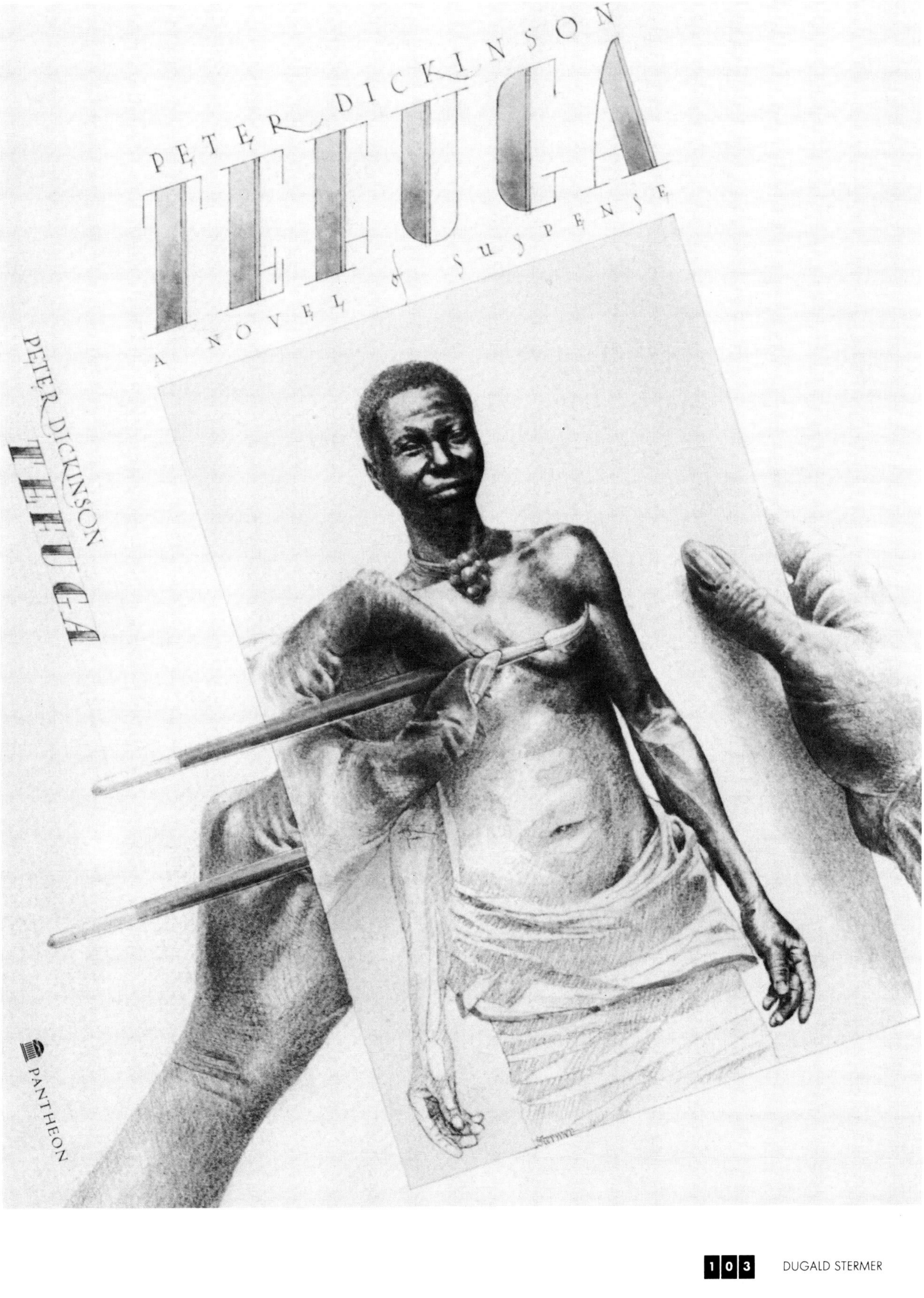
PETER DICKINSON
TEFUGA
A NOVEL of SUSPENSE
PETER DICKINSON
TEFUGA
PANTHEON

TURK WINTERROWD

From doing illustration for educational materials at the National Institutes of Health to designing background graphics for NBC's local and network television news shows, Turk Winterrowd has produced illustrative material that has had to be eye-catching yet no-nonsense: unlike their static cousins, television graphics are viewed for mere seconds. After apprenticing for designer Michael David Brown and illustrator Salvador Bru, Winterrowd designed book jackets and album covers and made illustrations for the *New York Times'* Op-ed and Living sections. A television graphics designer, he currently operates an image-processing computer, but the work discussed here, done for breaking news stories, was created the old-fashioned way, with scissors, paste, and hand.

COCKFIGHT
KNOCKOUT

On starting at NBC: I began as a freelancer, which is the way everybody on staff does it. Since the news never stops, the station needs artists on hand at all times. I was brought in to cover for staff members over vacations, Christmas, etc.

About the daily grind: The work is done at an exceedingly fast pace, requiring as many as four finishes in a day. The "Kidnapped" graphic, however, took a couple of days to produce. It is called a "generic," and can be used for any kidnapping story when actual news pictures are unavailable. This was also one of the last pieces of flat art I did before the introduction of computers. Everything is now done on videotape and computer chip.

Navigating around the clichés of television graphics: Because of the computer, the electronic airbrush now dominates the look of television graphics. I tend to rebel against such conformity and aesthetically prefer the kind of textures obtained with collage. With the "Kidnapping" and "Solidarity" graphics I wanted to return to something that was simple and strong—basically black-and-white with a newspaper feeling. The "Solidarity" photograph of protesting workers came from the Associated Press, where we get most of our images. I simply tore paper and added texture to the print. The hands for "Kidnapped" are speckled with an airbrush texture. The wrists are actually taken from a picture of someone's thigh and pasted together. I cut out the anatomical shapes from a piece of black paper, and then randomly played with white tape symbolizing ropes that tie the head and hands. Typographically I wanted a similar kinetic treatment. I did the headline using typewriter type. I also positioned it within the picture frame in such a way as to make the image appear boxed in. I had already done a kidnapped graphic before using the clichéd technique of cutting out various letters.

Television graphics must tap into the audience's collective memory. I have certain crutches, such as the use of figures, because people relate best to people. I also have to draw upon universal symbols, but since instantly recognizable imagery is a prerequisite, I try to break them down into the simplest elements.

Some influences: I've always been fascinated by strong poster images. The revolutionary Russian film posters from the 1920s are powerful collages, as are the political satires of John Heartfield, the German Dada montagist. Television shoots out so many images that the collage or montage method works the very best.

About "Cockfight Knockout": For a story on illegal cockfights in New York I was given a lot of boring source material. At the time I happened to have a pile of paper scraps on my desk and began playing with them to see what image I might conjure. Once the scraps resembled a cock, I applied some airbrush texture, threw in some Color-Aid paper, and scribbled across it with a grease pencil. I use press type because often a story changes either during the broadcast or over a few days if there are breaking subtopics. Hence, different titles are needed. Now all the type is done electronically—shot separately and keyed in over the top of the art.

On designing for different news show formats: The local NBC station has two different news formats: horizontal and vertical. The

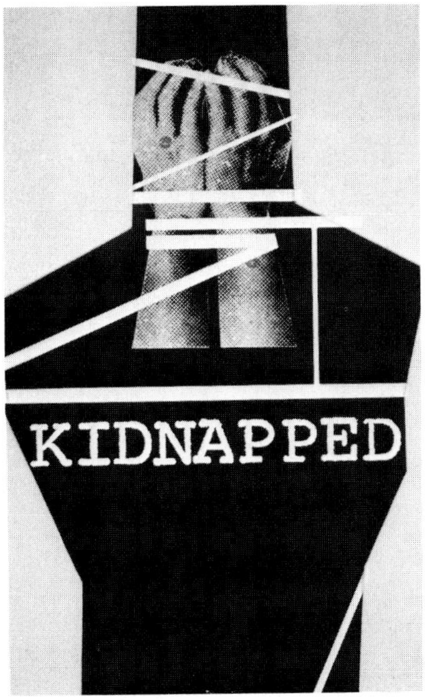
KIDNAPPED

SOLIDARNOŚĆ

KIDNAPPED (1986), *Television news graphic*
NEWS 4 NEW YORK/WNBC-TV, *Client*
TURK WINTERROWD, *Designer*
TURK WINTERROWD, *Illustrator*
BEVERLY LITTLEWOOD AND TURK WINTERROWD, *Art Directors*

SOLIDARITY (1983), *Television news graphic*
NEWS 4 NEW YORK/WNBC-TV, *Client*
TURK WINTERROWD, *Designer*
TURK WINTERROWD, *Illustrator*
BEVERLY LITTLEWOOD AND TURK WINTERROWD, *Art Directors*

COCKFIGHT KNOCKOUT (1985), *Television news graphic*
NEWS 4 NEW YORK/WNBC-TV, *Client*
TURK WINTERROWD, *Designer*
TURK WINTERROWD, *Illustrator*
BEVERLY LITTLEWOOD AND TURK WINTERROWD, *Art Directors*

MURDER IN
ATHENS

MURDER IN ATHENS (1984),
Television news graphic
NEWS 4 NEW YORK/WNBC-TV, *Client*
TURK WINTERROWD, *Designer*
TURK WINTERROWD, *Illustrator*
BEVERLY LITTLEWOOD AND TURK WINTERROWD, *Art Directors*

horizontal is used for the five o'clock show, and displayed behind the anchor person on an on-air monitor. The vertical is used for the six o'clock show. In fact, the early morning show has yet another configuration. Knowing this, it becomes very obvious when a graphic designed for one format is adapted to another—the image is there, but the type just doesn't quite fit. Often I design two pieces for each format or I might do it only once if the producer wants the story broadcast on only one show.

About "Murder in Athens": This story was about the assassination of a Greek government official. There was no time to get a photograph of the deceased, so I used a picture of a piece of broken Greek statuary that I knew would work symbolically. For a design element tying the type to the illustration, I placed the headline *Murder in* in a bar to pick up the red bar running from the eye. The photograph was airbrushed over to give it some tonal quality.

About computers: I made a fairly smooth transition from flat art to computer. My style is consistent and easily carried over. Drawing with the computer is like illustrating with light. This seems remarkable when viewing what appears to be a very tightly rendered piece of art. It's all an illusion.

Concerning the art direction of news graphics: At the time these graphics were made, the art director was Beverly Littlewood. She hired people whom she trusted enough to say, "Go with it." Given the speed with which these things had to be produced it would have been fruitless to do it any other way.

The direction changed, however, every time a new executive producer took over. There was a period, for example, when skulls were prohibited. This made it difficult to do a poison graphic, since the international symbol is a skull and crossbones. For a brief time splashes of red were prohibited because it looked like blood, and they did not want things to look too grisly. Then another producer came in and demanded that we use more blood in our graphics.

On failure: "What if I can't do it?" is always the nagging question. But incredibly I have always come up with something, I think because it is ultimately a team effort. Among the staff of artists someone is always willing to lend a hand. There have been times when a solution has not been appropriate, or didn't work, or became unsuitable after we received more information about the story so had to go to a generic backup. You have to illustrate with one hand and keep your fingers crossed with the other.

DESIGNERS WHO ILLUSTRATE

MICHAEL ARON

Having studied and apprenticed with Herb Lubalin and Seymour Chwast, the former a master of type and the latter a master of image, Michael Aron is a passionate advocate of the seamless practice of design and drawing. Although his preference is for collage, he is skilled in the methods of rendering; and this skill, as he notes here, gives him the freedom to create and the ability to precisely visualize the solutions to a variety of problems. The principal of a small New York design studio, Aron primarily does promotional work—direct to the consumer, rather than business-to-business—for educational institutions and real-estate developers, among others. Here he discusses two subway and billboard posters for LaGuardia Community College, which were designed to increase enrollment.

About the advantages of drawing: For some art directors the phone, not the pencil, is the primary tool. I know art directors who sit down, think of an idea, and just start calling illustrators. They never draw the idea themselves. I envy that method when it works, but I can't help thinking that when the two come together, it is really a one-in-ten chance that something terrific will happen. I find it hard to believe that an art director or designer cannot draw. The pencil is my tool. And the truth is that anyone can draw; it's just making marks on a page. These marks are one's own personal gestures: Lynda Barry has a different way of marking than has Jim McMullan or Bascove. My line might be fat, your line might be thin.

CUNY
LAGUARDIA
COMMUNITY
COLLEGE
OUR SECRET IS SUCCESS

About a preference for illustration: I am a designer, not an illustrator, but I have the ability to create images. When I went to school at Cooper Union I studied with Herb Lubalin and Seymour Chwast, and so drawing was just part of the education process. The former influenced my typographic sense, the latter my illustration—their messages entered my brain and came out through my hands as one unified approach. Also, the 1960s and 1970s were noted for extremely clever visual advertising and design, and for me it was the natural way for problems to be solved. Add to this my preference for visual humor, surrealism, and fantasy and you can see it would be unlikely for me to solve problems with austere still-life photography or stolid typography. I like to put images together that do not belong together.

CUNY
LAGUARDIA
COMMUNITY COLLEGE
OUR SECRET IS SUCCESS

There are certain styles I cannot do and certain images, such as realistic portraits, that another artist might draw better. Whenever I work as an illustrator, it is because my clients do not have the budget to hire one and I have already solved the problem using an illustrative approach. At that point I'm left with my own two hands, and that is also why I rely on found-imagery.

But a designer's imagination is not all that different from an illustrator's. When I design a cover for something, I visualize it in my mind and then draw it. I always design with images because the viewer can relate to an image on a personal level. Typography alone, or other designey textures, is usually cold and impersonal. It is also my natural inclination to draw the lettering as I'm drawing the overall image. Then I decide on what typeface I want. If no typeface is available, then I

LAGUARDIA
COMMUNITY COLLEGE
CUNY
OUR SECRET IS
SUCCESS

LaGuardia
Community College
¿HABLA ESPAÑOL?
CUNY
Our Secret is
SUCCESS

OUR SECRET IS SUCCESS (1986),
Mailer/handout to increase enrollment
LAGUARDIA COMMUNITY COLLEGE, *Client*
MICHAEL ARON, *Designer*
MICHAEL ARON, *Illustrator*
BILL FREELAND, *Art Director*

WHERE THE FUTURE WORKS (1984),
Subway poster to increase enrollment
LAGUARDIA COMMUNITY COLLEGE, *Client*
MICHAEL ARON, *Designer*
MICHAEL ARON, *Illustrator*
BILL FREELAND AND SEYMOUR CHWAST, *Art Directors*

WHERE THE FUTURE WORKS
START A CAREER IN COLLEGE!
LAGUARDIA
COMMUNITY
COLLEGE
626-5588

draw it. Rarely do I visualize a photographic solution to a problem; for the kind of work I do the process of photography is just too drawn out and expensive. I don't have time for it. If I get a job on Thursday it is likely that it will have to go out on Monday. Moreover, photography just doesn't offer me the same kind of challenges as illustration. I can control the feeling of a piece. There is a certain magic in drawn or found imagery. And an image that is new is always going to be more arresting for the viewer.

About realism: I practiced realism at school. In fact I excelled in realistic rendering of objects. It allowed me the freedom to play with space, perspective, and so on. But I was not interested in pursuing that ability into professional life. Collage is my preference.

On Doing the "Our Secret Is Success" mailer for LaGuardia College: This is the most complex kind of mixed media. The background is airbrush. The hand is a photograph that I took to give it a hyperrealistic look. The little woman riding the rocket is a drawing based on a photograph I took. In fact, I had a friend approximate that position by sitting on the ledge of my roof; the rocket on which she is perched came from an antique needle package. The type was hand-drawn at a time when I was doing a lot of hand lettering. I still rely heavily on drawing letterforms rather than modifying existing ones. I just sketch what I need and then render it. Incidentally, there are no curves in the lettering because it is less time-consuming to draw.

About the influences for this mailer: Anyone who is versed in the history of graphic design will notice that I borrowed from Russian Constructivist typography just as liberally as I swiped from Buck Rogers. The pennant shape is really a comic book way of depicting the future, but at the same time this style of lettering suggests school sports. I knew that would appeal to an audience, in this case high school students thinking about which college to attend. These kids are bombarded with MTV and record jacket images, and I thought this mailer would have much more impact than, say, a photograph of schoolrooms, students, or the campus—and LaGuardia, incidentally, has a rather unattractive campus. This same approach would not be appropriate for all schools. LaGuardia students are primarily Latin or black, and very hip.

On the evolution of the LaGuardia mailer: Originally I did a series of much simpler designs using conceptual ideas, such as a gameboard and a target. I wrote the headlines and came up with images to solve the problem, but the client asked that I push it further than I had gone. So my next step was to draw inspiration from books—I have about two thousand books on fine and applied arts at the studio and home, and everything I see becomes grist for the mind mill. So I looked through them and made lists of images, categories, colors. Then I rummaged through my imagination and made mental doodles. I started to play with scale. I drew something that should be big small, and vice versa.

About the "Future Works" poster for LaGuardia College: This poster was done while I was still at Pushpin. The client supplied us with a provocative headline that allowed for any number of visual solutions; how does one illustrate the future? Again I decided to do a collage. The head is swiped from an old ad and the sunglasses and hair were added to make it look contemporary. Without those elements the guy looks too old.

ART CHANTRY

From an interest in surfer and hot-rod culture, psychedelia, comic books, and monster magazines Seattle-based Art Chantry developed a graphic style that is at once charming and unconventional. Although he thinks of himself as a cut-and-paste artist, and thus differentiates his "mechanical" design from design that is more drawing-oriented, his illustration is nevertheless compellingly narrative. As a former art director for Seattle's *The Rocket*, a monthly alternative-culture tabloid, Chantry encouraged the use of cartoon as illustration. As a designer of theatrical posters, record covers, and book jackets, he throws together disparate elements creating surrealist juxtapositions and absurd graphic commentaries. Here Chantry not only discusses his iconoclastic method and how it enhances the posters he does for Seattle's cultural events, but also offers his point of view about design issues.

On design as a drawing versus a mechanical process: I don't agree with the conventional wisdom that design is an illustrated medium. It's a constructed medium, and drawing is only one small portion of what a designer has to deal with. Design is primarily based on the mechanics of typography. Much of what we know about layout stems directly from the physics of early movable type. And that, combined with the needs of what I call the folk art medium of advertising and the other requirements of merchant culture, gave rise to graphic design.

Concerning the difference between design and fine art: Fine art is the dialogue of an international elite who are not directly connected to the popular culture. Though they are influenced by their culture, their ambitions and involvement are in a fine-art aesthetic. I am very interested in the fine arts, but if I were to approach design from that vantage point, it would become a self-referential system that required the artist to reinvent the wheel every time. Still I'm basically an artist masquerading as a graphic designer; I have a degree in painting, though my teacher used to scream because I put type on my paintings. My preference has always been for interactive media, particularly the intellectual confrontation of Dada and Surrealism. When I got out of school in 1978 the punk scene was in full pitch; incredible posters by seasoned unprofessionals were plastered everywhere, and I thought, well here is someplace I can fit in. I originally began by doing rock posters because the punk style was akin to what I was doing for myself anyway.

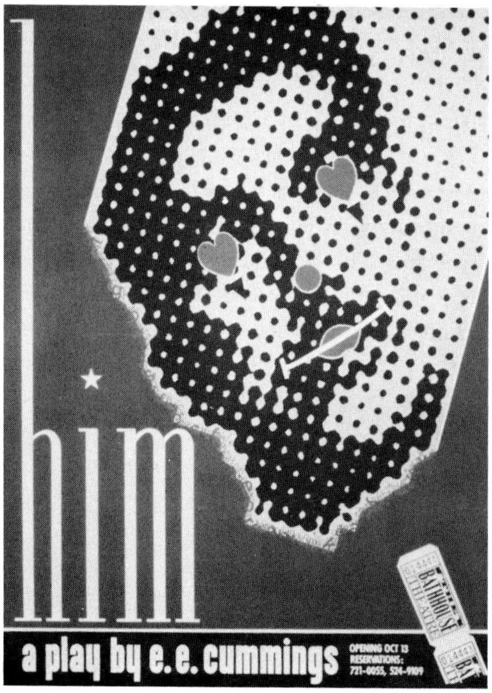
him
a play by e.e. cummings
OPENING OCT 13
RESERVATIONS:
721-0055, 524-9109
BATHHOUSE THEATRE

On a relationship with computers: I believe that when a culture thrives it is because it is being refreshed by bubbling underground subcultures that somehow affect mainstream thought. Yet now there are very few fresh ideas being shoved up from underneath. In fact no trash is being allowed in either, which I believe is a necessary factor to push on innovation. The computer revolution is perhaps the only bright spot. Although there will be a lot of very bad design, out of all that stuff will come some really neat accidents. The natural weirdos are going to be able to do good stuff because that is what they can do.

On the conceptualization process: I generally come up with a concept and sell the client on an idea. I recently became acquainted with the work of the late Robert Brownjohn [of Brownjohn, Chermayeff and Geismar], who during the early sixties was such a brilliant conceptualist that he could sell ideas to his clients over the telephone. He believed that if it wasn't good enough to talk out, then it wasn't good enough to take to completion. I try to get well versed with the client's needs so that my concepts fit the problem and I too can verbalize them before putting them to paper.

If a client demands a more visible interpretation I sketch things out, but most of composition is done in the mechanical stage. That's where I do my best work, because my art *is* the mechanical. When I depart from the direct, hands-on approach my work gets somewhat rote and sterile, but being that the mechanical is only a step away from reproduction it is fresher than other methods. It's like the nineteenth-century method of working directly on the litho stone.

BATHHOUSE THEATRE
MAY 6 - JUNE 7
Reservations: 524-9110
THE ADDING MACHINE

About type: When I started I did not have access to typesetting facilities and so generated my own type by Xeroxing it out of books, cutting it out letter by letter, and pasting it into place with glue sticks. Boy, I learned a lot about type spacing that way! Every early project I worked on had its own personality. Some were image-heavy/type-light and vice versa. Still other projects were all type and so I learned about the expression of different letterforms.

When I make type decisions that interplay with an image, they are usually based on gut reaction. I might scan all my old type books—or comic books and things like that—until I find something that just feels right. Sometimes I hit it right on the mark and I am convinced that my choice is the only one possible. But I can't tell you why that's so. It depends on the image. I try to avoid type that clashes with my image.

I realize, though, that when a designer takes something "gooey" and organic, like calligraphy, and places it against an austere grid, the contrast makes it look beautiful. People respond viscerally to the clash of textures. My more tightly designed pieces tend to have sloppier images on them. In fact, once you remove the image, much of my poster design is remarkably conservative.

Concerning theater posters in general: In Seattle there is considerable competition to do theater posters, because everyone here seems to be a graphic designer. It becomes a supply-and-demand thing: prices are usually low and quality must be high.

My approach is to stay true to the play and get as much input as I can without making the poster a literal interpretation. I reject the billboard school of poster design, which says the message should be given and received immediately. I don't think anyone is going to go to the play based on the poster anyway.

If the client trusts me I usually perform well. Generally, however, clients try to stick their fingers in the pie, and I try to nip that. I want to give my clients what they want, or rather what they need, because what they want isn't always what they need. I come up with the idea and present it as completely as possible. Invariably they want to change something, and I must consider whether their change will work or not. I've actually gone so far as to trick clients by including something in the design that is so obviously wrong that the biggest dunderhead would say, "I like it a lot, except for *that.*" Then I'll change it, and end up with what I had originally planned.

About the *Him* poster: This is a case when my process failed—well, it failed in my estimation at least, though the poster has received universal acclaim. The client wanted me to put the clown face on the really coarse halftone image. Originally I had nothing on the face at all, but they didn't think it evoked enough of the play, which is set at a carnival. Though it works okay, it was a half-baked idea—a cliché—and I wish I'd had

THE ADDING MACHINE (1982), *Theater poster*
THE BATHHOUSE THEATER, *Client*
ART CHANTRY, *Designer*
ART CHANTRY, *Illustrator*
ART CHANTRY, *Art Director*

HIM (1984), *Theater poster*
THE BATHHOUSE THEATER, *Client*
ART CHANTRY, *Designer*
ART CHANTRY, *Illustrator*
ART CHANTRY, *Art Director*

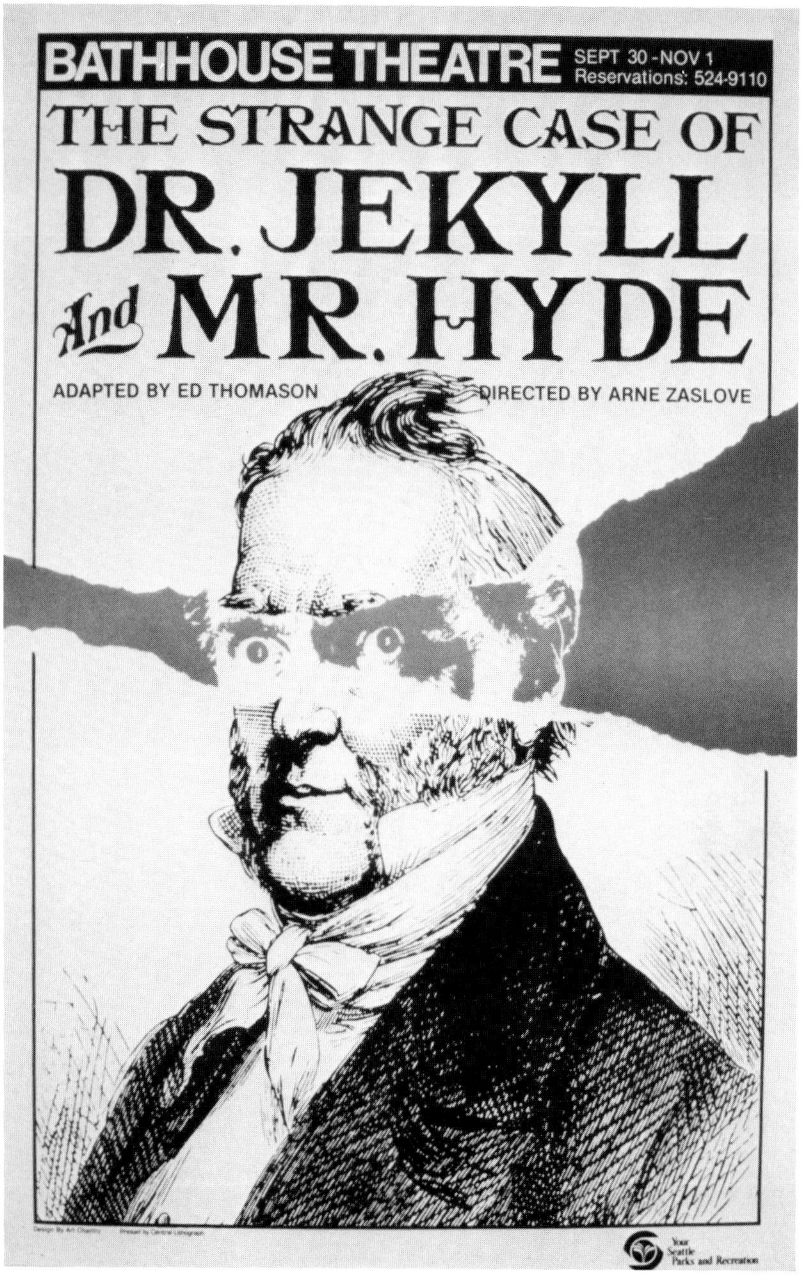

BATHHOUSE THEATRE
SEPT 30 - NOV 1
Reservations: 524-9110
THE STRANGE CASE OF
DR. JEKYLL
And MR. HYDE
ADAPTED BY ED THOMASON
DIRECTED BY ARNE ZASLOVE

DR. JEKYLL AND MR. HYDE
(1983), *Theater poster*
THE BATHHOUSE THEATER, *Client*
ART CHANTRY, *Designer*
ART CHANTRY, *Illustrator*
ART CHANTRY, *Art Director*

more time to think it over and do it better. You know, arts people are the worst clients.

About the *Adding Machine* poster: This play, one of the finest expressionist plays to be written in America, is about a milquetoast accountant who is replaced by a machine. His wife leaves him, and he dies and goes to accountant hell, which is run by machines. I concocted a face that's half machine in keeping with the character. For the background I made little numbers into a grid pattern. It was printed on the State Park's AB Dick 360 press with rubber-based Vanson inks, for a budget of, get this, fifty dollars. The unit cost was a joke, but it won six design awards.

On economy and the poster for *Dr. Jekyll:* Again the printing budget for this was nothing—the printer was paid off in beer, but he was basically very good. The image is a collage. Actually it's an old etching of John Quincy Adams; what I did was create a kind of violence that happens when the good Doctor transforms into the evil Mr. Hyde, by tearing the paper through the top of his face and having these wild animal eyes protruding out. The eyes, by the way, are a blown-up Xerox of Christopher Lee's Dracula. Xeroxes can turn a halftone into a wonderfully mottled texture. I love things that look like they have been on the bottom of the ocean too long.

The typeface is both representative of the period and imbued with an evil quality. But it is almost *too* overpowering, and clashes with the image. The trick to working with type and image is being able to push the edges to increase the strength of the message.

About the poster for *The Vampires:* I had worked with the director of this play before and he really loves my stuff—"the wilder the better," he says. So this was one of those dream assignments. The play is set in New York's East Village during the early 1980s art scene. The Jetsons, Flintstones, and day-glo graffiti art are prominent in the set design. The main characters are upwardly mobile yuppie types who are fake artists living the bohemian life-style. They are two frustrated, angry people who argue throughout the entire play until they come to the point where, like vampires, they start biting each other. My concept is a contemporary yin/yang, happy/sad theater mask thing. And I used fluorescent inks, which had not been used in Seattle for years—it was a real jolt on the walls. The zigzag design is based on some graffiti that I saw, and I added the teeth for shock value. I redrew it about a zillion times and finally ended up with a version done with a marking pen that was blown up.

Originally at the bottom I had a line of beautiful type made from an old rubber stamp kit. The contrast between the oldish letterforms and the new fluorescent colors provided great tension. Everyone loved it . . . until someone came

OKTOBERFEST AT THE SEATTLE CENTER
OCTOBER 14th (4-11), OCTOBER 15th (12-11), OCTOBER 16th (12-7) · SEATTLE CENTER FLAG PAVILLION
ADMISSION IS FREE WITH A DONATION TO THE SEATTLE CENTER'S NORTHWEST SECOND HARVEST
MUSIC, DANCE, ARTWORK, FILMS, CABARET, INTERNATIONAL CUISINE! · INFO 633-5005
SPONSORED BY WARSTEINER BEER, MUSCULAR DISTROPHY, AND THE SEATTLE CENTER

THE VAMPIRES
By Harry Kondoleon
The Empty Space
919 East Pike
Opens January Eleventh
Tickets 325-4443

OKTOBERFEST (1983), *Festival poster*
TERRY MORGAN/THE SEATTLE CENTER, *Client*
ART CHANTRY, *Designer*
ART CHANTRY, *Illustrator*
ART CHANTRY, *Art Director*

THE VAMPIRES (1984), *Theater poster*
JOHN KAZANJIAN/THE EMPTY SPACE, *Client*
ART CHANTRY, *Designer*
ART CHANTRY, *Illustrator*
ART CHANTRY, *Art Director*

into the room and said that according to the contract the playwright's name had to be 90 percent as high as the cap height for the play's title. Since the title I had designed was 3 inches high the name would have overpowered the image. But they insisted that I redesign it to accommodate that contractual obligation. The author, Harry Kondoleon, would not have cared if they asked him, but they were insistent. So I had to design a new typeface in a couple of hours. Somebody suggested using stars and stripes because that motif comes up often during the play. In my opinion the type is a disaster; and one of these days, if I ever get enough money, I will reprint it the way it should have been done.

Satirical posters for "Oktoberfest": The original idea for this series was to satirize different periods of German logo design—the 1890s, 1930s, 1950s, and so on, ending with a high-tech version. I did only two of the series, since they went bankrupt before I finished. The basic image was lifted from *The History of German Trademarks* book; I redrew the griffin's face so he would look like he was having a good time, and placed him off center with a beer stein and the logo of the beer sponsor. I often reconstruct (collage) letterforms, especially when I'm working with foreign alphabets such as this one, which do not have all our letters. I also try to work in things that have little jokes or subtle commentaries that people will not get until maybe the tenth viewing of the poster.

And a "haywire" one for "Bumbershoot": For this arts festival I was given a painting and told to make it into a poster. I went through and dug out the worst typefaces to spell out *Bumbershoot* and then overprinted it with a thin, clean type. The color breaks did not turn out the way I wanted, but as things went haywire the "artibility" increased. It looks like bad "artist" type. In fact the image and the type are essentially two illustrations side by side that want to cancel each other out. You can see how difficult it is to read against the illustration, but when you cover it up the type is more legible.

About the poster for the 1988 Pacific Northwest Art Exposition: Up to this point their posters had been dreadful because artists who do not know how to make posters had been doing them. When I received the commission I asked Carl Smool, an artist who does theater sets, paintings, and sculptures, to do the illustration. He has two primary styles: one is a dynamic scratchboard approach, which this is; in the other

BUMBERSHOOT (1984),
Arts festival poster
BUMBERSHOOT, ONE REEL VAUDEVILLE SHOW, AND SEATTLE ARTS COMMISSION, *Clients*
ART CHANTRY, *Designer*
T. MICHAEL GARDINER, *Illustrator*
ART CHANTRY, *Art Director*

1988 PACIFIC NORTHWEST ART EXPOSITION (1988), *Arts festival poster*
ROD STUART INC., *Client*
ART CHANTRY, *Designer*
CARL SMOOL, *Illustrator*
ART CHANTRY, *Art Director*

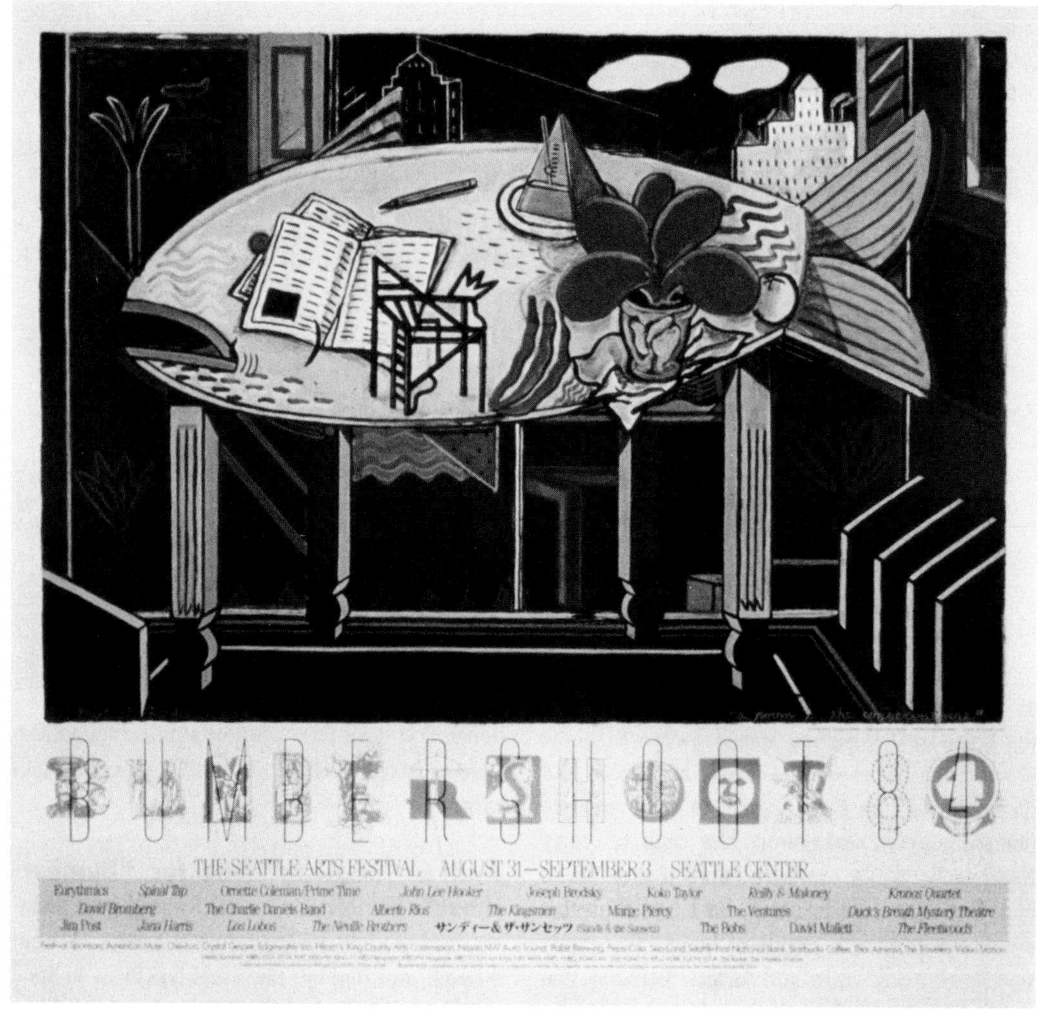
BUMBERSHOOT 84
THE SEATTLE ARTS FESTIVAL AUGUST 31—SEPTEMBER 3 SEATTLE CENTER
Eurythmics Spinal Tap Ornette Coleman/Prime Time John Lee Hooker Joseph Brodsky Koko Taylor Reilly & Maloney Kronos Quartet
David Bromberg The Charlie Daniels Band Alberto Rios The Kingsmen Marge Piercy The Ventures Duck's Breath Mystery Theatre
Jim Post Jana Harris Los Lobos The Neville Brothers サンディー&ザ・サンセッツ The Bobs David Mallett The Fleetwoods

he builds up texture with border tape and Zipatone screens. Carl knows how to work with a designer and I know how to work with him. This was a fine collaboration. In fact most of the time when I work with illustrators I give them free rein to show off. I am not trying to compete with them, but I understand that the design of the piece can accentuate their art.

I wanted him to splay out the buildings, which he agreed was correct. To emphasize it I made the bottom of the poster narrower than the top, the idea being to have something like a fountain going off. I insisted that he put a flying saucer in because the first UFOs were spotted over Mt. Rainier—just a little bit of Tacoma culture imposed on the rest of the world. My other big idea was to use phosphorescent inks that glow in the dark. Here's an interactive idea: turn out the lights and the poster (actually the lights in the buildings) will light up. You can do experiments with silk screen that cannot be done with offset.

And speaking about a bottomless bag of tricks . . . : Sooner or later the advertising function ceases and the poster remains as artifact. I've gone so far as to design posters that change over time—inks that fade to reveal other things, papers that deteriorate quickly. Sometimes they include thematic ideas that change with time. A particularly politically charged image shows up whenever there is a war scare or election crisis. I would love for my posters to have an archaeological function, so that twenty years from now, when people are researching certain aspects of this culture, my posters will be a reference to a historical moment.

ART-X-PO
1988 PACIFIC NORTHWEST ART EXPOSITION
OCTOBER 21,22,23 SEATTLE TRADE CENTER
ART EXPO
KNUA 106.9 fm
POSTER: IMAGE BY CARL SMOOL/DESIGN BY ART CHANTRY/PRINTED BY FINE PRINT STUDIOS, 2923 N. STEVENS, TACOMA, WA 98407 (1-752-4004)

SEYMOUR CHWAST

In the early 1950s four Cooper Union graduates, Edward Sorel, Reynold Ruffins, Milton Glaser, and Seymour Chwast, founded Push Pin Studios on the idea that design and illustration were a single practice and historical styles from the nineteenth and twentieth centuries were ripe for reapplication. Chwast's spare, linear style, which draws upon Art Deco, Art Nouveau, and comic art for inspiration, helped to define a distinctly American style of illustration; and his typography, derived from classical models, exemplifies an eclectic approach to design. A designer of hundreds of book and record jackets, advertisements, and posters, he is a master of the unified word and image. Here he discusses two of his recent and one of his classic posters.

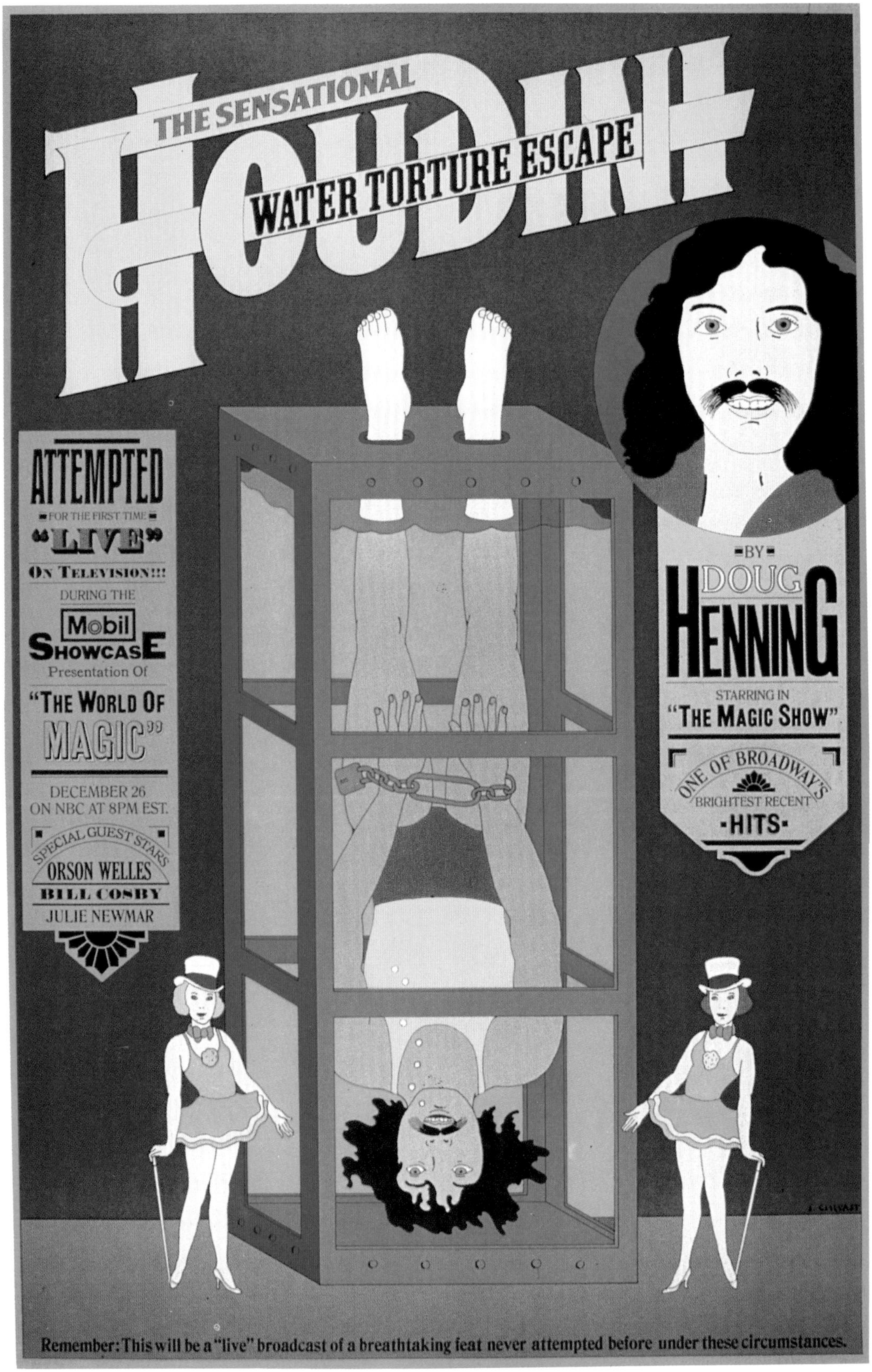

THE SENSATIONAL
HOUDINI
WATER TORTURE ESCAPE
ATTEMPTED
FOR THE FIRST TIME
"LIVE"
ON TELEVISION!!!
DURING THE
Mobil
SHOWCASE
Presentation Of
"THE WORLD OF MAGIC"
DECEMBER 26
ON NBC AT 8PM EST.
SPECIAL GUEST STARS
ORSON WELLES
BILL COSBY
JULIE NEWMAR
BY
DOUG HENNING
STARRING IN
"THE MAGIC SHOW".
ONE OF BROADWAY'S
BRIGHTEST RECENT
HITS
Remember: This will be a "live" broadcast of a breathtaking feat never attempted before under these circumstances.

On illustration versus photography: Designers and art directors are more comfortable with photography than with illustration. Photographers routinely shoot lots of film, whereas the illustrator may provide a sketch or two and one finish, which apparently limits some art directors in their involvement. Film represents "reality" no matter how abstract or surreal. Clients think it adds credibility to their product or service, but a good drawing doesn't need the imposition of a lens—it has a tactile immediacy that photography could never achieve. Photographs can be manipulated to achieve an effect but drawing *is*, by its nature, manipulation.

On the philosophy behind the early Push Pin Studios: We started out as a studio where each member was a designer as well as illustrator. We were unique because most illustrators did not care about typography or about how their illustration worked in relation to the design of the page. They didn't have to and weren't interested. I loved cartooning and drawing during my early school years, but fortunately I had a high school teacher who exposed me to those great European poster artists who worked with type and image. I consider myself a designer rather than an illustrator because the concept and the design of the surface are supreme.

On typographic fashion: I am fussier with type than with illustration, and I follow rather rigid rules. I admit to being swept along with some trends in type and ignoring others. Phototypesetting (and now digital setting) has freed designers to do much more than was ever possible with hot metal. Consequently, they do things that shouldn't be done; this freedom often leads to chaos. The look of letters developed from stone carvings and from writing that was cast in metal or carved into wood. Letterforms were designed to acknowledge origins and technological limitations. But some typographic rules—the ones that should not be broken—have something timeless to say about legibility and beauty. Good designers know when to bend the rules and perhaps redesign type so that it might work harmoniously with their more chaotic ideas.

Chaos or surprise?: We all want to be surprised if not astonished. The way to do that is with a well-crafted work that the world has never seen before. Okay, it's not easy considering deadlines and the appointment with the dentist. But discovery is what makes our work worthwhile. And it keeps us from being bored.

On satisfying the client and himself: If I do not communicate the client's message I face rejection. My job is to have all our concerns, interests, and obsessions resolved in creating the work.

About the "Houdini" poster: This was for a television special starring the magician Doug Henning, who was to re-create Houdini's famous escape from a tank of water. I chose to be influenced by the Victorian magic poster, but mine is not one hundred years old. The drawing and color are not particularly Victorian. However, the type is as close to the look of the period as I could make it. Styles of the past often add irony to a contemporary situation. In this case the use of Victoriana was obvious and inevitable.

I enjoy playing with the scale of elements. I put a large figure in the tank surrounded by tiny assistants partly to exert the proper impact but also to mock exaggerated claims through visual emphasis of all advertising. The type is taken from Victorian wood types popular in playbills and broadsides of the nineteenth century. The problem with this came when I had to incorporate the Mobil logo, which is in a decidedly modern typeface somewhere between Futura and Helvetica. Keeping it small, I was able to bury it so that it doesn't look incongruous among the other type styles—that is, unless one looks too closely.

Type is a tool to set the stage. It is often expressive and may make the use of image irrelevant. The choice of type style, layout, size, and varied type spacing can be used to express a certain spirit, to project different messages. In the "Houdini" poster, type surrounds the image. Those nineteenth-century printers who worked with wood type and engraved images had little interest in white space—I don't think that white

HOUDINI (1973), *Poster to promote PBS show*
MOBIL OIL CORPORATION, *Client*
SEYMOUR CHWAST, *Designer*
SEYMOUR CHWAST, *Illustrator*

ILLUSTRATION FROM *A BOOK OF BATTLES* (1957), *Hand-printed, hand-bound personal piece*
SEYMOUR CHWAST, *Designer*
SEYMOUR CHWAST, *Illustrator*

WAR IS MADNESS (1987), *Antiwar poster*
THE SHOSHIN SOCIETY, *Client*
SEYMOUR CHWAST, *Designer*
SEYMOUR CHWAST, *Illustrator*

space had been invented. The more that was crammed in, the better. The commercial use of lithography, however, in the second half of the nineteenth century freed the designer to integrate more drawing with type. Since the lettering and picture were printed on the same surface, they could touch or overlap with ease.

On a preference for posters: I have had trouble working on magazine covers where the masthead and cover lines dominate the page and my drawing is relegated to a half-page; I learned in art school that breaking the page in half weakens the impact. Generally I like to work with a large image and smaller type, but they can have equal impact on a page. Posters, packaging, and covers are forms where type and image are easily and naturally integrated, but the scale of posters enables us to play with both large shapes and the smallest details.

About "The Grand Game of Baseball" poster: This was for an art exhibit at the Museum of the Borough of Brooklyn on the theme of baseball. I attempted to create an atypical baseball image that expressed excitement for the game. Baseball is more prosaic and homey than, say, football, and I wanted to reflect that with my nostalgic and somewhat funny idea. The headline is a wood type and evokes a sense of tradition. I ran the lettering down the side rather than across the top because I wanted the figure to be as large as possible—and also because it was quirky. I contained the other type in neutral gray bands to avoid conflicting with the other colors and to make it more readable. Because it is readable I could keep it small and thus have more image area. The placement is pure layout. The type plays off the speed lines of the ball.

About the "War Is Madness" poster: This is a difficult, cliché-ridden theme for any designer. I decided to do a "tough" poster to counter the previous gentler and positive antiwar posters I had done.

The rough crayon drawing of the madman's face contrasts with the white bombs and the newspaper headline type. I tend not to use free-style lettering because of its lack of tension and the fear of conflicting with the "free-style" images. The straightforward, no-nonsense layout is appropriate and different from many posters on this subject that rely on graphic tricks.

On the process of ideation: I usually start sketching until I come up with something. If nothing jells, I will look in a book of old posters for a symbol, metaphor, or pun that generates the idea. It may come from the copy or title, or it may come in the morning when I wake up from a good sleep. Usually there are two elements to the message, that of the client and my own creative requirement. The way they are represented in one image (style, technique, scale, color, mood, spirit, and so on) determines the success or failure of every design.

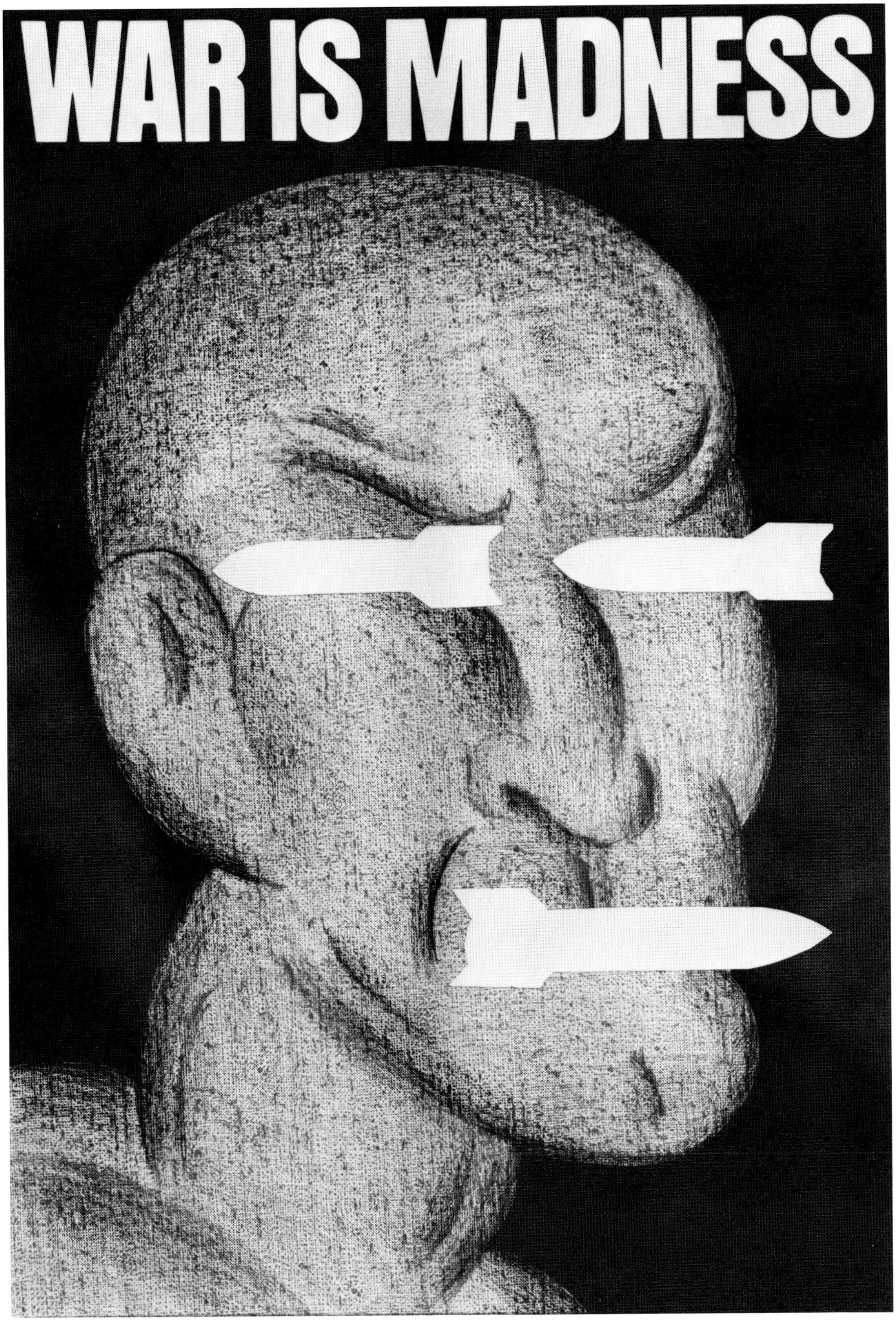
WAR IS MADNESS

THE GRAND GAME OF BASEBALL
...AND THE BROOKLYN DODGERS
APRIL 22 - JUNE 17, 1987
MUSEUM OF THE BOROUGH OF BROOKLYN
BROOKLYN COLLEGE, LA GUARDIA HALL, BROOKLYN, NY
MON, TUES, WED: 10-5, THURS: 10-8, SAT & SUN: 12-4
ADMISSION FREE. FOR INFORMATION CALL: (718) 780-5152

THE GRAND GAME OF BASEBALL (1988),
Poster announcing an exhibit of baseball art
THE MUSEUM OF THE BOROUGH OF BROOKLYN, *Client*
SEYMOUR CHWAST, *Designer*
SEYMOUR CHWAST, *Illustrator*

THE MUSEUM OF THE BOROUGH OF BROOKLYN   APRIL 22 - JUNE 17
THE GRAND GAME OF BASEBALL
LA GUARDIA HALL AT BROOKLYN COLLEGE   MON-WED: 10-5 THURS: 10-8, CLOSED FRI

THE MUSEUM OF THE BOROUGH OF BROOKLYN APRIL 22-JUNE 17, 1987
THE GRAND GAME OF BASEBALL
AND THE BROOKLYN DODGERS
BROOKLYN COLLEGE, LA GUARDIA HALL MON, TUES, WED: 10-5, THURS: 10-8, SAT & SUN: 12-4
CHWAST

MICHAEL PATRICK CRONAN

If an illustration is defined as a drawing (or for that matter another kind of pictorial image) that tells a story, then it might be argued that the work of Michael Patrick Cronan shown here is not illustration. Well, not in the traditional sense, at least. Cronan, the principal of his own San Francisco–based design firm, works with drawing, to be sure, but as a narrative not a symbolic tool. Nevertheless his symbols are storytelling devices. Postmodern by definition, the examples discussed here combine two converging sensibilities: the reductive and the decorative. Cronan uses drawing and collage (hand work) to create spare yet provocative graphic messages; in totality they are more than mere design ornaments—they subtly and often humorously imply, if not actually spell out, a larger significance.

About the poster for Mercury Typography: Within the confines of what a particular job must convey, we imbue much of our work with a sense of humor or lightness. The brochure was a simple idea to describe the five least-used letters of the alphabet. The idea comes from a method of cryptology whereby to break a code one replicates the symbols that are repeated most and least often, giving the two ends of the alphabet. It's a silly idea, but I decided to dress up the letters with decoration—to mix my metaphors, they were made to look like candy. And then Jon Carrol, a wonderful San Francisco columnist, wrote fictitious histories of these letterforms. The piece is a trifle. It doesn't teach anything or convey specific information, but through the combination of design and illustrative elements it draws attention to the typesetter.

On designing for other designers: When we are designing for *ourselves* we should challenge ourselves, make mistakes, and do things that are so weird only *we* understand them. But I agree with the critique against those who design for themselves despite the clients' needs so they can get into shows and win awards from peers; it's the wrong way to approach work. Yet there are certain targeted assignments that are meant to appeal only to our peer group, and *those* should test and push our sensibilities.

About the Stanford design conference poster and mailer, which was just such a piece: In contrast to the typesetter's promotion, this poster is about serious communication; it conveys a lot of necessary information for conferees that I've woven into the pattern of the entire design. The basic design is simple: horizontal with four folds. The first quarter—the cover, if you like—shows a circular pattern. Around it are twenty-four cryptic puppies [small graphic icons] that I categorize as type, but not in the roman sense; more like hieroglyphs, they all have little meanings, or at least implied meanings. One could say that the icons each represent a speaker or event, but actually they do not, because the positioning is arbitrary. The idea was to be at once whimsical and thought provoking. It doesn't really matter what anybody thinks it means; the clues are not real clues. But if the visual game is to be enjoyably played, one could say that the sewing machine translates into industry; the chair, hospitality; et cetera. Decode the symbols, learn the alphabet, and make your own meaning.

The little images were manipulated from an antique Japanese book filled with the most beautiful illustrations showing step-by-step how to draw a soldier, a bee, a wrestler, and so forth.

I made no rules to follow. The client wanted something that conveyed nuts-and-bolts information; I wanted something that would provoke a second look. The illustration of the Stanford University campus is done roughly but is an accurate representation. It appears in contrast to the scattered icons which imply a certain "officialdom" or order. The handwritten headline was just a nice contrast but does have a relationship to the large drawing. My purpose was to load this up with as much suggested reference and random meaning as I possibly could.

On illustration and typography: In the early days I couldn't afford to hire illustrators, so I became good at doing airbrush illustration. Well, I thought I was good, but in reality only my ideas were good, and I couldn't hold a candle to the true virtuosos of the medium. I would work for two or three nights in a row on some $300 job and screw it up right before finishing. It was hell, but I kept my finger in the process, and over the last few years I've had to illustrate more, because of client limitations.

My typography, particularly for annual reports, is usually very straight because I want to make contrasts, and the image is usually where the risks occur. I've done a lot of posters that are handwritten and part of the illustration; when the drawing is tight and the lettering is not, there is terrific tension.

About the Group I identity: This program was done for a commercial film production company, so their clients were advertising agencies. The goal was to tell the creative people at these firms that this production company would sort out their ideas and give them a terrific product.

FORGOTTEN LETTERS (1987),
Poster for typographer
MERCURY TYPOGRAPHY, *Client*
MICHAEL CRONAN, *Designer*
LINDA LAWLER, *Illustrator*

Ad agencies are manipulators of clichés, and so we decided to out-cliché them. But how does one do that with dignity? We took a humorous but not sarcastic tack: for example one of the collateral pieces reads, "Very few things are important. Air is important; love and children and adequate medical insurance are important. That is all. Wait, one more thing: receptionists with British accents. Very, very important."

The whole thing had an air of the ridiculous, but it wasn't really. The company called itself Group I; in fact it was a collective of five to eight film directors each known for different skills. So we decided to make a heraldic symbol out of dollar bills and stock certificate borders that emphasized the number one. Then we developed individual promotions for each member of the group, but we never visually referred to film. We also developed their motto: *E Pluribus Unum*, which, of course, means "from many, one." With that motto it seemed logical that they could have their own government; their office could be their own nation, state, or city. We gave them their own postal system and actually designed a sheet of postage stamps that had a few logo variations. The text for that component read, "Before the invention of postal stamps (1810), citizens were required to glue coins to the outside of envelopes using a substance made of equal parts lanolin and grain husks. In rough frontier regions, postal

STANFORD
1987

STANFORD CONFERENCE ON DESIGN (1987), *Announcement*
STANFORD ALUMNI ASSOCIATION, *Client*
MICHAEL CRONAN AND ROZ ROMNEY, *Designers*
MICHAEL CRONAN, *Illustrator*

PROMOTIONAL IMAGE FOR A FILM PRODUCTION COMPANY (1988)
GROUP I, *Client*
MICHAEL CRONAN AND LINDA LAWLER, *Designers*
MICHAEL CRONAN AND LINDA LAWLER, *Illustrators*

workers (often part-time laborers with seasonal jobs as ski instructors) would steal the coins and use them to buy junk jewelry for 'sophisticated ladies of the afternoon.' "

None of this material dealt directly with what Group I does because their publicity machine had been churning out releases on the formation of the group a few months before we finished the identity. All the principals are well known in their fields anyway, so we felt confident that the trade knew what they did. It's not your conventional hard-sell identity. And we obviously did not have the normal client-designer relationship. I also recommended that the architect Jim Jennings design their office space. With our collaboration the floor plan echoes a portion of the identity image. When we brought our schemes together we knew we were on the right track.

JOE DUFFY

Joe Duffy started his own design firm in 1984 in conjunction with the Minneapolis advertising agency Fallon McElligott. However, the relationship was not the traditional one in which a design studio is subcontracted to do collateral work. From the outset the Duffy Design Group worked with certain clients from the agency's roster as well as servicing their own. But more important, Duffy insisted that the group's own design style be permitted to emerge. In 1985 he hired Charles Spencer Anderson (who is now out on his own), a graphic designer with a strong illustration background, and together they forged a Duffy Group design personality that combines Anderson's taste for vintage American graphic art and an acute understanding of printing technology. The Duffy Design Group includes two senior designers, a writer, a production artist, and others. Here Duffy discusses a few of their assignments and why the illustrative process is so consequential in their work.

About using a variety of materials and techniques: From the outset Chuck and I sought out unusual media and complex printing techniques that in conjunction with our illustration style would engage and surprise an audience regardless of the subject. In general our work is layered, using different patterns, textures, and backgrounds to communicate on a number of levels. We want a point-of-sale piece or a poster, for example, to be striking from a distance; but we also hope that when the viewer is up close, he or she will be absorbed by the other things going on, such as an enticing illustration or hypnotic pattern. Anything that causes people to spend more time with the piece will make the client's message more memorable. Our experimentation with different production techniques is intended to provide more than a flat surface of information. We have used thermography [a raised glazing process], embossing, foil stamping, and other finishing techniques so that the design has a physical depth even though it is printed on a two-dimensional surface. And we work with a few printers who are always willing to bend a bit when it comes to things like longer press time or making changes to improve the job. We stay loyal to those who are willing to expend the extra energy, and in return they get some unique samples.

About the collaboration process: Virtually everyone in the office has some input in the design process. Someone might come up with the design approach, and another might suggest things like a color palette or border style. Usually Chuck, Sharon Werner, or I take the lead on a project, which we discuss with our account executive; but that decision really depends on who is least busy at the time or who is most suitable for the job. Then we meet with Chuck Carlson, our writer, to discuss concept directions. And finally we have a brainstorming session involving other people in the office during which we throw around everything from general ideas to specific decisions, like who will do what.

From my experience in advertising, one of the toughest things to do is become comfortable enough with one's colleagues to throw out ideas—be they dumb or brilliant. We, however, have a conducive environment in which no one is inhibited about contributing—so much so that it really is difficult to recall after the fact who contributed what. With the Dickson promotion book, for example, I do not remember who came up with the idea, but at one of the meetings someone said, "Why not do stamps?" And that was the perfect solution because this printing company is a specialist in stationery.

On type and image: We administer the whole design of a project. Too many times the type treatment on a poster, cover, or whatever is an afterthought—or it appears that way. Someone comes up with a great idea for a visual, and then the designer or art director feels that's it, it's complete. This is unfortunate, because unless that image is framed or woven together with all the other elements, it is not a total design. Though we have been criticized for *overworking* things, I would rather err on that end than not work a design to its fullest.

Once we've decided upon a format, we spend a lot of time trying out different typefaces—sometimes a dozen or more during the course of a

project. And we fiddle with them in different positions until the correct balance is achieved. The easiest thing to do is get a great illustration or photograph, give it white space all around, and then slap some type on top or bottom. The best design, however, is where all the elements are interconnected; where if you take one element away the whole falls apart. For us, the design process is a matter of trial and error. Sometimes, given the right configuration, a type treatment that would never have seemed to work is made harmonious. That is why we must experiment and continue to try various alternatives until something pleasing clicks.

It takes more time and we make less money, but experimentation in general is definitely worth it. Even if we fail a few times—and do not crank out as much work—when we finally do come up with a solution that is completely new, it ultimately earns greater attention; the client is obviously pleased with the results, and we are happy.

On typographic preference: More often than not we use classic typefaces. I am not fond of many of the new faces, nor of the adaptations of the classics where the x-height has been altered or otherwise given a modern look. We've recently been using a lot of hot metal. I love to get the type proofs back with that kiss showing on the paper. In fact, we found a shop in Fort Worth, Texas, called Linotypographers, that still employs the old craftsmen working with metal. All the French Paper work—the swatch books, brochures, and letterhead—are set in hot metal. We also use hand lettering, or create our own typefaces when necessary.

About the lettering for the Classico pasta sauce labels: Sometimes we've used handscripts. For the Classico label I did a little hand-lettered script that ran up the side of the comp. When Chuck saw it, he reduced it on a photocopier and then blew it up again to get a real crusty look.

More about the French Paper project: French Paper is the company that offers Speckletone. Every designer who has ever done an annual report knows that brand, but they do not necessarily know about French. Indeed their corporate identity is overshadowed by this one product. We convinced them that if they wanted to have better recognition in the design market, they should upgrade their image and then introduce new products under the French banner. Chuck is responsible for the design of the project. He started by designing a trademark, which is the face of a guy from a 1930s engraving book. Chuck took it out of its original context and redrew him to make him look French.

The mill is in the center of a small town where time really has stood still; it's called Niles, Michigan. We've tried to capture that nostalgic sensibility in the overall identity. The copy is a tongue-in-cheek slice of Americana, and the imagery is based on those "We Aim to Please" signs from the 1940s and 1950s. Each sample book has a running story about the mill; and rather than conform to the typical swatch books, we've tried to make these into resources for de-

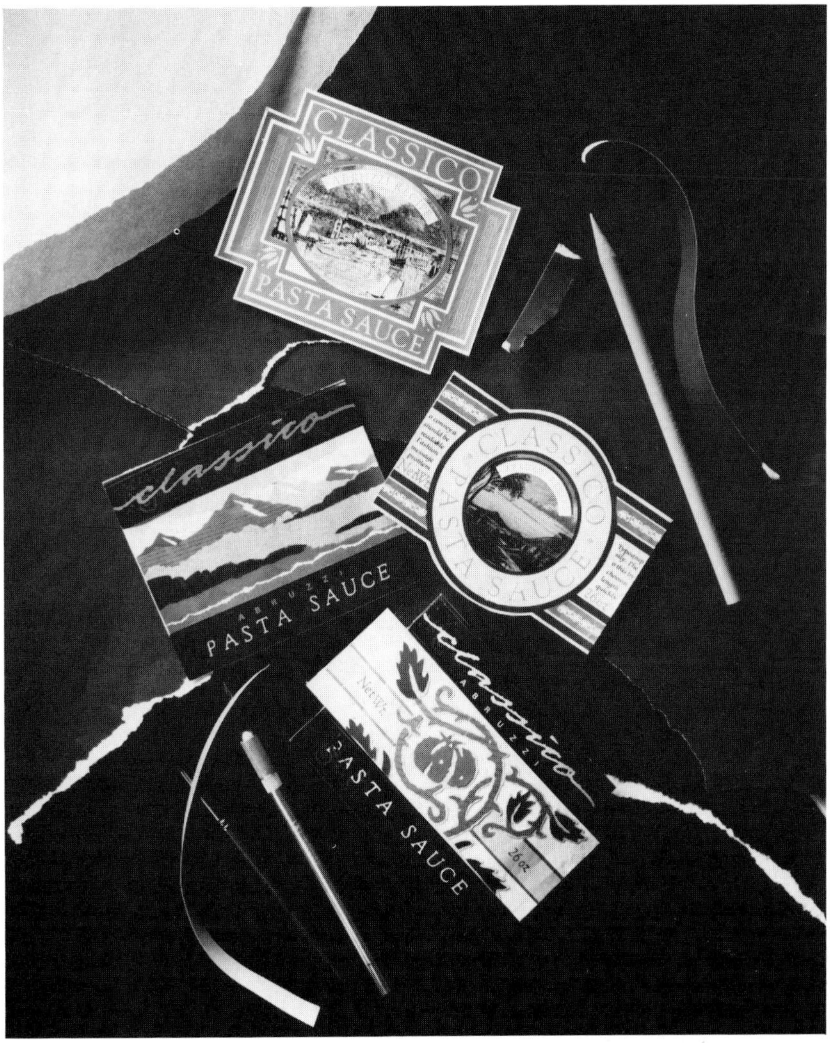
CLASSICO
PASTA SAUCE
classico
ABRUZZI
PASTA SAUCE
CLASSICO
PASTA SAUCE
classico
ABRUZZI
PASTA SAUCE

CLASSICO LABELS (1986)
PRINCE FOODS, *Client*
JOE DUFFY AND CHARLES S. ANDERSON, *Designers*
JOE DUFFY AND CHARLES S. ANDERSON, *Illustrators*
JOE DUFFY AND CHARLES S. ANDERSON, *Art Directors*

DICKSON'S STAMP 5 (1987), *Capabilities brochure*
DICKSON'S INC., *Client*
JOE DUFFY, *Designer*
JOE DUFFY, *Illustrator*
JOE DUFFY, *Art Director*

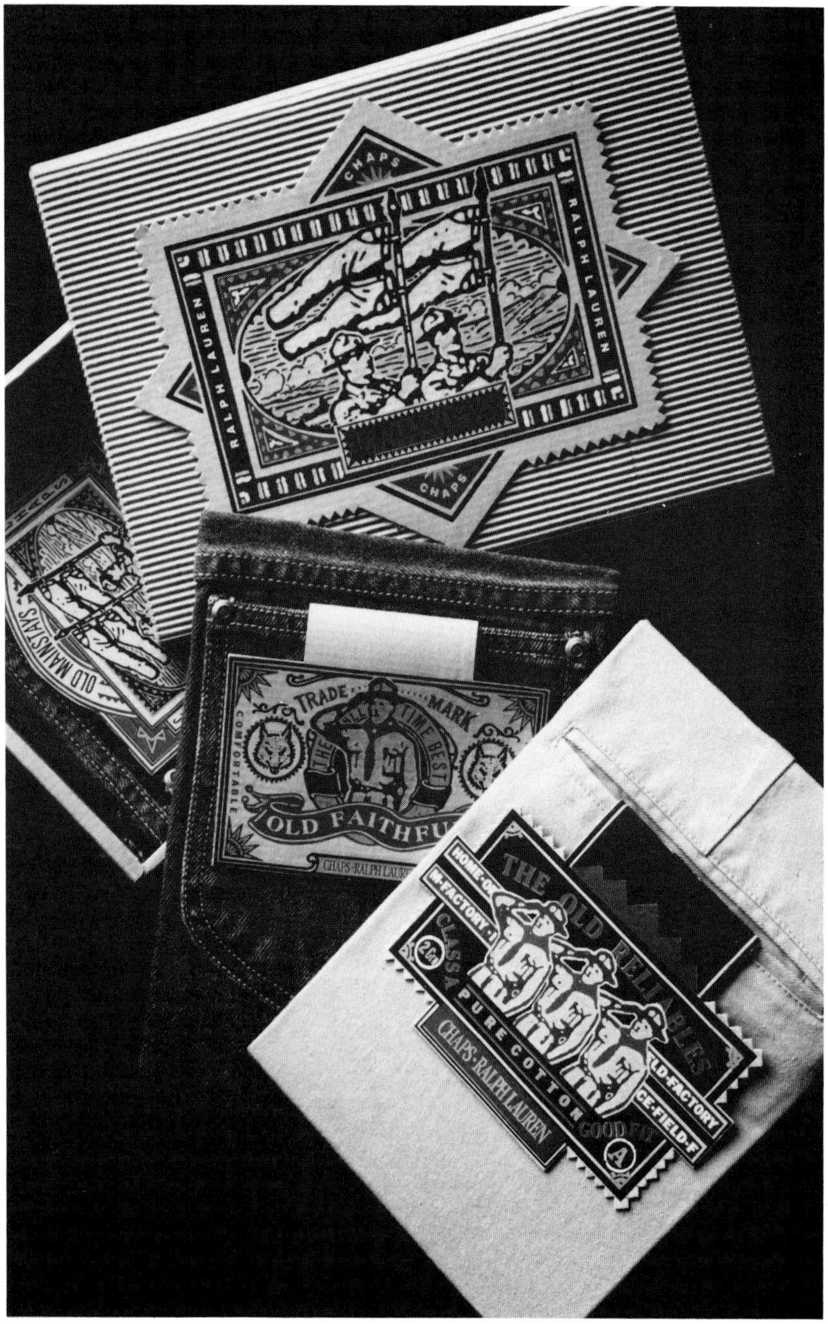
CHAPS
RALPH LAUREN
TRADE
MARK
OLD MAINSTAYS
CLASS A
PURE COTTON
CHAPS·RALPH LAUREN

CHAPS POCKET BILLBOARDS (1987), *Sales tags*
CHAPS/RALPH LAUREN, *Client*
CHARLES S. ANDERSON AND SARA LEDGARD, *Designers*
CHARLES S. ANDERSON AND LYNNE SCHULTE, *Illustrators*
CHARLES S. ANDERSON, *Art Director*

signers—something that might stay on a desk and keep French's name visible.

About the identity for Ralph Lauren's Chaps: We decided to use a scout as the identity image for this line of casualwear because the entire line is nostalgic: chambray shirts, denims, khakis—natural-fiber things. Our character was not a Boy Scout, rather an Indian scout, and Chuck made the illustration from an old photograph he found of one of these guys. Most Ralph Lauren ideas come from the past; and just as we wanted the imagery to have an old-fashioned look, we wanted the materials we printed on to have an old, crusty, worn-out feeling. For instance, we printed the shirt band on corrugated cardboard, and the other hangtags and labels were silk-screened or lithoed on rough chipboard. For the Chaps showroom displays, we produced porcelain signs and found a company in Dallas that makes them by baking the silk-screened image of porcelain crystals onto the metal. We also silk-screened wooden boxes to hold swatches and designed blankets and ties for the sales people to wear.

About the Circa project for Fox River Paper: Circa is a line of uncoated paper used primarily for covers and stationery. We convinced the client to let us do a piece that designers would find memorable not only for its graphic form, but also for its content. This includes a poster, collector cards, video, and book. We came up with a "mystery" plot featuring a character named Max LaPointe, a graphic designer from the 1940s who is always seeking out new scrap on which to base his ideas. Max is in the library one day and meets Marion the librarian, who has a time machine and can send Max into the future so that he can find his graphic treasures. Along the way he meets various people who show him new kinds of paper and printing techniques. He meets a printer in the 1950s, a hippy photographer in the 1960s, and a designer from the year 2020. The book will be printed on all grades of Circa paper and elaborately produced.

We hired Charles Burns, an "underground" comic artist, to develop the character and do all the illustrations. We originally took a few of his own comic characters as models for what we wanted to do, then pieced them together as a comp for the clients, to give them some indication of what the final art would look like. Finally we gave Burns a description of each character in the story so that he could do rough sketches.

Burns is sensitive to design, and was great to

CIRCA
THE VOYAGE OF ALL TIME
FOX RIVER PAPER'S CIRCA PAPERS: WHERE GOOD IDEAS APPEAR RIGHT ON TIME.
SURVIVES, HE MAY BECOME THE GREATEST DESIGNER EVER. BUT THAT'S A BIG IF.
IS THE BRAINCHILD OF LIBRARIAN MARIAN, A CLOSET NUCLEAR PHYS-ICIST. IF MAX
MAX LEFT THE 40'S WORLD OF GRAPHIC DESIGN, ONLY TO BAT-TLE TOE-TO-TOE WITH AN UGLY FUTURE.

CIRCA (1989), *Promotional booklet for Circa paper*
FOX RIVER PAPER CO., *Client*
SHARON WERNER, *Designer*
CHARLES BURNS, *Illustrator*
SHARON WERNER, *Art Director*

work with. His illustrations are perfectly harmonious with Sharon Werner's design, and the result is more like a storybook than a comic strip.

About being a draftsman: Each designer in the Duffy Design Group has the ability to draw, but we do not expect that everyone will illustrate their own work; in fact we are now trying to use more outside artists on some projects. We do want our designers to be able to clearly present their ideas, however; and without drawing skills I think that is impossible.

SPECKLETONE I (1986), *French Paper promotion*
FRENCH PAPER CO., *Client*
CHARLES S. ANDERSON, *Designer*
CHARLES S. ANDERSON AND JOE DUFFY, *Illustrators*
CHARLES S. ANDERSON, *Art Director*

SPECKLETONE
GRADE
APPROVED
MATCHPRINT
SPECKLETONE

Enjoy
Our
FRENCH
PAPER
You'll Enjoy
French
OK
SPECKLETONE

French Paper (1988),
Promotional portfolio
French Paper Co., *Client*
Charles S. Anderson, *Designer*
Charles S. Anderson and
Lynne Schulte, *Illustrators*
Charles S. Anderson, *Art Director*

TIM GIRVIN

Known for his elegant and colorful calligraphy, Tim Girvin has built his Seattle-based design firm on a variety of graphic approaches. Yet calligraphy—what might best be described as the illustrated letter—serves as the basis for much of his typographic and illustrative design. Born of this expressive form of lettering are design solutions that have audible as well as visual qualities. Here Girvin discusses approaches to work that range from calendars to film and clothing logos to a Bloomingdale's special merchandise campaign.

First, a little background: I studied to be a marine biologist and comparative physiologist; I was interested in how organisms live harmoniously on the planet yet my interest was in terms of the beauty of life rather than of a pure scientific orientation. In college the study of beauty is secondary to knowing the internal workings, and I just wasn't equipped to deal with the dissecting, slicing, and dicing we did on all those marine creatures. Realizing I was not going to be another Jacques Cousteau, I put more energy into drawing than lab work. (My mother is a painter, and as a kid I often used to draw alongside her in her studio.) I spent more time working on the design of my lab notebooks than their content. The illustrations became bigger, and I experimented with different ways of laying out the text on a page. As they curiously took on a Middle Ages look, I became fascinated with the history of the medieval book and the theory of the Golden Section. While still in college, I decided to pursue this newfound interest in type design and calligraphy. I learned about the classical approaches but was even more interested in early-twentieth-century book and type design in Germany, France, and England, where I next spent time meeting and studying with the masters.

I understood that type could be an illustration of language, not just a series of characters that meandered horizontally across the page. Type could be imbued with enough vitality that the characters themselves became part of the message. If one extrapolates that idea into the whole design process, things begin to have an expressive character. I used letters as illustration, and also began to see how I could use the same energy that was applied to the design of letterforms—the color, texture, gestural elements—as a method of illustration. Combining the calligraphic with the pictorial is the perfect unification.

About the Manpower calendars: Every year this international personnel firm hires a different artist to do a signature treatment on a calendar. I've done two. The budget did not allow for highly evolved illustrations, however; so I had to come up with something that was strong by using full-color reflective art, process colors, and metallics. For each month I did an abstract illustration intended to be both fun and surprising. The first calendar was more lettering-oriented, which is what they wanted. But they had a pretty biblical treatment in mind that I told them would not work, at least not if they wanted to use me for the job. In turn I suggested an approach that combined interesting type treatments with abstract illustration. The calendars were distributed internationally, so naturally I had to revise the holidays for the different countries—the Fourth of July, for example, would not go over big in Great Britain.

On working with the client: I was commissioned by an East Coast advertising agency. Working with an agency is a rather interesting proposition; often many of the people are very responsive, and I attribute this to being involved in the early stages of a problem, before the idea is locked in stone. In this case we talked a bit, and I sent them some samples of jobs the studio has done. There was not much budget for roughs, so we sent over thumbnails with PMS chips—just to give them an overview.

THE UNTOUCHABLES

STREETS OF FIRE

the Hunger

JAGGED EDGE

JULY

MANPOWER CALENDAR (1984), *Promotional calendar*
MARCUS ADVERTISING, *Client*
TIM GIRVIN, *Designer*
TIM GIRVIN, *Lettering*
TIM GIRVIN, *Illustrator*
RUTHANN PRISTASH, *Art Director*

THE UNTOUCHABLES (1987), *Identity for film*
PARAMOUNT PICTURES, *Client*
TIM GIRVIN, *Designer*
TIM GIRVIN, *Lettering*

STREETS OF FIRE (1984), *Film logotype*
UNIVERSAL STUDIOS, *Client*
TIM GIRVIN, *Designer*
TIM GIRVIN, *Lettering*

THE HUNGER (1983), *Film logotype*
MGM/UA, *Client*
TIM GIRVIN, *Designer*
TIM GIRVIN, *Lettering*

JAGGED EDGE (1985), *Film logotype*
COLUMBIA PICTURES, *Client*
TIM GIRVIN, *Designer*
TIM GIRVIN, *Lettering*

The mechanical process: From there we had to go immediately into mechanicals. I would do the strokes, the drawing, the spatter, cut paper or the assembly, and then have someone in the office put the mechanical together. I indicated what colors I wanted, and an assistant determined what the process tints were going to be.

August

The creative process: Much time was spent thinking about what would be an interesting way to illustrate, let's say, the Fourth of July. I happen to have a house that overlooks a section of water over which a huge amount of fireworks is displayed every Fourth; they provided a great image. For August I just used symbols that convey the spirit of that time—earth, sun, heat. But I don't ponder these solutions for very long; the entire process goes quickly, and I can tell right away if it doesn't work. When I see an opportunity I go for it; therefore it's really very difficult to dissect and intellectualize afterward. But I can say this: I do try to develop design foils that balance each other. For example, I may position a wild typographic treatment within a restrained environment, but ultimately it has to be appropriate to the message at hand.

On the expression of type: It is rare that I will find an existing typeface that works perfectly. Therefore I modify it: blow it up, redraw it, develop my characters. Or often there are parts of a letterform that I don't like, so I customize. I believe that type can be made to emotionally and

Un Bleu Choix (1987),
Logotype variations
Generra Corporation, *Client*
Tim Girvin, *Designer*
Tim Girvin, *Lettering*
Tim Girvin and Anton Kimball, *Illustrators*
Tim Girvin, *Art Director*

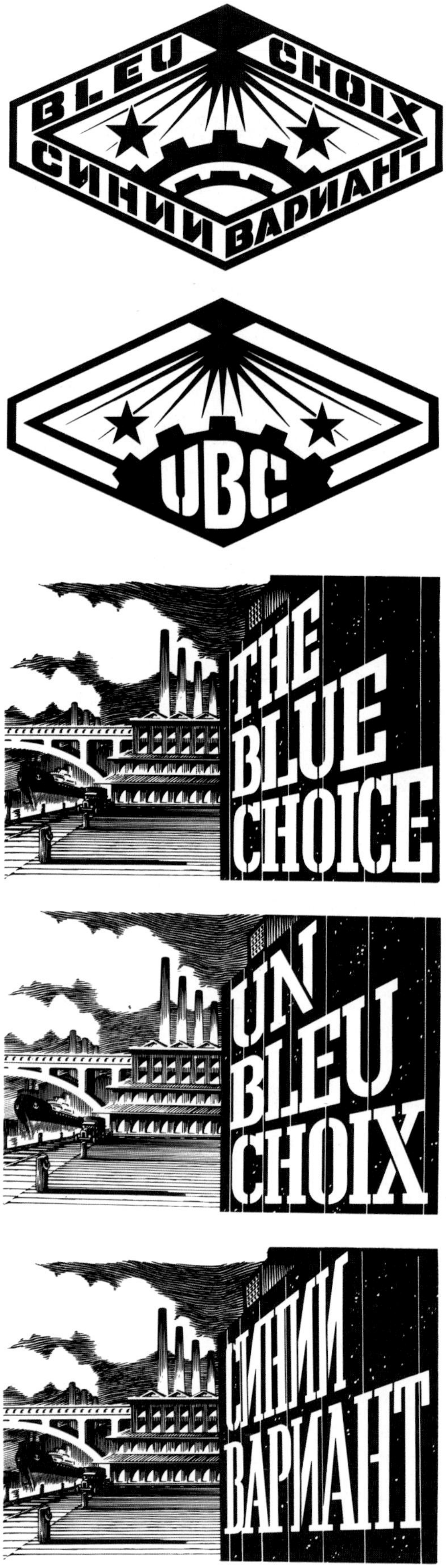
BLEU CHOIX
СИНИИ ВАРИАНТ
UBC
THE BLUE CHOICE
UN BLEU CHOIX
СИНИИ ВАРИАНТ

symbolically convey meaning. This is evident in what we've done for movie identities. So many movie logotypes appear to be randomly designed, suggesting that they are unimportant elements in a campaign; yet when one is looking over a newspaper page at the movie ads, especially in the second and third week of advertising, it is the logotypes that generate an impact, develop in the reader a memory of the film. Those that we've done—*The Hunger*, *Streets of Fire*, *The Untouchables*, and *Jagged Edge*—try to induce the message through lettering, and do so, I believe, as a more pictorial illustration.

About the logos for Un Bleu Choix: It was suggested that a French approach for this line of clothing by Generra was a way of positioning the product for the youthful consumer. The graphic presentation obviously derives from a thirties style. We worked directly with one of the founders of the corporation, who both appreciated and understood our ideas and was open to other suggestions, like the industrial images with Cyrillic lettering.

One reason for this approach is that Seattle has a fairly ongoing program of peaceful activity with the Soviet Union. It is also fashionable, these days, to use Soviet graphic forms, and as a design consideration, the characters are interesting to play with. We also toyed with the idea of power and energy—some industrial and space-age images are used here. The overall sensibility, however, is based on German symbolic logo design of the twenties, such as that of Peter Behrens, who did the identity for the AEG [once Germany's leading producer of electrical services and industrial products]. The linear quality of these illustrations was predicated on the fact that they would eventually be used as labels. The engraved factory-scene illustration for the Un Bleu Choix logotype was drawn by our senior designer, Anton Kimball.

About the South China Seas campaign for Bloomingdale's: We've worked often for John Jay, the art director at Bloomingdale's, who will call us with the concept and the design direction for a merchandise campaign. Sometimes

SOUTH CHINA SEAS
thailand
indonesia
bali
philippines
singapore
malaysia
brunei

SOUTH CHINA SEAS CAMPAIGN (1987), *Promotion*
BLOOMINGDALE'S, NEW YORK, *Client*
TIM GIRVIN, *Designer*
TIM GIRVIN, *Lettering*
TIM GIRVIN, *Illustrator*
JOHN JAY, *Art Director*

SOUTH CHINA SEAS

SPICE ISLANDS

he will have a thumbnail or a very loose sketch; other times, if it's a logo problem, we will just go back and forth using the Fax, until he decides on a specific design direction. The South China Seas campaign began as a sub-promo for Generra; they were doing a new line using batik patterns which they decided to premiere at the Bloomingdale's event. I sent John an example of what we were doing for Generra and he asked us to take part in the overall plan for the larger store promotion. Such an identity must be fairly self-contained, and adapted throughout the store without much difficulty. We came up with the ideas for a logo that used tiny illustrative elements because it is rather unclear what the South China Seas really are (it's actually a large body of water encompassing many different nations, cultures, and islands). The overall design uses a lot of different batik patterns for borders, which we applied to advertising, bags, banners, border treatments, and, of course, large maps to identify the location of the area.

MILTON GLASER

In the early 1950s, after a short apprenticeship in Italy, Milton Glaser returned to the United States and joined several former Cooper Union classmates at Push Pin Studios. Glaser brought a newly acquired European sensibility to the mix, applying an interest in history to the requisites of commercial art. He was not tied to any single approach, so his numerous book jackets, posters, and magazine and record album covers were a conceptual smorgasboard that nonetheless had the distinct imprimatur of one maker. Glaser left Push Pin after twenty years to start Milton Glaser Inc. and practice different approaches. He now designs magazines and supermarkets. His restaurant designs are akin to environmental posters, and he even conceives the furniture, lamps, and uniforms. Yet with all this branching out, Glaser continues to create posters at a prodigious rate. Here he discusses four of them.

BACH
JOAO CARLOS
MARTINS
"HIS TECHNIQUE SENDS FIREWORKS IN ALL DIRECTIONS...HE DOES EVERYTHING WITH EXTRAORDINARY ELAN."
—Harold Schonberg, New York Times
The Complete Keyboard Works, Recorded Digitally On Tomato.

On the purpose of illustration: At the heart of our approach at Push Pin was the idea of narration. At that time nobody seemed interested in telling stories, because when you're concerned with formalism and purity, as were designers in the early fifties, you end up dealing with abstraction. So what emerged was nonnarrative, abstract work that was supposed to be appreciated at the highest platonic level. The use of visual material to tell stories was the fundamental difference between our work and what others were doing.

Providing information is an important part of design, but narration has a different kind of resonance; I don't think it can be achieved very often. The most interesting thing about illustration is finding a particular image that is sufficiently provocative or mysterious or incomplete. In that way the viewer basically participates in the creation of the story.

We also recognized the danger of losing drawing as an essential element in design. To control your idiom you have to make objects that are understandable. However, if you remember back to the sixties, it was almost impossible to convince art students—forget about designers—that the drawn image had any validity. As a result, a whole generation of people could not represent their ideas through drawing. That may be why found-objects and collage became such dominant techniques.

About the pitfalls of theory: If you come to design out of a theoretical rather than an illustration or painting background, you don't have the experience of physically making things in color—seeing what happens to the edges and so on. That's a big loss and one of the reasons students' work in graphics is all based on black-and-white imagery and primary colors. There is little experience dealing with tonality in grays and hues. After all, where does that experience come from?

About content: I am very interested in iconography and mythology. Symbols with historical or literary content have great impact in the sense that they evoke recurring events in human history—there is no way of getting past them. That's why naturalism can recur in painting, why it will never disappear or become abstract. Painting is about the difference between what is seen and how it's represented—it's basically an instrument for making you aware of what is real. Once you eliminate references to the real world by moving into pure abstraction, you've lost one of painting's great functions.

I have always believed that to give up the representational image is to constrict one's ability to move people. And for what? Abstract and formalistic work is absolutely appropriate for certain things, but to reject all imagery that has a basis in observation of reality is crazy. The idea that painting is made obsolete by the photographic revolution is a nonsequitur. Painting is not photography. In painting you make a moral judgment about what you're painting. Like all art, it comes out of an idea about what is good and bad.

A place for abstraction: In the hands of individuals, one form is, of course, better than another. El Lissitzky was a genius at making powerful, fresh things in his particular medium. But take a tenth-rate practitioner copying the formalism of art and you get watered-down crap. It depends not so much on the theory behind what one is doing as on the skill and passion of the practitioner. Futurism, for example, is a wacky idea for painting, but actually there are a couple of very wonderful Futuristic paintings. It's not the school that counts; good work can be produced in any area.

On overcoming the "unfashionable": I object more than anything else to the dismissal of modes of thought because they are unfashionable—and at mid-century it became unfashionable to use representational imagery. Fashion is a generational thing. With the endless promotion of novelty in America and elsewhere there is a quick repudiation of anything that establishes validity. Once the height of abstract painting and design were established there had to be the budding of a new expressionism. Every fashion now—and illustration is certainly susceptible—has its counterrevolution within a five-year period.

FUGUE SUITE BACH (1989), *Promotion*
TOMATO RECORDS, *Client*
MILTON GLASER, *Designer*
MILTON GLASER, *Illustrator*
MILTON GLASER, *Art Director*

C H A R V O Z

CHARVOZ (1987), *Point-of-sale poster*
CHARVOZ, *Client*
MILTON GLASER, *Designer*
MILTON GLASER, *Illustrator*
MILTON GLASER, *Art Director*

About changing style and method: I simply do something intuitively for a while to see whether it works. Yet most of my work has been pragmatic; I've tried to see what I could bring to the table that didn't look exactly like everything else around.

Sometimes my approach depends on what interests me at the moment; sometimes it's what I'm capable of doing at the moment. If I am trying to do a drawing and that drawing doesn't make any sense, I'll change materials or change attitude. Perhaps I'll cut paper. I try to respond to my own capacity at a particular time as well as appropriately reflect what I'm dealing with.

On inspiration: If you are a professional, ideas come about in a thousand different ways. Sometimes there is no inspiration—you're just doing your job and the solution is obvious. Somebody wants a picture of Lena Horne and gives you the photographic reference. That's it. However, the best ideas, the most resonant ones, come from the unconscious. They seem perfect, but you don't understand the genesis. All of a sudden what we call inspiration forces its way through your will and comes to the surface. You may have set the stage by telling yourself the problem, but it still comes from nowhere.

A Bach re-invention for the *Fugue Suite Bach* poster: I don't know where this image came from. I can rationalize it now, the idea being if Bach were alive today he'd be this outrageous guy who would wear a crazy suit and look supercilious, not anything like the grand Old Master we imagine him to be. Since I didn't have a reference I didn't know how to create a suit pattern that would be convincing. Moreover, I wanted to do some nonpatterned, geometric, fugue-like dancing shapes that were related to the Bach in my mind. The image resulted from both the lack of reference and the desire to reflect something about the quality of the music and the personality.

A range of techniques in the poster for Charvoz: I approached this logically. The company makes a variety of art supplies, so I asked myself in what setting do they find their expression? The answer, of course, is a drawing board or tabletop of some kind. First I considered making a landscape out of all the objects on the table. Then I thought I could do each in a different technique to reflect the variety of materials the company sells. I could show the colored pencils by drawing them with colored pencils, and so on. (It's an idea that has worked for me before.) My hope was that the elements would make a congruent landscape; and actually, when you see the elements together, you're not conscious that the techniques are different. Finally I made a puzzle out of it—a little rebus where all the objects spell the name of the company. When viewers feel they are sharing some kind of joke with you the experience becomes more memorable.

About control: Doing the whole process is a means of controlling your work, but it inevitably varies with your own ability and success. The first thing is to demonstrate to the client that by virtue of the way you think and work their product will be enhanced or their objectives achieved. Then you have to be smart about what you're doing; you have to understand the client's needs sufficiently so that your work is not an egocentric exercise.

I am not interested in doing things that don't accomplish the objectives of my client, but I also want to do them in the freshest and most imaginative way possible. I have reached a point in my life where it's difficult to simply take somebody's sketch and render it. I'll do it, but I prefer not to. There are good art directors and designers around who are better typographers than I am; it's more important to have the whole thing as a single vision, to have my work represent me. If it only half-represents me, it's only half as good.

About the bus shelter poster for the two hundredth anniversary of George Washington's inauguration: Every once in a while you get an idea that you immediately know you're going to use. This was one of them. The first thing I thought of was to make Washington's head out of fireworks. The logo was done by Ivan Chermayeff, and my problem was to integrate it with the image. The biggest question, however, was whether I could get something through an agency of city government that was worth doing, and in this case there was no problem at all. Originally they wanted to hang it in the subway, but I said it would be better as a bus shelter poster because the illumination would give it a special glow.

I give a little talk called "light and lightness" that questions why it is possible to recognize something or someone out of a few dots, a squiggle, or a line. I'm interested in the idea that you can make things like little dots of color stand for fireworks, and that people will understand your intentions. Then, just by varying the intervals between those dots, you also can create a recognizable person. I have never been able to get over the relationship between imagery and recognition.

On creating the San Diego Jazz poster: Everybody in San Diego knows this bear at the San Diego Zoo, so I thought I'd have him playing the saxophone. It seems like a rather unlikely thing, but for the primary audience it defines a certain relationship. Others who don't know about the reference have to do the anthropology to find out what the imagery means.

The formal idea for this poster came from a book on Japonism. I lifted the idea of making the whole plane almost like a dimensional foreground, with an object—in this case, the bear—behind it. It's not a very complicated idea, but I'm intrigued with it as a graphic device. It was rendered with a little cross-hatching. The lettering, however, is too hard to read. In retrospect, I should have controlled it better by making it bigger and changing the color. If I had had a good art director, undoubtedly he or she would have sent it back because it was illegible—that's what most art directors do.

About his mother the art director: In high school I had to do a travel poster—I think it was the first poster I had ever done—for an assignment called "From Africa to Alaska." It had a big African head in the foreground and behind it an Eskimo in a kayak. The lettering went up the side. I was working at it very late, and by two o'clock in the morning was so overcome with fatigue that I fell asleep. When I woke up in the morning, my mother, trying to anticipate what I would do, was sitting at the kitchen table painting in the spaces I had left. Of course, she didn't have any idea about it and totally destroyed the bottom half, but I was overwhelmed with the idea that she had gotten up at four o'clock in the morning to finish it because she knew it was due the next day.

SAN DIEGO JAZZ (1982), *Promotion and announcement of jazz festival*
SAN DIEGO JAZZ FESTIVAL, *Client*
MILTON GLASER, *Designer*
MILTON GLASER, *Illustrator*
MILTON GLASER, *Art Director*

San Diego
Jazz Festival

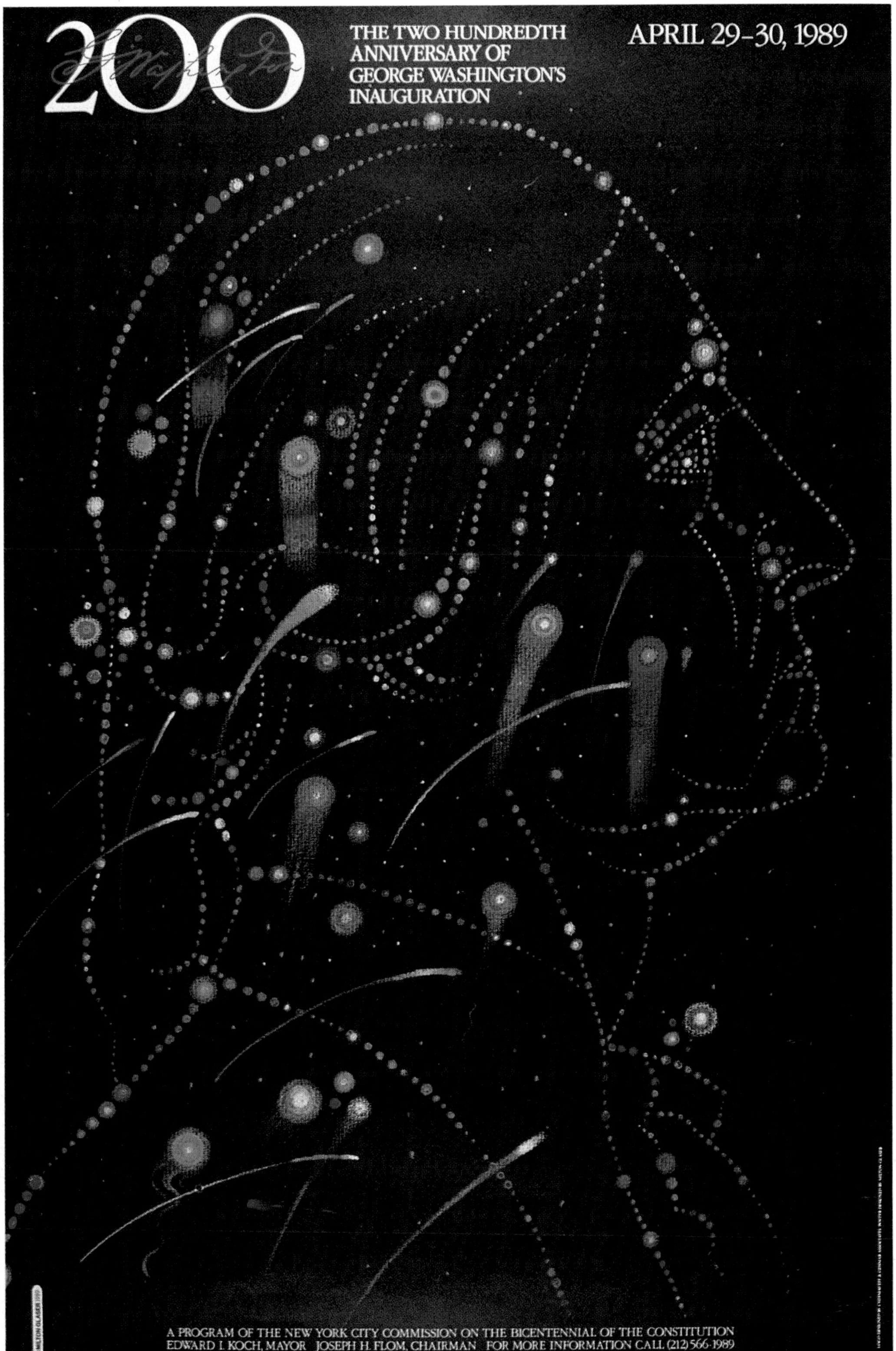
200
THE TWO HUNDREDTH ANNIVERSARY OF GEORGE WASHINGTON'S INAUGURATION
APRIL 29-30, 1989
A PROGRAM OF THE NEW YORK CITY COMMISSION ON THE BICENTENNIAL OF THE CONSTITUTION
EDWARD I. KOCH, MAYOR JOSEPH H. FLOM, CHAIRMAN FOR MORE INFORMATION CALL (212) 566-1989
©MILTON GLASER

WASHINGTON FIREWORKS (1988),
Poster announcing the celebration of the bicentennial of George Washington's inauguration
THE NEW YORK CITY COMMITTEE ON THE BICENTENNIAL OF THE CONSTITUTION, *Client*
MILTON GLASER, *Designer*
MILTON GLASER, *Illustrator*
MILTON GLASER, *Art Director*

MICHAEL MABRY

Architecture was the foundation of Michael Mabry's design education. Today he runs a successful design firm in San Francisco whose clients include Esprit, the trendy sportswear company; Il Fornaio, the legendary Italian bakery-turned-restaurant; and Pacific Rice, for whom Mabry has created a series of delightful package designs. Here Mabry discusses these three distinct design/illustration problems.

On combining illustration with design: It started because of a lack of budget. During my junior year at the University of Utah, I took a job in the graphic design department of the Division of Continuing Education. There was little budget allotted for anything but type and mechanicals, so any visuals had to be produced in-house; thus began my side career as an illustrator.

I've always used my own drawing when financially strapped and that's still the case today. Clients are starting to relate to me as an illustrator, but that was never my intention.

About his method: When I think it appropriate, I take very simple ideas and make them work by twisting reality. I put a person or an object in an unusual context and make it seem like a logical thought. This is something that you cannot do with photography. Drawings of funny people become symbols, and using symbols gives you greater creative latitude.

About the Esprit sport club T-shirts: T-shirts are great display items because they graphically express a mood or theme. I work for Esprit on a very concentrated basis, providing the stores with garment designs that change every two weeks. The graphics represent specific seasons: early spring, spring, late spring, and so on. Recently we've been doing parodies of sport clubs by creating funny logos for imaginary clubs, such as tennis and wrestling, yachting and bowling, mountaineering and golfing, soccer and fly fishing. In formulating what the collection was going to be we remembered a Tyrolian winter sweater—you know, the kind with reindeers on them—but instead of the reindeer, it had a guy on a surfboard. When working on the project with the creative director at Esprit we talked about how good the Japanese are at making things with a lot of English words thrown together that don't make sense but nevertheless have a lot of charm. We decided to make our own collection of odd juxtapositions. I worked on the core symbols and brought in John Hersey to supplement them with computer-made graphic patterns. The Esprit people made certain suggestions and we invented the images. At one time they were interested in using

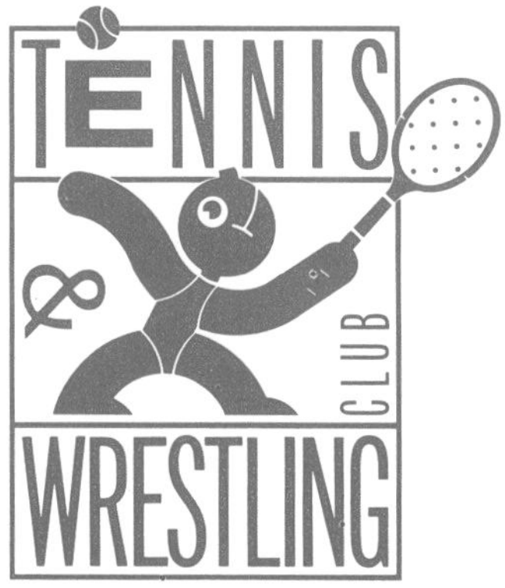
TENNIS
&
CLUB
WRESTLING

MOUNTAINEER
GOLFING TEAM

FLY
CLUB
FISHING
SOCCER

YACHTING
CLUB
BOWLING

Ciao
Saturday was Rome. Sunday,
Nice (nice) Monday. the Loire
Valley. Tuesday, Paris.
Wednesday,
Amsterdam.
tomorrow,
London and then
home...
I feel like
I'm really getting
to know Europe
1989
ESPRIT·SPORT
Love, Conchetta
x x o

CIAO . . . SATURDAY WAS ROME (1988),
Summer 1989 T-shirt placement for Esprit Sport
ESPRIT DE CORP, *Client*
MICHAEL MABRY, *Designer*
BONNI EVENSEN, *Lettering*
MICHAEL MABRY, *Illustrator*
SUE COPELAND, *Art Director*

ESPRIT SPORT CLUB LOGOS (1986),
Spring 1987 clothing placements
ESPRIT DE CORPS, *Client*
MICHAEL MABRY, *Designer*
MICHAEL MABRY, *Illustrator*
SUSIE TOMPKINS AND JIM NEVINS, *Art Directors*

type as a texture, so we did large scarves and shirts with typographic images.

On his process: I start with an image and then add type by Xeroxing, cutting, and pasting until there seems to be a relationship that works. Sometimes I alter the image to fit the type, and sometimes vice versa, until the problem seems to resolve itself. The only thing I was specifically asked to do was change the *E* each time, because that stresses Esprit. This is a case where the illustration and typography are integral, because type is used as one element of the illustration.

About the Esprit travel T-shirts: Travel is definitely a spring idea, and Esprit wanted to do a series of shirts that were akin to hand-drawn and written postcards showing a fanciful scene with some copy fragments such as, "I don't need a vacation, I need an adventure." The images, however, don't relate a whole lot to the words. We've juxtaposed copy about the tropics with images of France. The hope, of course, is that these will be provocative.

About the Il Fornaio identity: For this I used my own illustration, while the Il Fornaio script was done by someone else—it was the only given. My waiter on the menu is rendered in an Art Deco/Cubo-Futurist style and will change when used on other products. On the coffee package he will carry a big cup, and on pasta boxes he will hold a big fork. These characters are used to maximize display. The concept is based on the look of cafés in Europe. Many of them have been around for decades, some in a baroque setting and others in Art Deco. I wanted to work within the illustration style of the thirties and forties, mixed with Spencerian typography and baroque patterning, and have tried to make all these illogical juxtapositions into something that's believable.

QUICK'N CREAMY (1984),
Hot rice cereal package
PACIFIC RICE PRODUCTS, *Client*
MICHAEL MABRY, *Designer*
MICHAEL BULL AND NOREEN FUKUMORI, *Illustrators*
MICHAEL MABRY, *Art Director*

PACIFIC RICE PRODUCTS, INC.
QUICK'N CREAMY
HOT RICE CEREAL
COOKS IN 30 SECONDS
NET WT. 28 OZS. (793.8 G)

Il Fornaio

On the Pacific Rice Products package: This company originally sold their product wholesale to their food processors. When they became more established they decided to enter the marketplace directly and needed packaging for the consumer. We started with the logo for their stationery, and I induced them to let us do the packaging too. They really didn't have a great deal of money to develop a packaging system, so I recommended using the logo illustration of the egret. The egret is known in Asia as the rice bird because it sits in the fields and eats bugs; it is almost sacred. They originally wanted something very hard edged, like the Japan Air Lines logo, but I felt it should be something warm that would feel comfortable in the kitchen. We asked Michael Bull to do the egret illustration and then we dropped the hard-edged rice behind it.

I convinced them to have us design the Rice Flour package. It was going to other manufacturers, and they had planned to just have a printer put something together. I felt it was a crime to let such a large posterlike shape be used poorly, and they finally relented. I was sent a number of bag styles to choose from and selected the ribbed paper. I decided to use the logo in the rectangle as the dominant motif. It's a versatile image that has functioned for them on a variety of products.

The Quick'n Creamy package no longer looks like our original design; a "glamour" photograph replaced the illustration. And I regret to say that they have not stayed with the egret image either.

Il Fornaio

IL FORNAIO BAKERMAN LOGO, PASTA BOX, AND SHOPPING BAG (1988)
IL FORNAIO RESTAURANTS AND BAKERIES, *Client*
MICHAEL MABRY AND MARGIE CHU, *Designers*
MICHAEL MABRY, *Illustrator*
HILARY WOLF, *Creative Director*

MICHAEL MANWARING

A leading exponent of the San Francisco aesthetic, Michael Manwaring has wed an interest in strict European Modernism with an eclectic spirit that bespeaks his colorful surroundings. As the principal of The Office of Michael Manwaring, he works on environmental signage, retail-store identity, and magazine and poster design. Here he reveals some of the influences on a logo for Heffalump, a store specializing in European toys for children; on an autumn theme cover for *Metro* magazine; and on the signage for the San José Historical Walk.

On Italian Mannerism: The Heffalump logo comes from a desire to incorporate my enthusiasm for Italian Mannerist architecture, specifically those very flat facades that are made up of numerous graphic panels. Each is a symbolic, usually grotesque figure—either an animal or human head—often flanked by two other panels with completely different symbology and then divided by an ornamental panel, frieze, cornice, or whatever. It's wonderful how they stack these symbols together to make a whole. As a graphic designer I see it as an additive process that begins at the center and works out. I found it so wonderful that I started doing logos like that for certain clients. Unlike the Italian versions, which exhibit a self-assured awkwardness, my early attempts were not so self-assured.

Today we are not trained to appreciate this approach. It's hard for us modern people to really understand the beauty of complexity. Moreover, we don't know what all those symbols mean anymore—we don't have the rich Mannerist forms in our own vocabularies. Therefore my symbols are still somewhat on the neutral side; I'm trying to discover more interesting images that mean the same thing to me as they do to you. I am determined to see how these forms can work in contemporary American graphic design.

In praise of complexity: Reduction was part of my educational background, but as beautiful and efficient as Swiss design is as an educational process, I realized that it doesn't have a lot to do with living in California, or America. This method was developed in a culturally stable and tradition-

H
EFFA
L•U•M•P

bound European country. It was too tidy and polite for America. It also bothered me that it was not indigenous. I became more interested in the psychedelic poster artists like Kelly and Mouse. What these guys were doing was part of America—big, dynamic, and out of control. Though I still start with the structural principles of Swiss design, I could never go back to that. I draw constantly. Compared to most graphic designers, I am a draftsman. But compared to a Renaissance painter, I am not.

About conceiving the Heffalump logo: I did this in one afternoon. That is not the way I usually do logos; all the planets were in alignment. Everything happened on that one piece of paper, and I knew that when I did the next twenty logos I would be thinking, "Why isn't this happening like Heffalump?"

I wanted it to be a toy, but I didn't want it to be a rendering of one. I thought of it as a little person—a doll. Heffalump is an elephantine character from *Winnie the Pooh,* but I didn't want to do the *Winnie the Pooh* character either. It had to be appreciated by children and adults, and therefore I didn't think readability was important if the symbol was interesting enough. You can give up readability if there's an equal payback. Indeed, people are not frustrated by the broken word because, like a child's voice, it says "Ha . . . effa . . . L-U-M-P. It's a pleasant puzzle to work out; it is playful and a little magical. Most important it has some reference to nature and to play.

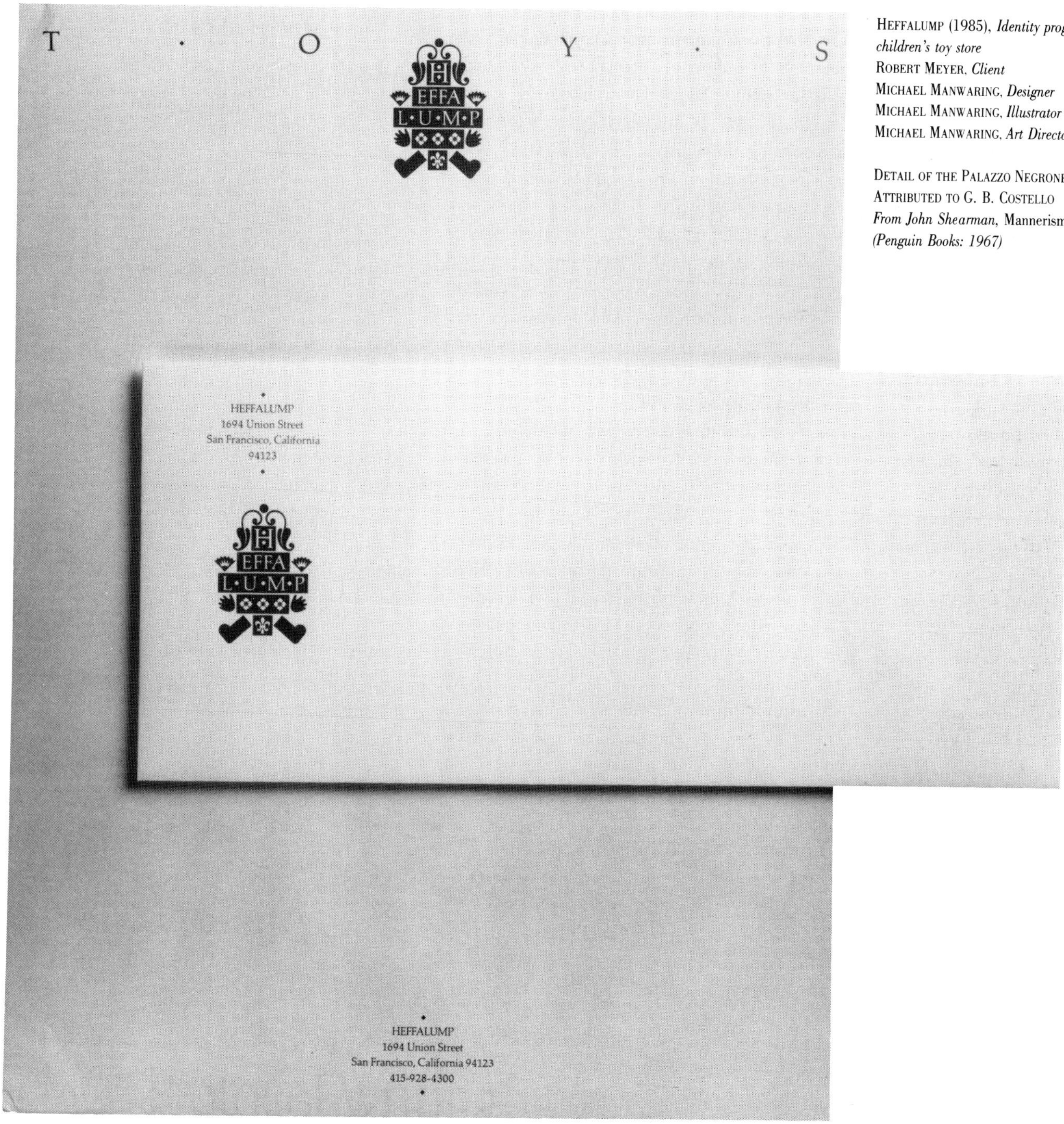
T · O · Y · S
HEFFALUMP
1694 Union Street
San Francisco, California
94123
HEFFALUMP
1694 Union Street
San Francisco, California 94123
415-928-4300

HEFFALUMP (1985), *Identity program for children's toy store*
ROBERT MEYER, *Client*
MICHAEL MANWARING, *Designer*
MICHAEL MANWARING, *Illustrator*
MICHAEL MANWARING, *Art Director*

DETAIL OF THE PALAZZO NEGRONE,
ATTRIBUTED TO G. B. COSTELLO
From John Shearman, Mannerism
(Penguin Books: 1967)

About the San José historical signs: If you are going to do a sign it should not only be utilitarian but contribute to the environment. The best example of this kind, and certainly my inspiration, is Hector Guimard's Paris Metro signing. If anyone tried to take those out of Paris, people would be outraged because they are more than signs; they're part of a culture. If you are going to do signs that will be around for ten to forty years, they should be done with the same love of materials and consciousness of environment as Guimard had. For the San José redevelopment agency we did thirty-eight metal-cast historical markers that are 10 feet high, beautifully made with leaves and sunbursts as their ornamental motif. They do not stand out in the environment as some kind of freak but as an integral part of the city.

SAN JOSÉ
HISTORY WALK
CITY OF SAN JOSÉ
CALIFORNIA
FOUNDED 1777

SAN JOSÉ HISTORY WALK (1985), *Self-guided marker system to identify historical landmarks*
SAN JOSÉ REDEVELOPMENT AGENCY, *Client*
MICHAEL MANWARING, *Designer*
MICHAEL MANWARING, *Illustrator*
MICHAEL MANWARING, *Art Director*

AUTUMN (1981), *Magazine cover*
METRO MAGAZINE, *Client*
MICHAEL MANWARING, *Designer*
MICHAEL MANWARING, *Illustrator*
MICHAEL MANWARING, *Art Director*

Concerning illustration: I call this illustrative signing. And there's nothing new about what I'm interested in—complexity and ornament are not new. It's trying to go back and find out what's good and what's missing from contemporary design. Illustration is narrative drawing; design can be illustrative, and illustration can be design-oriented. I am interested in using pictures to tell a story. Even in typography. For example the Swiss approach is to use type as a formalist device to carve up two-dimensional space, as opposed to Herb Lubalin, who used type to express an idea and make a picture. Lubalin's approach was more suitable for America.

About the *Metro* cover: I think I'm better at making pictures than at making type designs. With this cover I originally used some kind of sans serif type across the bottom, but it didn't seem right. When I scribbled the word *autumn* as a formal complement to all these jagged shapes, that seemed better. It had nothing to do with the meaning of autumn; it was purely a formal decision. I wanted something spindly, weak, and slightly out of control against all these sharp points. There was no historical reference here, as with the others. In this case I picked a form that was kind of arbitrary and just started working with it. At first I was thinking grape harvest, and the romance of the harvest—and it was trite. I had to think of the opposite. (When I am stumped, I try to think of something that is just the opposite of what I've been doing.) I decided to use a cigarette—it had nothing to do with anything, so I drew it and put lips around it. What did it mean? I put the eye in, and the hat shape . . . so what? A woman smoking a cigarette. I'd better throw some grapes in there. No, not grapes, a leaf. How do I get a leaf in there? I thought, it's a dry leaf on fire and she's lighting her cigarette. And I thought, God, that's so cynical. I mean, taking an autumn leaf and lighting a cigarette with it. But I kind of like it.

METRO
MAGAZINE
FREE
Autumn

DON SIBLEY AND REX PETEET

Don Sibley and Rex Peteet met at a small college "in the piney woods of east Texas," where they took illustration classes together. After Rex transferred to a different school, they reunited in Dallas. There, both took jobs in agencies and design firms, including Dennard Creative and The Richards Group, where illustrative graphics were routinely practiced. They founded Sibley/Peteet to test their own talents, and in so doing continued the Texas illustration tradition. Here they discuss how drawing plays a major role in much of their work, especially advertising for real-estate developments and retail malls, and how their eclectic approach is determined.

About the Texas look: The tradition for illustrative design in the Dallas design and advertising firms developed in part because of the clients themselves. For example The Richards Group created looks for shopping centers, and rather than a cool Swiss design these clients required a fashionable poster look. Richards developed a design style that was unlike any other retail advertising. Soon all the studios began doing illustration because the clients preferred approaches that were not staid or conservative. Texas has been labeled as the capital of frivolous and fun graphic work. Although it may have been true eight years ago, we have matured. Still, everyone wants a distinctive look, and illustration allows for that more easily than photography.

How the term *illustrator* applies to Sibley and Peteet: We do not consider ourselves illustrators because most of the images we do are really stylized design. A true illustrator is somebody who exclusively renders and is concerned with the nuances of drawing, such as mottling, shading, and dimension. What we try to do is simplify, reduce images to their basic geometry—create depth by using drop shadows or through the choice of color. We are, in fact, stylists.

About becoming graphic designers: Neither of us really understood what a graphic designer did until we left college. We both loved the process of drawing and making pictures but felt that our capabilities as renderers were not best suited to earning a living as illustrators alone. Solving an entire design problem was certainly more attractive than specialization. Indeed, now we also write the copy for most of our projects.

As designers our styles have evolved much quicker, perhaps, than if we had devoted ourselves to one speciality. As designers we deal with size and proportion; whether to use type, photography, or illustration. This affords us flexibility. We can make decisions about type and image size that an illustrator who is contracted only for his speciality is unable to make, and therefore we customize our illustrations to each problem.

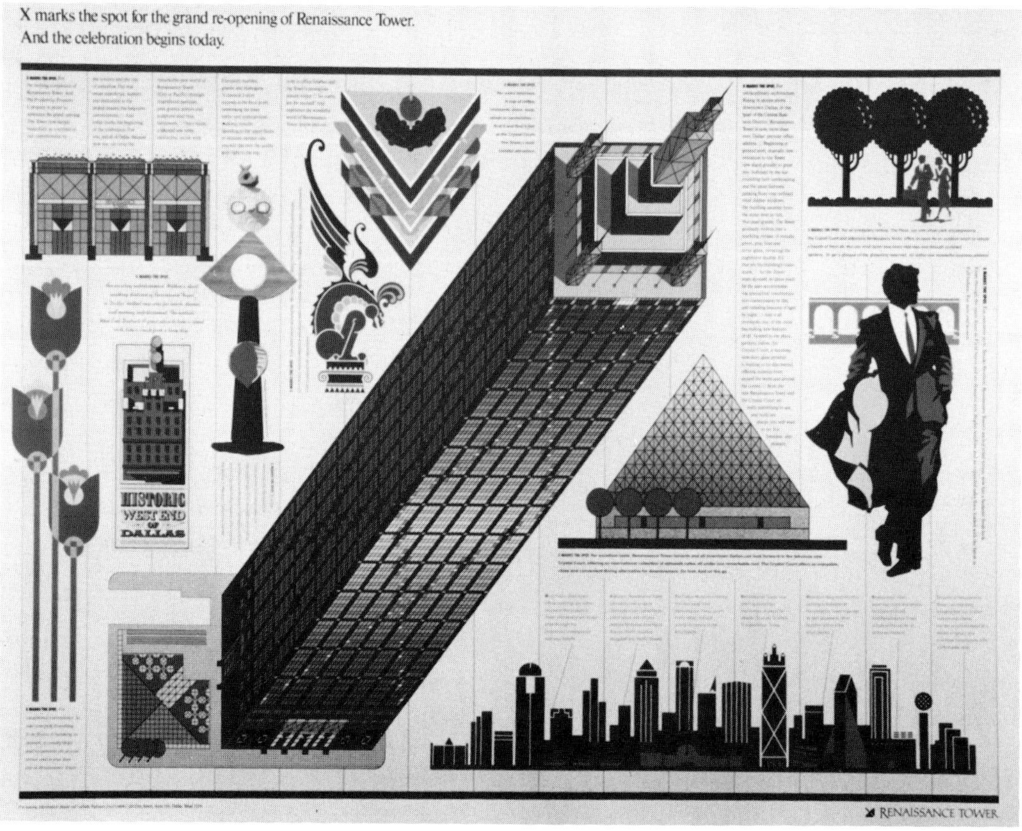
X marks the spot for the grand re-opening of Renaissance Tower.
And the celebration begins today.
HISTORIC WEST END OF DALLAS
RENAISSANCE TOWER

About type: While with The Richards Group we did a lot of illustrative trademarks that hearkened back to the antique and offered a great opportunity to really discover type and all the possibilities of uniting it with an image. Moreover, we were always fiddling with type in some way: instead of setting a block of text to go under an illustration, we would try to integrate it. We created illuminated characters to lead off paragraphs that were in the spirit of a particular illustration, and so on. We were—and are—eclectic. In fact, today some of the work we do involves four or five illustration approaches and weds a variety of typefaces to the illustration style. Type is one aspect of design where the more you use it, the better you get at it.

Concerning the process: Seldom do we create a piece of art that can be framed. We specify various screen combinations, providing Pantone or Zipatone comps. A lot of what a *real* illustrator goes through in the process happens for us when we cut and paste comps together. Our general style lends itself very well to large areas of flat color. But depending on the specific direction, there is a stage when we also sit down and draw with a brush, pencil, or Rapidograph. Lately we've been making photo-collage illustrations. But the final work usually happens at the printer.

We are often surprised at how little knowledge traditional illustrators have of the reproduction process. We have worked with Scitex, and so have the ability to create effects pure drawers cannot. That understanding influences the way we illustrate.

More about computer technology: The Scitex and the Gerber are helpful because, with the latter, images can be reduced to their geometric forms, specifically regarding architectural renderings or stylizations of buildings. We also work with the engravers to achieve a number of our techniques. Since we often provide simple keylines, once we get it on a system it is easy to manipulate.

About the advertisement for Renaissance Tower: This vividly represents our eclecticism. The ad is for the opening of a grand building and the constituent retail emporia. We decided on the rebuslike design solution because of the many diverse stories that could be told about the building, such as its revitalization and the development of a new arts district nearby. This variation gave us an opportunity to use different typefaces. We selected Times Roman because it has a kind of reverence and sophistication, and it related well to the architecture. For the entertainment centers, however, we used typefaces that are more fun. And we selected a more historical face for the monuments, such as the old red courthouse. The building had a plaza with a glass tetrahedron as its centerpiece, under which was a food court. Since the illustration for this was hard and rigid, it lent itself to a face like Helvetica. Despite this typographic smorgasbord, we are concerned that the typography be compatible and always keep in mind how it will look when color is applied. For example, we would never select a teeny-weeny serif to be reproduced with screen-mixed color.

Our careful setting of type—that is, the consistency of leading and of the rags—as well as

GOOD EARTH
LUNCHEON

GOOD EARTH MENU (1984)
GOOD EARTH RESTAURANTS, *Client*
REX PETEET, *Designer*
KEN SHAFER, *Illustrator*
REX PETEET, *Art Director*

RENAISSANCE TOWER (1987), *Double-page advertisement*
LASALLE PARTNERS/RENAISSANCE TOWER, *Client*
DAVID BECK, JULIA ALBANESI, REX PETEET, PAUL BLACK, AND JOHN EVANS, *Illustrators*
REX PETEET, *Copywriter*
REX PETEET, *Art Director*

Villa Linda Mall, Santa Fe

VILLA LINDA MALL (1985), *Poster*
HERRING MARATHON GROUP/VILLA LINDA MALL, *Client*
DON SIBLEY, *Designer*
DON SIBLEY, *Illustrator*
DON SIBLEY, *Copywriter*
DON SIBLEY, *Art Director*

the color choices tie the ad together. Although all the drawings were done by several people in our studio, Don did the lion's share, while the others inked and colored them.

About the menu for Good Earth: With the Good Earth menu we got several illustrators—including Jerry Jeanmard, whose style is compatible with ours. Good Earth Restaurant was founded in the mid-1970s when people were very health-oriented, so everything is natural. We believed a good way to convey this thought and bring it into the 1980s was with the seed package idea. Each illustrator had to do a seed package design according to a list of food categories in a different style. The client wanted us to make our approach a little more contemporary than we had originally planned but not lose the roots of the antique, which is why we used a sans serif face.

On the announcement for Villa Linda: This piece was just one from an entire campaign done for a Sante Fe shopping mall. Santa Fe is an arts-conscious community, which is something we had to be aware of when deciding upon a solution. In fact, the client requested that we *not* make it look as if a big-city developer had done it. So we decided on a very low-key approach, using a festive Southwest palette. The illustration required only a small amount of type. Although

FEBRUARY 6-16, 1988
MARDI GRAS
GALVESTON
CARNEVALE DI VENEZIA

GALVESTON MARDI GRAS '88
(1988), *Poster*
GALVESTON (TEXAS) PARK BOARD
OF TRUSTEES, *Client*
DON SIBLEY, *Designer*
DON SIBLEY, *Illustrator*
DON SIBLEY, *Art Director*

Lovers West
Where fashion becomes fine art. Expressive. Imaginative. Displayed by an exquisite collection of select boutiques. Opening Fall '84 at the corner of Lovers Lane and Inwood. Some call it Dallas' answer to Rodeo Drive. We call it marvelous. For leasing information, contact Thomas E. Brosseau, President, Swearingen/Brosseau Development Company. 214-922-8700
Lovers West. The Fine Art of Fashion.

LOVERS WEST (1984), *Advertisement*
SWEARINGEN/BROSSEAU, *Client*
DON SIBLEY, *Designer*
DON SIBLEY, *Illustrator*
PHIL TERRY, *Photographer*
DON SIBLEY, *Copywriter*
DON SIBLEY, *Art Director*

it is used fairly small, the typeface, called Ad Lib, has a hand-cut feel to it, which is appropriate for the paper-cutout look of the illustration.

About the Galveston Mardi Gras announcement: This event has a different theme each year; this year was Carnivale de Venezia. We researched the period and found that the hard-edged style of drawing was right for us. Even the borders are directly influenced by some posters that were printed in the late nineteenth century. Our poster was silk-screened. The smaller type is hand-drawn in the style of the time, while the headline is an existing face from the period. Making each letter different gave it the festive feeling.

Concerning their preference for various drawing styles: Illustrators tend to create one style that they stay with for a long time, in part because they want a niche that is marketable. Perhaps, also, they are just not as influenced by the range of things we see. Because we find ourselves getting bored doing the same sort of stuff, we continually try to push it. We also influence each other, so that our collective graphic style is a synthesis of approaches we may use individually. With all the activity in our studio it's hard not to be influenced by a colleague.

On collaboration: Sometimes we will come up with an idea that we both think is terrific, and will build upon it. Other times a problem will come in, we will talk for a while, and each of us will come up with ideas separately. With the Good Earth restaurant the client actually chose different elements from a number of ideas, and we were able to make them work together.

About the Lovers West ad campaign: This was for another Dallas retail strip, whose developers were trying to position it between Rodeo Drive and Fifth Avenue. The ads ran in *Vogue* magazine, which was a unique challenge because *Vogue* has page after page of wonderful images, and we wanted to do something that would dramatically stand out. As much as anyone can, we purposely went looking for something that would be innovative yet communicate the elegance and sophistication this center wanted to have. The graphic approach, combining photography with a loose illustration style, was a trick that turned out well. Don did one of the illustrations, and we farmed the other to Jerry Jeanmard because we do not work with pastels.

We were trying to capture the essence of fashion as an art. We wrote the headline, "The Fine

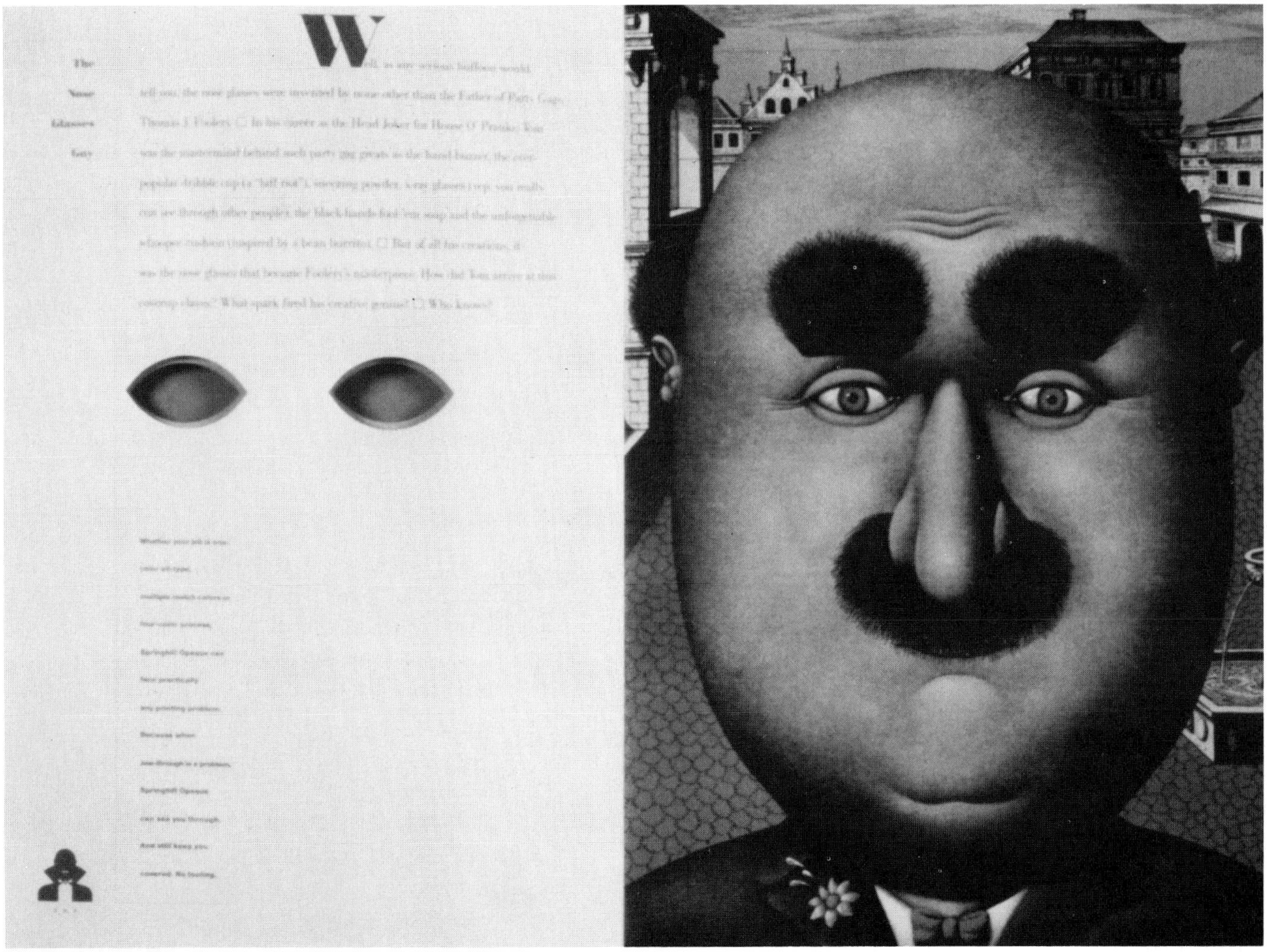

Art of Fashion" after coming up with the visual idea. The typography was kept fairly quiet because nothing should compete with the graphics—it's a soft sell, and the lettering is not so much a headline as a title.

About the promotion piece for International Paper: The purpose of this was to sell a line of lightweight opaque paper. The paper is used for direct-mail promotion not only because of its opacity, but because it can be covered with a lot of ink and remain lightweight. So we devised the "cover-up" idea; and the quintessential cover-up is the false nose and glasses. We commissioned a number of illustrators; the cover, which is supposed to show the "inventor" of the nose and glasses, was done by Tom Curry—he has a good sense of humor and a very similar sensibility to our own. But his original art was not as brightly colored as I wanted, so we put it on the Scitex system and changed the colors to meet our requirements. We beg the indulgence of those illustrators who resent our tampering, but Tom was really accommodating and said, "Rex, I'm glad you can do that with your machine, because I do not want to redo it."

INTERNATIONAL PAPER OPAQUE (1988), *Promotion*
INTERNATIONAL PAPER CO., *Client*
REX PETEET, *Designer*
JACK UNRUH, JERRY JEANMARD, TOM CURRY, REX PETEET, AND JOHN EVANS, *Illustrators*
REX PETEET, *Art Director*

MICHAEL VANDERBYL

Owing to his architecturally inspired graphic design, Michael Vanderbyl typifies one of the leading design styles of the eighties—the Pacific New Wave—for which the return to drawing is a significant departure from the Modernist ethic. His images are symbolic rather than narrative, iconographic rather than representational, a combination of the disciplined Swiss grid and the witty illustration of Push Pin. As principal of his own San Francisco design firm, he has expanded the role of graphic designer into a three-dimensional arena that includes "illustrative" showrooms for clothing and furniture concerns. As dean of the School of Design at the California College of Arts and Crafts, he tries to integrate the design and illustration disciplines.

About personal influences and the San Francisco style: The designers in San Francisco are primarily illustrative—very graphic, but also quite figurative—and this defines my approach too. Perhaps not surprisingly the Bauhaus and Push Pin Studios were the two strongest influences on my work. My instincts fall somewhere between the abstraction of the former and the illustration of the latter; I use recognizable images and icons rather than pure abstract forms. Yet I am also influenced by certain formal disciplines of the International Style represented by Armin Hofmann and Josef Müller-Brockmann. My Swiss side says that form follows function. However, if the job is romantic I will use images that are appropriate to the need. Transplantation of the strict, rational Swiss approach to the United States is bound to fail because the style is void of humor and warmth. I prefer witty, humanistic, and approachable methods. I've always wanted people to smile at my work. Moreover, I dislike the practice of design in the pseudo-intellectual way. As an elitist function, design is totally useless. Icons and images should be used which *people* comprehend, not only designers.

On the inevitability of style: There is no way a designer can avoid having a look. I try not to have one, but my influences are definitely visible. For example my work is somewhat architecturally inspired, though less so than it often appears. My most visible work—that reproduced in shows and annuals—is a series of posters for an architectural lecture series; it is, of course, architectural but this has less to do with style than clarity of purpose.

Visual clarity: A visual idea should be expressed immediately and clearly. I always find an illustration is better because people identify with pictures. With a drawing the viewer perceives the message faster than with type alone.

About the poster for California Public Radio: This was the first graphic I did that delineated modernist (or abstract) from pictorial image making. It is based on the Swiss idea of abstraction—using flat colors and planes—but it

CALIFORNIA PUBLIC RADIO
RADIO PUBLICA DE CALIFORNIA

also has a figurative element that can be easily understood. Moreover, it is an interpretation of two abstract ideas: hearing and speaking. It was the first time I was able to combine the two forms and apply my skill of axonometric drawing.

About the poster for Modern Mode: This was an announcement for the opening of a furniture company's showroom. Ironically, it has also become an icon of California design, representing a kind of Pacific New Wave sensibility. The funny thing is that the wiggly things with the drop shadows were not just gratuitous decoration, but placed precisely, for function. The family that owns the company is Italian, and they were going to throw a spaghetti feed to celebrate the opening of "Space Apple," their first showroom in New York.

Conceiving posters for an architectural lecture series: I have the most fun with the poster form because the problem is one of interpretation. Normally I begin with the words: in this series there was always a title such as "Art × Architecture," "Reflections," and so on. The "Peripheral Vision" poster announced a lecture by architects who were doing work outside of the mainstream, and the illustration symbolically ties

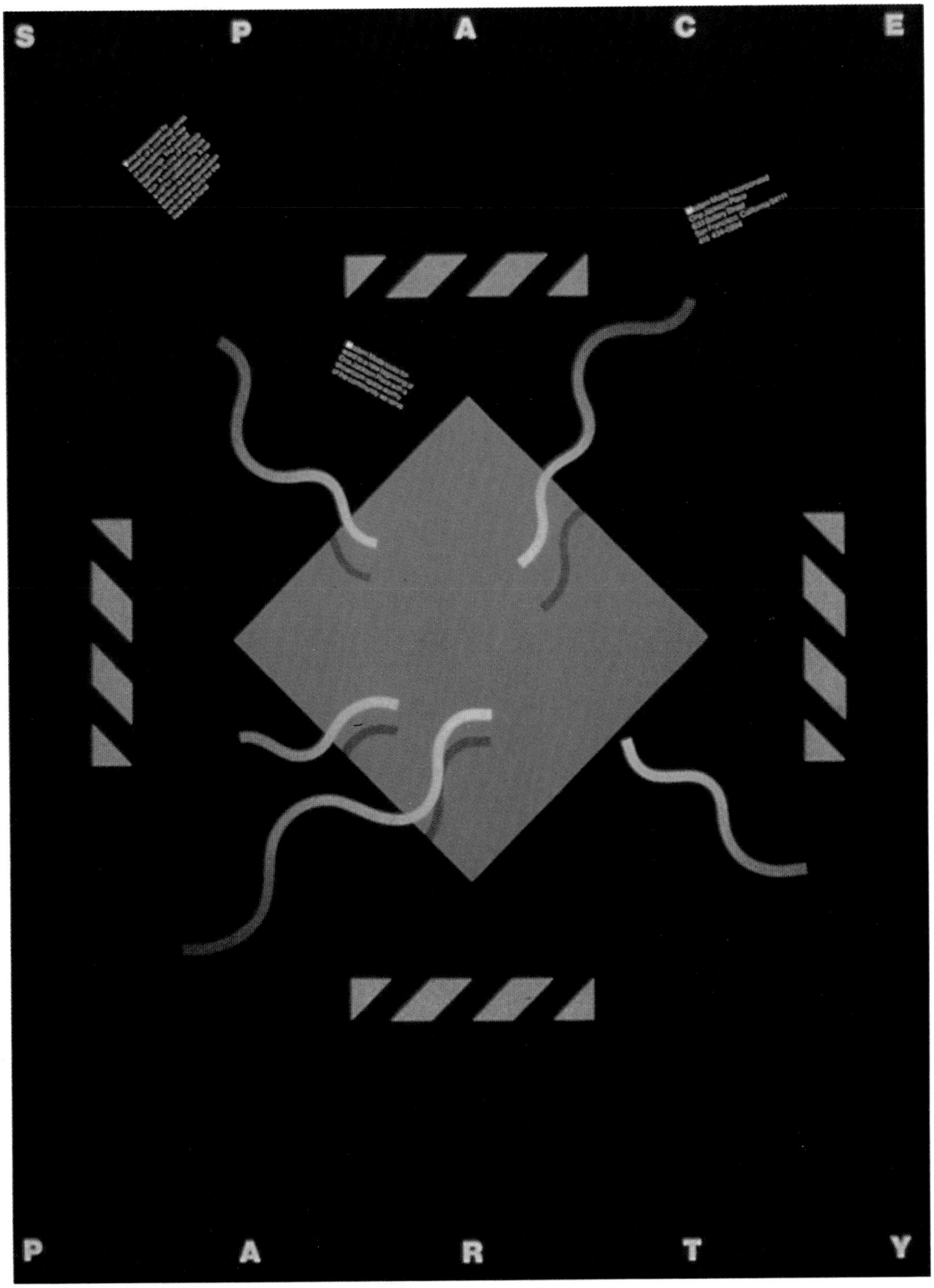
S P A C E
P A R T Y

SPACE PARTY (1976), *Promotion for showroom opening*
MODERN MODE INC., *Client*
MICHAEL VANDERBYL, *Designer*
MICHAEL VANDERBYL, *Illustrator*

CALIFORNIA PUBLIC RADIO (1980), *Promotional poster*
CALIFORNIA PUBLIC RADIO, *Client*
MICHAEL VANDERBYL, *Designer*
MICHAEL VANDERBYL, *Illustrator*
MICHAEL VANDERBYL, *Art Director*

these disparate fringe architects together. The type treatment on the bottom was done because not all the type would fit under the image, so we put the names on the side—what the hell, I thought; the readers can turn their heads a bit. It became a leitmotif for the series. It was also a means to diminish the impact of the type so that the image was dominant, and it reflects the illustration's verticality.

About the poster for Simpson Paper Company: For the "Connections" series Jim

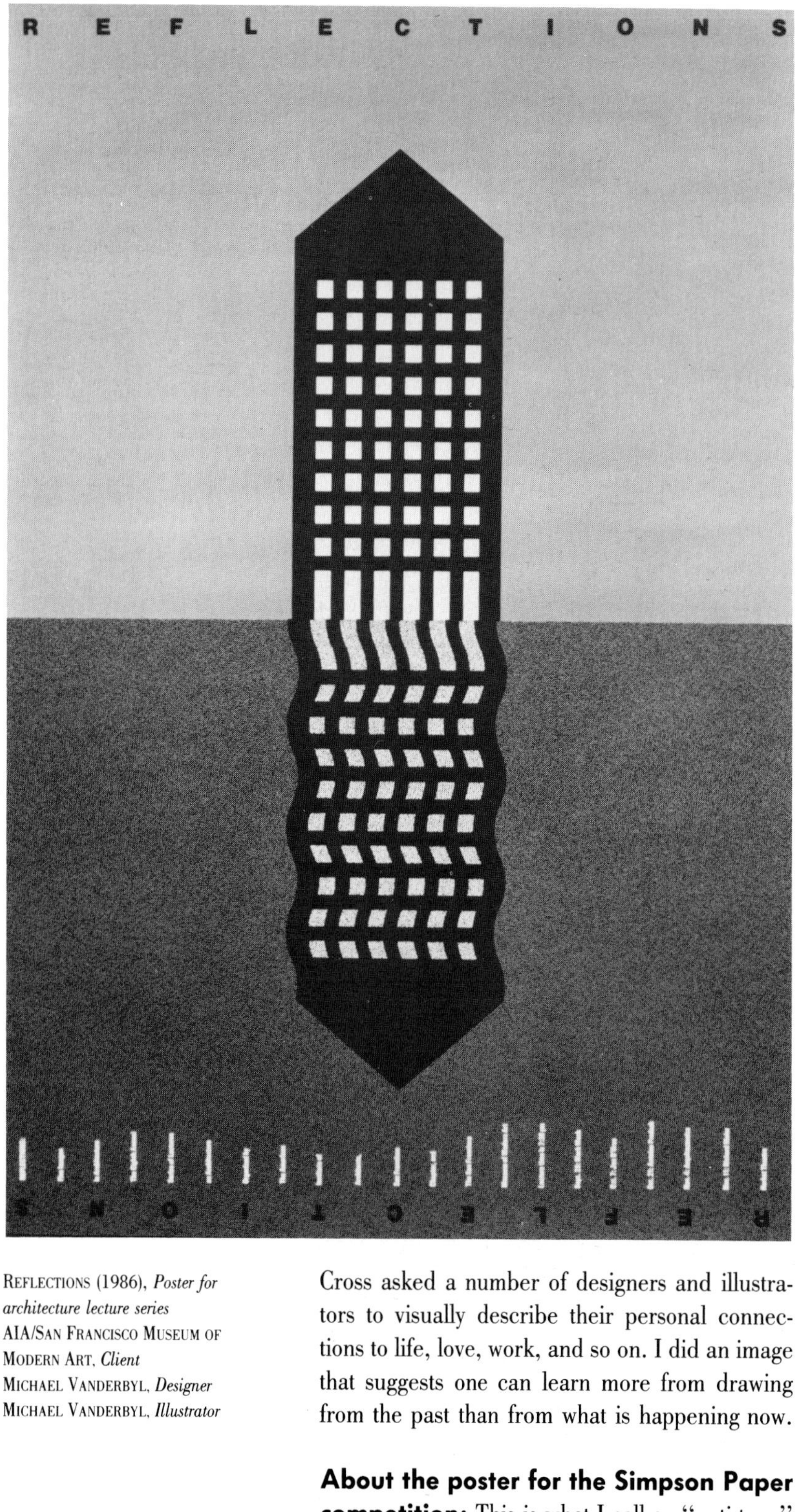
REFLECTIONS

REFLECTIONS (1986), *Poster for architecture lecture series*
AIA/SAN FRANCISCO MUSEUM OF MODERN ART, *Client*
MICHAEL VANDERBYL, *Designer*
MICHAEL VANDERBYL, *Illustrator*

Cross asked a number of designers and illustrators to visually describe their personal connections to life, love, work, and so on. I did an image that suggests one can learn more from drawing from the past than from what is happening now.

About the poster for the Simpson Paper competition: This is what I call an "anti-type" solution because I wanted the type to appear as a pattern or texture rather than to communicate

LASCAUX

specific information. I used Helvetica for its heavy weight, and the word spacing allows readability. But the primary idea was to emphasize the power of the printed image. I did the sketch using cut paper symbolically because Simpson is a paper company.

Concerning logo design: My logos are pictorial; I believe the problem with most "modern" trademarks today is that they do not reveal the company's purpose. Logos using random geometry are too cold; they should be humanistic, like a really fine letterform.

Creating an identity for the restaurant Lascaux: The restaurant is housed down in a large basement of a beautiful old terra-cotta building in San Francisco. Hence, the owner wanted to call it La Cave. I said it's bad enough that this is a basement—and attention should not be drawn to that fact—but people will probably use the American pronunciation of the name. So they asked me to come up with another one. Finally all those art history classes paid off. After coming up with Lascaux it became very obvious what the symbol should be. Instead of copying a real bison, I developed my own. I did the drawing and then traced my own hands for effect. But it looked too nice, so we made a stat of it, scratched it with the edge of a metal ruler, wrinkled it, and made another stat. I used the typeface called Onyx because it is very "bistro" looking.

On illustration versus illustrative solutions: I always render the images myself, but I will not call it illustration. *Illustrative solutions* is perhaps a better rubric because I do not accept

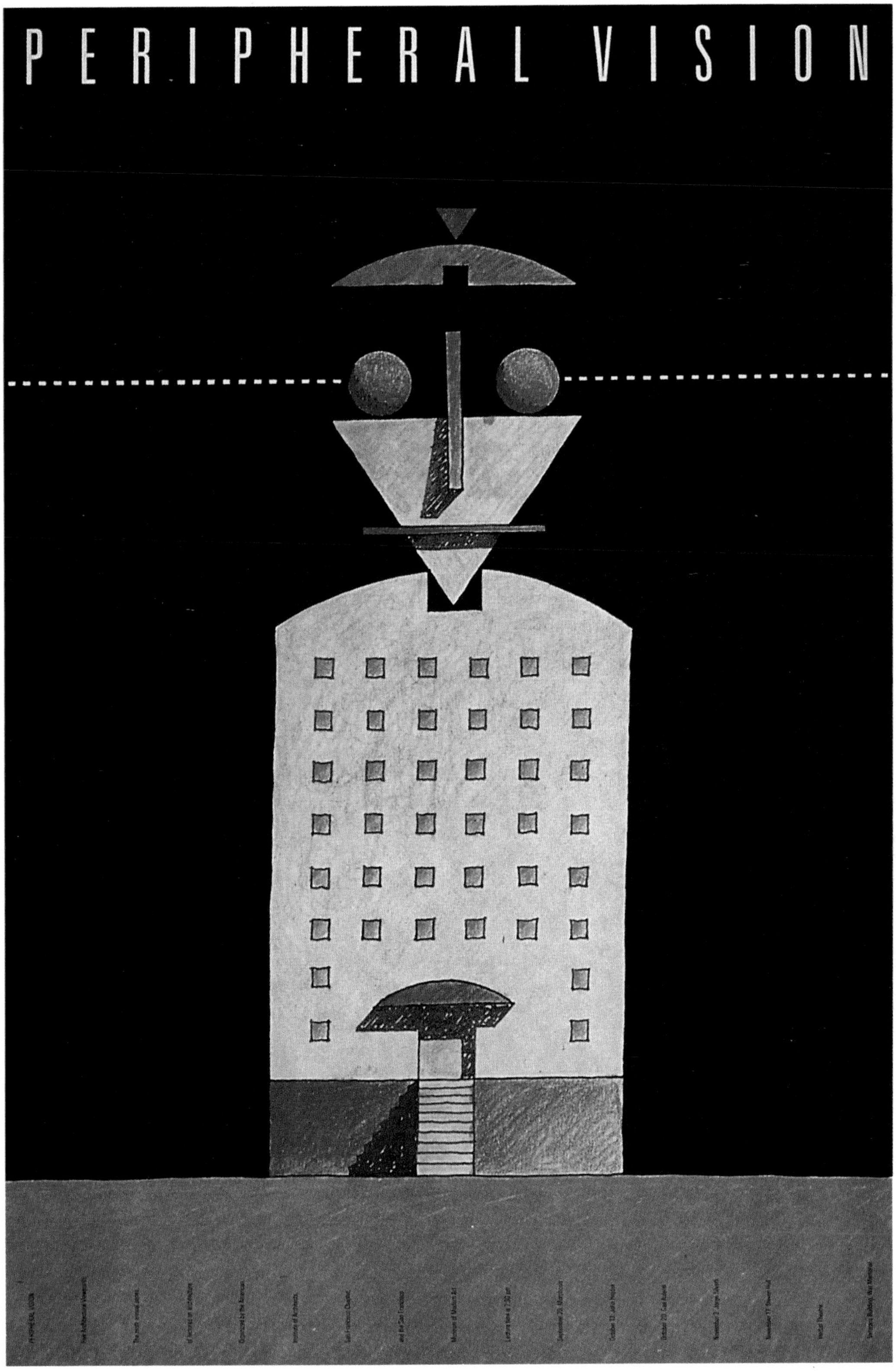
PERIPHERAL VISION

PERIPHERAL VISION (1987), *Poster for architecture lecture series*
AIA/SAN FRANCISCO MUSEUM OF MODERN ART, *Client*
MICHAEL VANDERBYL, *Designer*
MICHAEL VANDERBYL, *Illustrator*

LASCAUX RESTAURANT LOGO (1988)
LASCAUX RESTAURANT (SAN FRANCISCO)/ BEDFORD PROPERTIES INC., *Client*
MICHAEL VANDERBYL, *Designer*
MICHAEL VANDERBYL, *Illustrator*

C O N N E C T I O N S
Simpson

Simpson

CONNECTIONS (1980), *Promotion for paper company*
SIMPSON PAPER CO., *Client*
MICHAEL VANDERBYL, *Designer*
MICHAEL VANDERBYL, *Illustrator*
JIM CROSS, *Art Director*

SIMPSON PRINTED PAPER COMPETITION '87 (1987), *Call-for-entries poster*
SIMPSON PAPER CO., *Client*
MICHAEL VANDERBYL, *Designer*
MICHAEL VANDERBYL, *Illustrator*

that illustrating and designing are separate processes. Of course there are many illustrators who know nothing about design and many designers who do not know how to work with illustration—that is why the marriage of the two fails. I tell my illustration students not to be illustrators, but to study both disciplines so that they can control the results. Instead of being called in to enlarge someone else's thumbnail, or color someone else's idea, or steal another's style, they should be able to conceive and manage the entire process. Being a designer means being able to do things that are visual, and drawing is integral to that process.

On the animosity between designers and illustrators: When I assumed the post of dean at the School of Design at CCAC, the illustration students hated the graphic designers because of an inherent caste system that has developed. I told them if they did not understand what a graphic designer does, life would be really miserable. First, it is the designer who hires the illustrator. Second, if the illustrator does not know about typography, the designer can mess up the illustration. Few images stand alone; every illustration will have type on or near it. The illustration students were convinced that ignorance is not freedom, it is actually servitude.

ART DIRECTORS

DOUG AKAGI

A native of San Francisco, Doug Akagi has over twenty-five years of experience in the areas of marketing, communications, corporate identity, and environmental graphics. The principal of his own design firm, his clients include Pacific Bell, California First Bank, and Tandy Computers. Here he discusses how drawing plays a role in his design style in general, and in his work for architectural clients specifically.

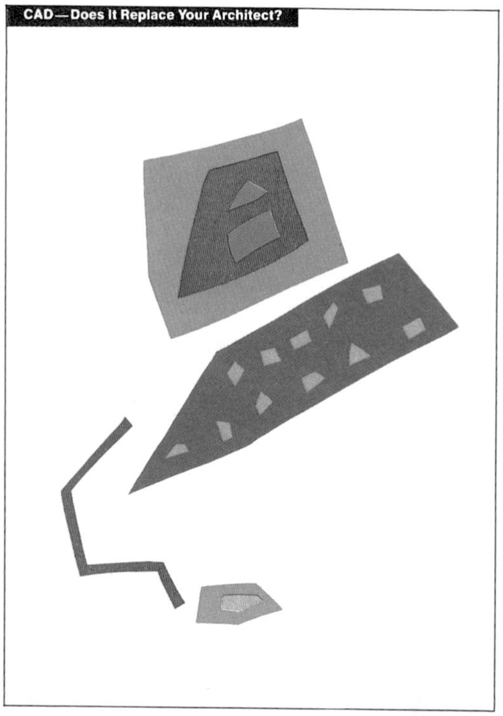
CAD—Does It Replace Your Architect?

Hospital Lighting—Too Much of a Good Thing?

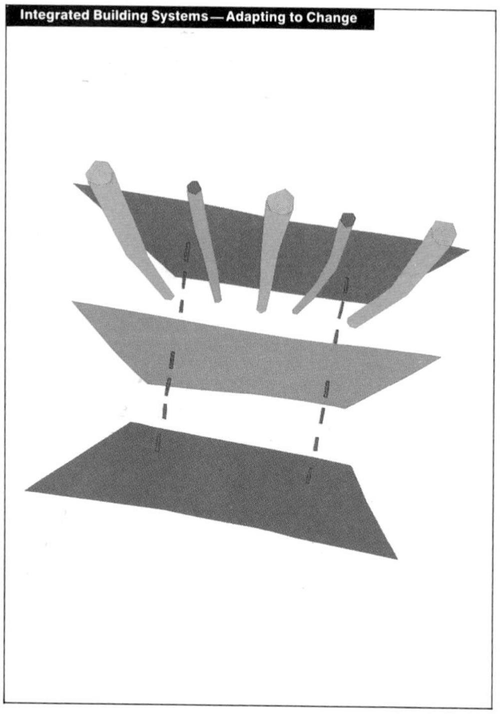
Integrated Building Systems—Adapting to Change

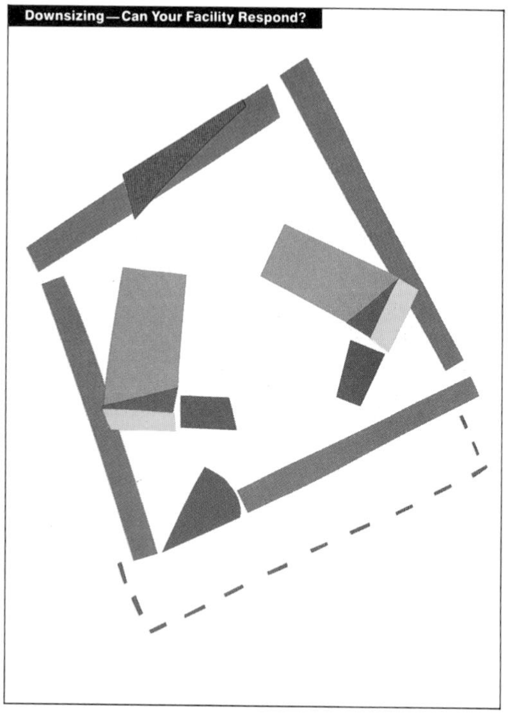
Downsizing—Can Your Facility Respond?

About operating a design firm: I heavily art direct everything, but I do not dictate or sketch everything and then have people execute: I give people a chance to design. Much of what we do is collaborative—it is difficult to say where I end and another designer begins.

On designing postcards for SMP: This architectural firm came to us with a problem: since they had been around for a long time they were perceived on the outside as being stodgy. Yet most of the original partners had retired—indeed they had a lot of young architects as principals—so their goal was for us to help them look more contemporary. Although hospital design is the firm's primary activity, they wanted to branch out, and they wanted to produce a series of monthly postcards to announce that. We were given a low budget—at least one that was too low to do twelve excellent cards—so I suggested doing a card every two months instead, allowing for more time and money on each. The first six (all concerning health care) were apparently so successful that we did another series the next year (half on health care and the rest on other areas).

They were the only client that upon presentation of the initial idea asked us to make it *more* far-out. We originally did axonometric drawings, sort of flat, distorted pieces that looked three-dimensional. They were pretty wild, but the client wanted it even wilder. I would have an idea of the concept, crudely sketch it out, and give it to a designer in my office. She would come back to me periodically and I would suggest, say, more lines in one or a simpler design in another. Reversing the type out of black in the corner allowed for a strong headline without using huge type. I wanted the type to become part of the whole composition to avoid conflict with the illustration.

About the style: Though the results might differ from piece to piece our illustration approach is basically constant. We've applied this to the mailer for the AWH Convention (which takes place in The Circle Gallery, designed by Frank Lloyd Wright); the "Collection of Favorite San Francisco Restaurants" (in which we did symbols for a number of international foods); and a die-cut 1987 Christmas card for Stone, Marraccini and Patterson. The latter is conceptually similar to the rest, though in that case we dealt with overlapping silhouettes.

A preference for classic type: Our first rationale for any type decision is an existing corporate style. If a typeface is already being used we try to adhere to it. If not, we choose type by how it feels. I like comparing design to language—visual language—so choosing the right typeface, the right illustration, and the right color is like choosing the right words and putting them together in understandable sentences for the most efficient communication. The more creative one is, the more eloquent.

I use Helvetica a lot, although I am somewhat tired of its sterility. Yet that is also a virtue because Helvetica can be used with anything and remain neutral. If I were to characterize my philosophy of type I would have to quote Massimo Vignelli's statement that there are only seven

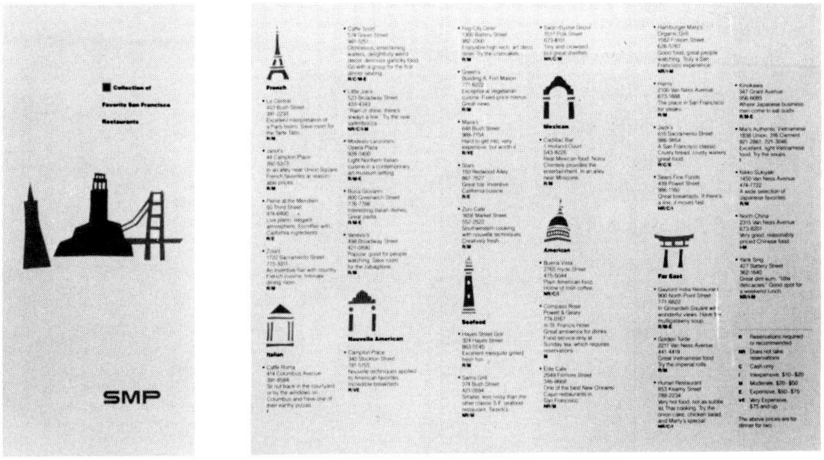
SMP

(above)
SMP San Francisco Restaurant Guide (1987)
Stone, Marraccini and Patterson, *Client*
Doug Akagi and Sharrie Brooks, *Designers*
Sharrie Brooks, *Illustrator*
Doug Akagi, *Art Director*

(left)
SMP Christmas Card (1987)
Stone, Marraccini and Patterson, *Client*
Doug Akagi and Karen Ann, *Designers*
Karen Ann, *Illustrator*
Doug Akagi, *Art Director*

(opposite)
SMP Postcard Series (1987), *Direct-mail campaign*
Stone, Marraccini and Patterson, *Client*
Doug Akagi and Sharrie Brooks, *Designers*
Sharrie Brooks and Gwen Terpstra, *Illustrators*
Doug Akagi, *Art Director*

S E A S O N S G R E E T I N G S
B A C K E N, A R R I G O N I & R O S S, I N C.

typefaces in the universe. While my menu changes from time to time, I tend to stick to the classics.

About the Christmas card for Backen, Arrigoni & Ross: This card for an architectural firm was done with the silhouettes of some of their best-designed commercial buildings. The one with the clock, for example, is the Jordan Winery in the Napa Valley—a very famous structure. We also did a card showing their residential buildings. Of course, the commercial card had to be vertical and the residential was horizontal.

Although it is difficult to distinguish the design from the illustration process in the commercial piece, I can say that the decorative triangles on top were a design element inspired by one of my favorite buildings. It is a former garage over in the Richmond district of San Francisco, which was converted into offices and has these beautiful inverted triangles embossed into the concrete face, much as you see it on the card. That is often how ideas come: you see something you like and then wait for an opportunity to use it.

About trends: However, I am also a slave to fashion. I can't help being influenced by the context of my life. And I am also influenced by other designers and design disciplines. Moreover, there are just certain looks that *feel* good, and I'll adhere to them for a while. For instance, several years ago, when condensed faces were popular, the studio used them extensively for body copy and headlines. But, you know, today I'm uncomfortable looking back at some of the things I did then. Perhaps I am becoming less responsive to trendy solutions.

About the brochure for Yosemite National Institutes: This nonprofit organization teaches children about the outdoor sciences, so the directive from the client was to make it young and playful. I thought that drawing would be the most appropriate method, and it's worked. They use these images on T-shirts, sweatshirts (which they sell by the bushel), and all of their signage and stationery. Most important, it was a coup for a nonprofit corporation to print a four-color letterhead.

About photography: Lately I've become interested in photographs as illustration. The photographers I hire are using the tool less to document than to conceptualize.

A hidden agenda for illustration: Illustration is a form of interpretation, and an illustrator is trying to get the viewer to see something in a very special—often personal—way. One of my strengths, and perhaps a weakness too, is that I want everything my way. Even when I am using the work of an artist or photographer, it is a way of manipulating the image so that it expresses my vision.

YOSEMITE
NATIONAL
INSTITUTES

YOSEMITE NATIONAL INSTITUTES (1986), *Brochure*
YOSEMITE NATIONAL INSTITUTES, *Client*
DOUG AKAGI AND SHARRIE BROOKS, *Designers*
SHARRIE BROOKS AND KAREN ANN, *Illustrators*
DOUG AKAGI, *Art Director*

BAR CHRISTMAS CARD (1985)
BACKEN, ARRIGONI & ROSS INC., *Client*
DOUG AKAGI AND SHARRIE BROOKS, *Designers*
SHARRIE BROOKS, *Illustrator*
DOUG AKAGI, *Art Director*

JERRY BERMAN AND NICOLAS SIDJAKOV

The San Francisco–based marketing and design firm of SBG Partners was founded seven-and-a-half years ago to fill a void in the packaging-design field. For many years packaging had had a generic feeling owing to preconceived limitations by marketers on the tastes of the consumer and the marketplace. Hand lettering was the dominant design element and style; quality illustration and photographs were used in very limited applications. Today the traditional tools of poster and advertising design are more integrated into the package designer's repertoire. And SBG Partners has been pushing the tight boundaries of this field. Jerry Berman, with a background in advertising and graphic design, and Nicolas Sidjakov, with a background in graphic design and illustration, discuss some successful work from the past and their philosophy of package design for the nineties.

CHASE& SANBORN COFFEE
FOR ALL COFFEE MAKERS
CHASE& SANBORN COFFEE
NET WT. 39 OZ. (2 LB. 7 OZ.)
FOR ALL COFFEE MAKERS
CHASE& SANBORN COFFEE

About package design today: What is revolutionary about today's packaging is that it has retreated from emphasis on the huge brand marks and the idea that people pledge allegiance to a product simply because of its brand name. Just because a package says *Sara Lee* or *Del Monte* no longer ensures its sales success. And what is forcing that to change, in part, is the introduction of all kinds of new products combined with the public's new buying habits.

In addition to increased appetite appeal (photography, illustration), more consumers read labels today because everybody has taken a greater interest in product ingredients, taste, and health value. This has resulted in a new, more aesthetic approach to package design. Better design is now revolutionizing the packaging industry.

Since the packaging industry is so market-driven it is a difficult area for aesthetic creation. Regardless of how pretty it is, if a product does not sell, out it goes. Package design is result-oriented: the results are quantitatively measured. On the average, it can take eight months from the time a package is designed to when it appears on the shelf. It could even be in test market for up to a year.

More on appetite appeal: Appetite appeal is the *perception* of what the finished product looks like. We have to interpret that perception. Photography is very effective. The photographers we use are the best in the business: they shoot for advertising agencies and gourmet magazines and can make food—even unpleasant-looking food—appear very, very tasty. Appetite appeal beseeches the senses; you can taste it, feel it, touch it. Also, given a clear container of soda or juice, the appetite appeal is the liquid.

About image: Packages that do not use appetite appeal have *image.* This is often where illustration comes into play, creating a pleasing, albeit decorative, environment. Take coffee, for example. Coffee cans are basically symbolic. Chase and Sanborn coffee comes in a can designed both to separate it from the competition and present a distinct identity that bespeaks tradition. That's image.

Designing the package for Welch's Orchard juices: We used illustration because it is difficult to get a photograph of perfect fruit without any blemishes. The centerpiece design is a *target*; it has a bull's-eye effect on the consumer. It also suggests an image of something very special. This is a "value-added product," because it is 100 percent concentrated juice. The oval and the wonderful Garamond typography are designed to exude the sense of quality and purity. Welch's Orchard became the most successful product introduction in Welch's history.

About the packaging for MacFarms of Hawaii: The solution for packaging macadamia nuts is found in the total image. Macadamia nuts are expensive. Together with MacFarms, we figured out a way to sell them so that MacFarms macadamias are considerably less expensive than the competition. We utilized foil packets, which are sold on peg boards, caddies, or display bins. Our task was to make a premium item. This approach gave MacFarms' foil packets a certain *quality factor* that does not come across on the competition's more pedestrian jar.

We felt that an illustration—a steel engraving, actually—of a farm scene worked better than a photograph because it is more romantic and has a certain intrigue. The type style and illustration are harmonious as decorative elements.

On working with illustrators: Unless there is something specifically dictated by the client, we will let the illustrators have freedom and fun with a project. Within the constraints of the project we are more interested in the technique and the feeling than in saying specifically what the image has to be. The difference between pack-

SINCE Welch's 1869
WELCH'S ORCHARD
100% Juice
No Sugar Added
100% NATURAL
Grape Juice
WELCH'S ORCHARD
100% Juice
No Sugar Added
100% NATURAL
Apple-Grape Juice
SINCE Welch's 1869
WELCH'S ORCHARD
100% Juice
No Sugar Added
100% NATURAL
Harvest Juice Blend

WELCH'S ORCHARD (1988), *Packaging*
WELCH FOODS, *Client*
JAMES NEVINS, *Designer*
GREGG KEELING, *Illustrator*
NICOLAS SIDJAKOV AND JERRY BERMAN, *Creative Directors*

CHASE & SANBORN (1985), *Packaging*
HILLS BROTHERS, *Client*
JAMES NEVINS, *Designer*
DAVID STEVENSON, *Illustrator*
NICOLAS SIDJAKOV AND JERRY BERMAN, *Creative Directors*

MACFARMS
of HAWAII™
Macadamias™
Kauai
Niihau
Oahu
Molokai
Lanai
Maui

MACFARMS
of HAWAII
Macadamias
NET WT. 3½ OZ. 99 GRAMS

aging and other media that use illustration is symmetry: there's much more in packaging, particularly on a round container.

About the creative limits of packaging: In most packaging, as in advertising, there is little or no creative concept but there is design concept. It is very difficult to reach a conceptual level because there are so many other merchandising requirements. In advertising there is a headline. In packaging it's a brand name and product definition. One can strive for integration, taste, and visual perfection, but it is difficult to go much further. Some taboos are falling away, and perhaps eventually a package design will be more like an ad with a product benefit.

About typography: Twenty years ago the printer threw typography in for free as an extra benefit. Some printers still do that. The main difference with typography in packaging today is that it has rejected the sixties look, when hand lettering was dominant and type was ignored because something hand-drawn was more "proprietary." At that time the designer would fragment the package to make the brand name look proprietary and the rest of the package ended up virtually "generic." Today, the total package design is becoming proprietary.

Design and buying habits: The eighties have brought us smaller households, single-parent families, and working mothers—a fast-paced society with less time to shop. An average shopping trip shrank from thirty to twenty minutes in the last ten years. Yet stores get larger and stock more items: a typical supermarket averages 40,000 square feet and offers over 25,000 products. At the same time, more people are arriving at point-of-sale without a firm purchase decision preconditioned by traditional advertising. The present popularity of VCRs and cable TV has slowly reduced the viewing of commercials. What all this means is that the battleground for the consumer has shifted from the media to the supermarket; therefore the package has to stand out to be noticed.

In some cases, the designer has to realize the package should be different from those of similar products. Yet if a design is too different, consumer perception may be jeopardized. For example, all the products in the detergent category look somewhat alike: they are bright, bold, colorful, and screaming for attention. If a package does not conform to the rest of the detergents, the consumer might not perceive it as being in that category.

About the package for Effie Marie's: With each package design project we adhere to a list of design and marketing objectives. The primary objective for Effie Marie was to design a package that would project a high-quality, expensive image with a built-in tradition. Different flavors were also an important factor. Appetite appeal was not. We had to develop a strong "story line." Many hours were spent trying to determine what Effie Marie should look like: young, motherly, grandmotherly, petite, and so on. Considering all the objectives, the cameo was perfect. The backgrounds were inspired by cocoa leaves and vanilla beans, and the illustration and typography work in total harmony.

Effie Marie's
SUTTON CAKES
EFFIE MARIE'S
CHOCOLATE FUDGE
RUM BUTTER CAKE

EFFIE MARIE'S (1988), *Packaging*
HERITAGE KITCHEN SPECIALTY FOODS, *Client*
BARBARA VICK, *Designer*
CAROLYN VIBBERT, REBECCA ARCHEY, AND KAREN MONTGOMERY, *Illustrators*
NICOLAS SIDJAKOV AND JERRY BERMAN, *Creative Directors*

MACFARMS MACADAMIAS (1982), *Packaging*
MACFARMS OF HAWAII, *Client*
JAMES NEVINS, *Designer*
MICHAEL BULL AND COLLEEN QUINN, *Illustrators*
NICOLAS SIDJAKOV AND JERRY BERMAN, *Creative Directors*

BOB DENNARD

A year after beginning his first job, at the Bloom Agency in Dallas, Texas, Bob Dennard joined The Richards Group in 1965, where he remained for eleven years. He developed his skills as a graphic designer and marketing person while working in all areas of advertising for clients such as Hyatt Hotels, Pepsi, Red Lobster Inn, and Quaker Oats. In 1977 he opened his own design firm, which combined traditional advertising techniques with more adventuresome applications of typography and illustration. Through the examples discussed here Dennard charts his evolution from illustrator to communications expert and explains how the basic knowledge of drawing continues to underscore his method.

About drawing: I remember teachers in school literally rapping my knuckles with a ruler and saying, "Stop drawing, Bob. Pay more attention." Well, I *was* paying attention, but drawing was my natural way of doing so. It was a form of concentration over which I had no control.

I am an artist and it is pretty instinctive that when I start putting down my thoughts and ideas I draw them rather than write them out. Indeed the first thing I want to know when I hire someone for the firm is whether he or she can draw. If the answer is yes, then I feel they will be better designers, because drawing, in my opinion, is what we call *talent.* Design can be taught and learned—it is playing positives and negatives against each other. But talent means one has a sort of built-in system for knowing why things are big or small and why they work well together on a page. A good drawing ability reinforces the design sense. Just think what Michelangelo could have done with a PMS book, a roll of tape, and an X-Acto knife. He would have been great, because the whole design process starts with drawing.

On becoming a designer: I was a good designer right out of school, but I couldn't *think.* I couldn't tie my hand to my head, which is a necessity in the advertising business. I even wangled a job at an ad agency as art director, but sat there for a year before admitting that I just did not have what was necessary to be effective. So I enrolled in the Art Center in Hollywood, California, for a year, and in the first three months I accomplished what I set out to do: I worked with agency people and was taught how to use my mind. Mario Donna was a big help at that time. Design became a tool—a means to an end. Moreover, and perhaps more related to illustration, the legacy of Push Pin Studios had a tremendous impact on my approach—one that can still be seen in my work.

About advertising: In the early seventies I went to work for Stan Richards, who had a good-size design firm–ad agency in Dallas. In those days there was no market in this city for being just a designer; but one could be a designer–art director and ply one's craft at advertising, especially because Richards not only wanted his ads to read better but to *look* better than the competition. Indeed an art director also had to be part copywriter and photographer in this city. I think that the "Dallas look" took root in the early 1970s with advertising; but a distinctive look is not so evident now because of the proliferation of big agencies, most of which have become no different from those in any other big city. I run a design firm today because I realized at The Richards Group that in order to be in the agency business today, one has to forfeit too much creative fun for the corporate life.

An unusual ad campaign for Broadway Square: Richards had a client who was opening a shopping center. We were considering a campaign that used photography, but I could see in my mind's eye that Broadway Square could benefit from a different approach, an illustration approach. I convinced Richards to show two different campaigns—the photographic approach and the illustrative. I got these excellent illustrators named Ron Sullivan, Woody Pirtle, and Larry Sons to do drawings in the manner of Seymour Chwast and Milton Glaser, promising them—in the carrot-and-stick tradition—that this campaign would be so good that it couldn't fail to be selected by the *CA Annual.* So we approached the problem through symbolic illustrations à la Push Pin (but equally influenced by the innovative Neiman-Marcus advertising of the sixties). The first ad was a cardinal that completely filled a broadsheet newspaper page. In this context one is accustomed to seeing black-and-white photography, so such a bold splash of red on an unexpected image had sensational impact, and the illustration *became* the headline. The ad was the first to announce the countdown toward opening day of Broadway Square. The cardinal represented the beauty of the place. The next day another ad appeared with the drawing of a drummer at a parade beating a big bass drum, suggesting the celebratory atmosphere. Another had a rabbit jumping out of a hat announcing the magical environment of the shopping center. And yet another was a huge bouquet

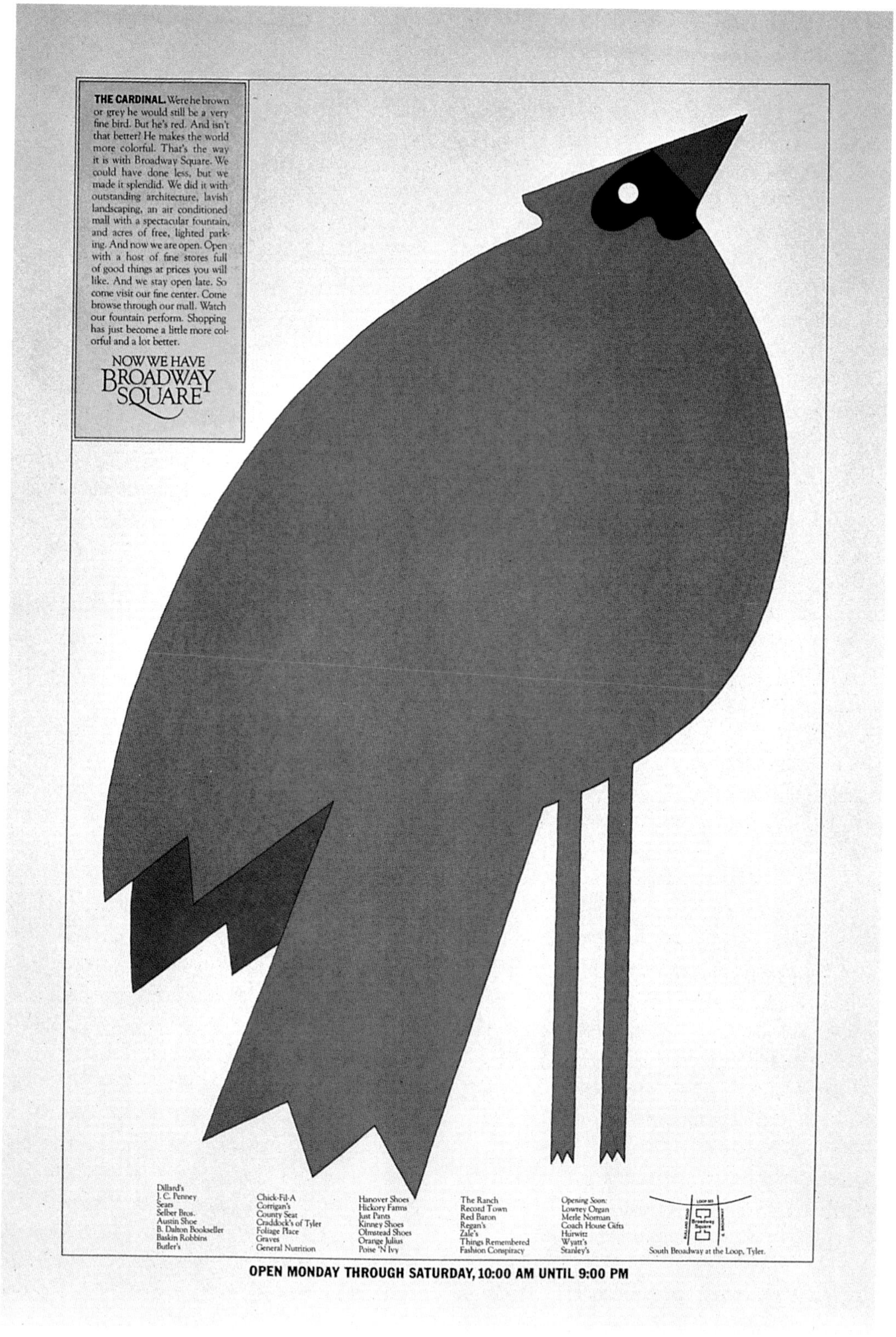

THE CARDINAL. Were he brown or grey he would still be a very fine bird. But he's red. And isn't that better? He makes the world more colorful. That's the way it is with Broadway Square. We could have done less, but we made it splendid. We did it with outstanding architecture, lavish landscaping, an air conditioned mall with a spectacular fountain, and acres of free, lighted parking. And now we are open. Open with a host of fine stores full of good things at prices you will like. And we stay open late. So come visit our fine center. Come browse through our mall. Watch our fountain perform. Shopping has just become a little more colorful and a lot better.
NOW WE HAVE
BROADWAY SQUARE
Dillard's
J. C. Penney
Sears
Selber Bros.
Austin Shoe
B. Dalton Bookseller
Baskin Robbins
Butler's
Chick-Fil-A
Corrigan's
County Seat
Craddock's of Tyler
Foliage Place
Graves
General Nutrition
Hanover Shoes
Hickory Farms
Just Pants
Kinney Shoes
Olmstead Shoes
Orange Julius
Poise 'N Ivy
The Ranch
Record Town
Red Baron
Regan's
Zale's
Things Remembered
Fashion Conspiracy
Opening Soon:
Lowrey Organ
Merle Norman
Coach House Gifts
Hurwitz
Wyatt's
Stanley's
South Broadway at the Loop, Tyler.
OPEN MONDAY THROUGH SATURDAY, 10:00 AM UNTIL 9:00 PM

CARDINAL (1975), *Broadway Square shopping mall newspaper ad campaign*
RAYMOND D. NASHER CO., *Client*
BOB DENNARD, *Designer*
RON SULLIVAN, *Illustrator*
BOB DENNARD, *Art Director*

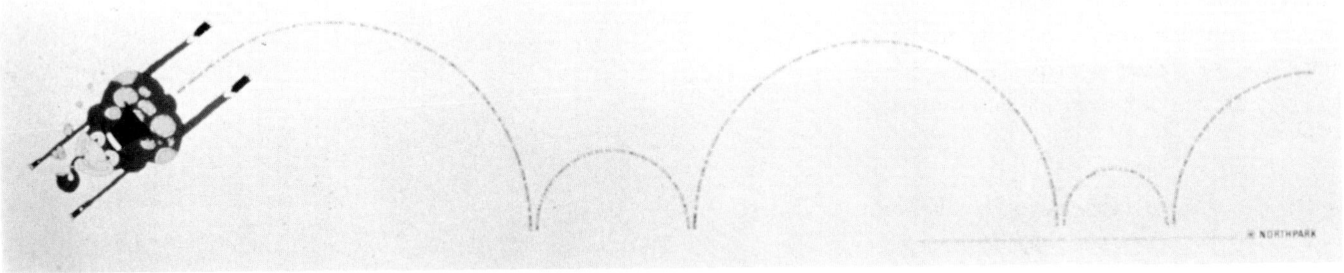
NORTHPARK

FROG (1982), *NorthPark Center newspaper ad campaign*
RAYMOND D. NASHER CO., *Client*
REX PETEET, *Designer*
REX PETEET, *Illustrator*
BOB DENNARD, *Art Director*

of flowers, because the center is beautiful, colorful, and refreshing. What does a bouquet do for you? It makes you happy. And that's a pretty good reason to use illustration over photography—at least in this campaign.

Stan presented his idea for the photographic campaign first, and the client loved it—he was sold. But to Stan's credit he showed the client mine. He told me later that if he hadn't done that he couldn't have lived with himself. The client's wife was immediately seduced by my approach. It was as if we did a market test on the spot. Indeed women really liked the campaign.

I was too insecure to do the illustrations myself. I suppose I could have, but it might have taken two weeks more than we had; I couldn't afford the time. I also felt that it was so important that I should not have been given the chance to muck it up. I knew, however, exactly what it should look like and who could do it best. That is the art director in me, and that is what an art director does. None of this would exist if I hadn't had the idea.

About art direction: I usually do thumbnails that really hum. They are not comps, but do not leave much room for interpretation: they show the size and style. Sometimes I will ask an illustrator to come up with an idea that is within my parameters. I don't say, "don't think," but I do have definite ideas about what I want the work to be. If the illustrator or designer can show me something better, great! But show me what I want first!

Being a good art director with an illustrator is developing a team relationship. It is not necessarily going to be done exactly the way the illustrator wants, but when it is done he or she will be happy with the result. It will not be all mine either; I cannot do it without the illustrator, just as the illustrator cannot do it without me. My role is as leader, and so the illustrator must follow and submerge some ego because I'm going to take advantage of that ego and talent. I know how to do it because I am one of them.

About the advertisement for North Park shopping mall: The marketing director asked us to do an Easter promotion but could not afford three or four full-page ads. We thought, What can be done on a limited budget and still make a bell ring? If I had had color, I could have done something fantastic. Imagine a ladybug flying the length of one newspaper column, with a spot of color and with everything else in black and gray surrounded by all the white space. Where is the eye going to go when one opens that page? The type and image are so captivating in that context that we compel people to read the ad. We even had a frog jumping across the bottom of two pages. We had to literally beg the paper to let us to do it because they don't sell space that way.

I believe these were the first illustrations that Rex Peteet ever did without using a T-square and triangle. I was playing the "agency art director," telling him to finish it quick so we could collect the fee. I told him to stop drafting every single time-consuming line and learn to be looser, because that can look good too. Owing to his insecurities I had to force him to work freehand, and it worked. The excellent copy treatment was Rex's idea.

On designer versus painterly illustration: I call very flat drawing *designed illustration* as opposed to the narrative approach by the likes of Mark English or Jack Unruh. The designer-illustrator of the former will handle space much differently than the painter-illustrator. Graphic designer illustration usually considers and/or includes type (or a place for type). A designer is like a concert master making all the pieces work together.

About the advertisement for the Killeen Mall: I had the idea for doing the copy treatment and the big illustration, but the drawing and the design is by Don Sibley. It echoes an idea I did for Faneuil Hall when I was with the Richards Group. Indeed, sometimes I wonder whether I repeat myself too much. I wonder if my clients are as aware of it as I am. My way of thinking is like a thread that ties many things I've done. The simplification of things began with the cardinal, and the silhouette illustration in this context represents my "style"—I rather feel like I invented it.

On doing thumbnails versus comps: I try very hard not to do a comp because roughs or thumbnails are every bit as effective. I also do not care to waste money or time. If you are the client paying me $1,000 to come up with an ad, I'm not going to burn up that money in cutting and pasting comps. I would rather spend the time coming up with more ideas. I'll show you thumbnails, and if you don't trust my judgment I'll say you've got the wrong guy. But I do try to show you lots of ideas.

About Pizza Inn "Pick Talkers": This device is a way to "cross-merchandise" four new hoagie sandwiches that Pizza Inn introduced. For each one we created a little logo to be stuck into the customer's order. If he ordered an Italian Beef Hoagie, it would say so on one side, while on the other it would say "Next time try our All-American Beef Hoagie." I roughed them out, and Jan Wilson, an illustrator–designer, saw them through.

About other Pizza Inn promotions: Originally five people in the shop worked creatively on Pizza Inn materials—from table tents to posters to place mats. Everyone put their ideas down on a table in thumbnail form and we eliminated what we did not like. The initial direction was to do something in the Push Pin style, but I let the designers take it from there. Once a design direction was established I would go back and fine-tune things, including typography. The team captained by Chuck Johnson and Blyn Powell worked very well together.

In the "Pizza by the Slice" we could have made all the type the same size, but thanks to designer-illustrator Chuck Johnson, we made the menu fun. The words *pizza-by-the-slice* have a rhythm. So we reprised the 1800s circus poster approach, when printers had fun with words and

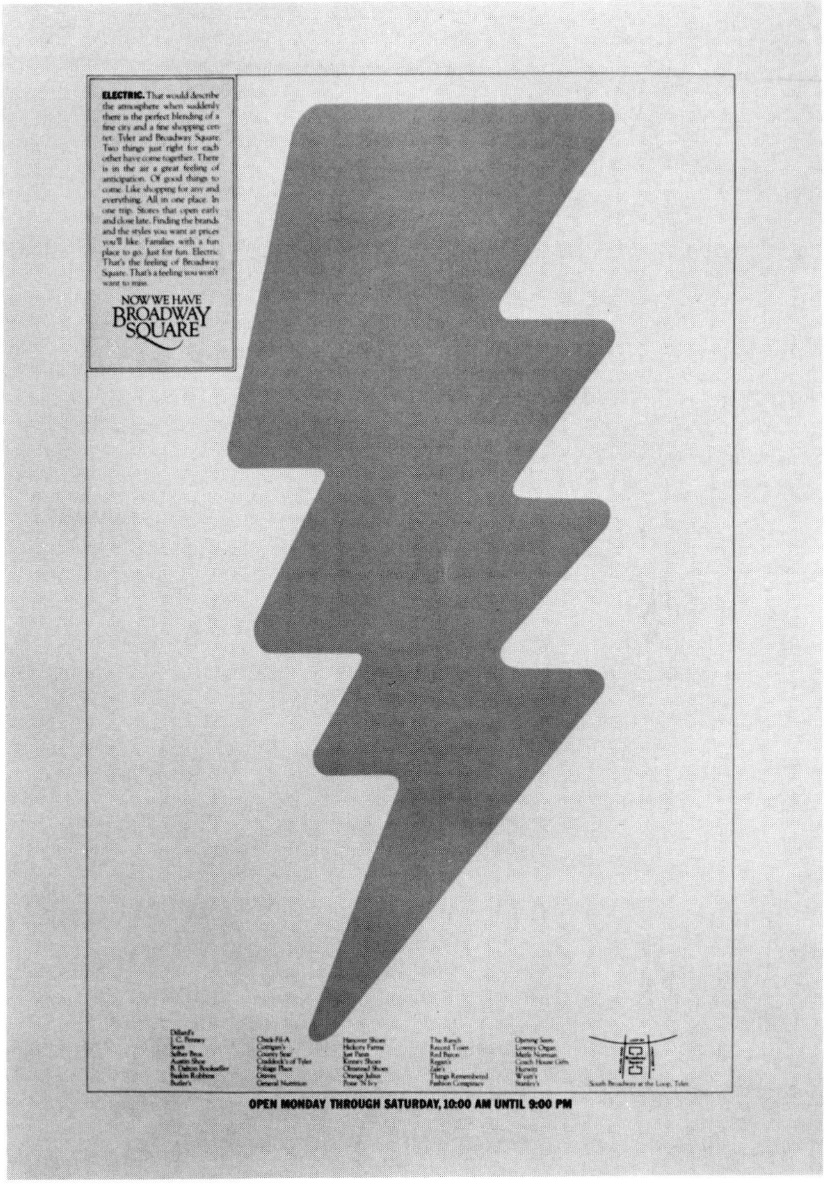

ELECTRIC. That would describe the atmosphere when suddenly there is the perfect blending of a fine city and a fine shopping center. Tyler and Broadway Square. Two things just right for each other have come together. There is in the air a great feeling of anticipation. Of good things to come. Like shopping for any and everything. All in one place. In one trip. Stores that open early and close late. Finding the brands and the styles you want at prices you'll like. Families with a fun place to go. Just for fun. Electric. That's the feeling of Broadway Square. That's a feeling you won't want to miss.
NOW WE HAVE
BROADWAY SQUARE
OPEN MONDAY THROUGH SATURDAY, 10:00 AM UNTIL 9:00 PM

LIGHTNING (1975), *Broadway Square shopping mall newspaper ad campaign*
RAYMOND D. NASHER CO., *Client*
BOB DENNARD, *Designer*
LARRY SONS, *Illustrator*
BOB DENNARD, *Art Director*

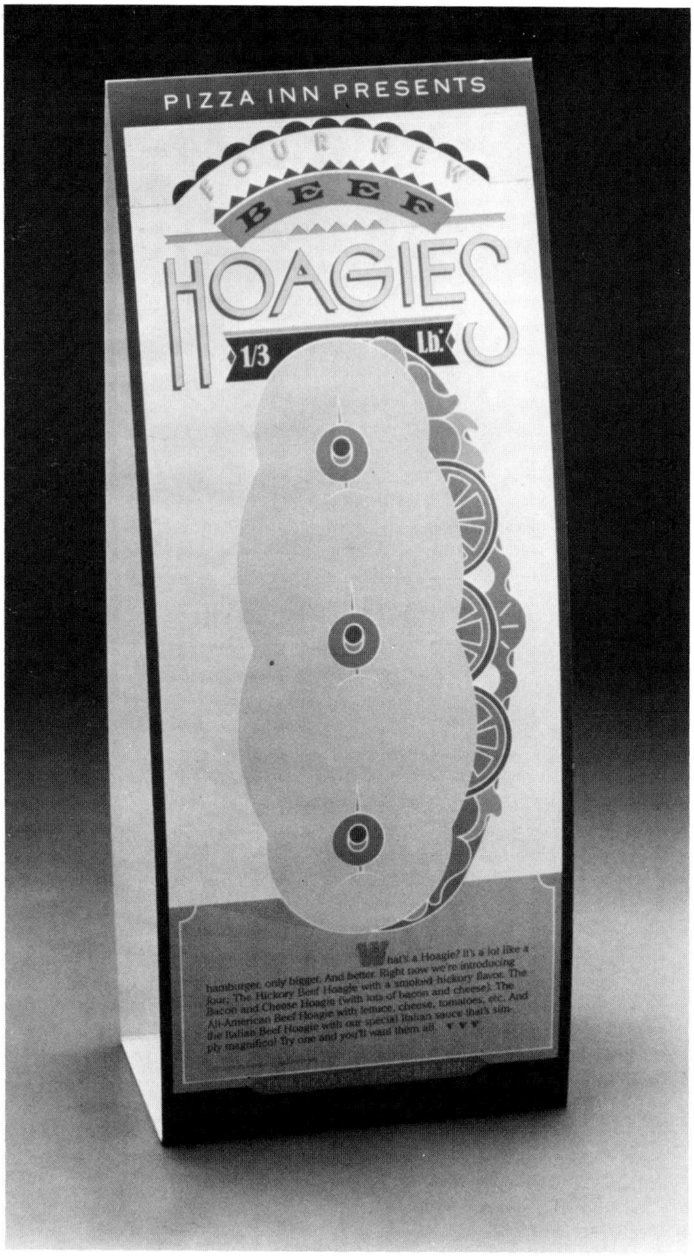
PIZZA INN PRESENTS
FOUR NEW
BEEF
HOAGIES
1/3
Lb.
What's a Hoagie? It's a lot like a hamburger, only bigger. And better. Right now we're introducing four; The Hickory Beef Hoagie with a smoked-hickory flavor. The Bacon and Cheese Hoagie (with lots of bacon and cheese). The All-American Beef Hoagie with lettuce, cheese, tomatoes, etc. And the Italian Beef Hoagie with our special Italian sauce that's simply magnificent! Try one and you'll want them all.

HICKORY
BEEF HOAGIE
ITALIAN
BEEF HOAGIE
BACON
BEEF HOAGIE
THE ALL AMERICAN
BEEF HOAGIE
ITALIAN
BEEF HOAGIE

images. The graphics here are saying eat, drink, and be merry. It's pizza, it's not serious food. Even the stories on the place mats are pure comedy. I write them and encourage others in the studio to do the same. And for Pizza Inn this was a radical change.

We had previously done this approach for Bennigan's and Friday's, and Pizza Inn had a marketing director who wanted to try something new. I thought that we did fine, but Pizza Inn is such a big company and so assembly-line-oriented that I do not think they knew how to use the materials to their best advantage.

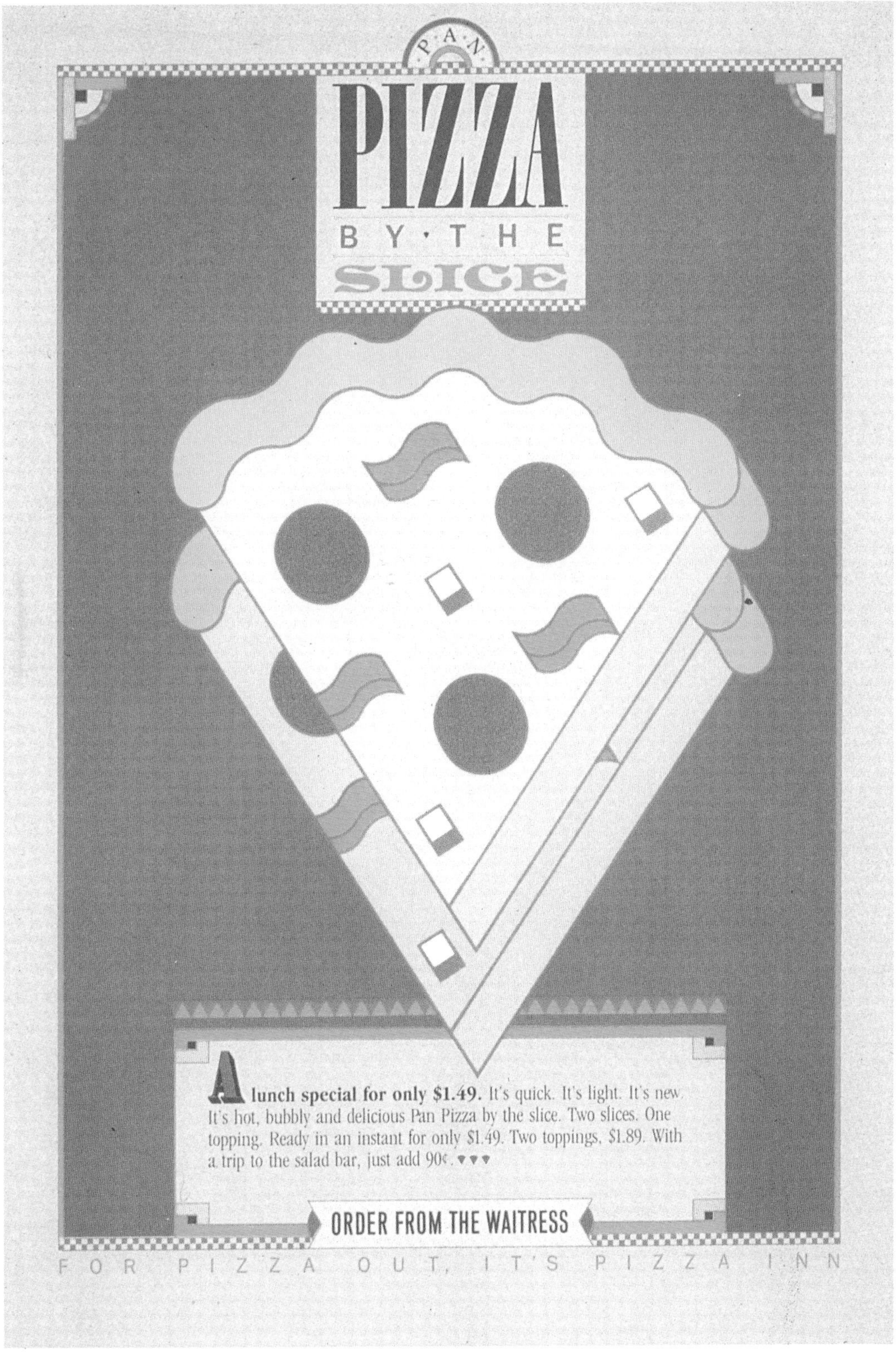
PAN
PIZZA
BY·THE
SLICE
A lunch special for only $1.49. It's quick. It's light. It's new. It's hot, bubbly and delicious Pan Pizza by the slice. Two slices. One topping. Ready in an instant for only $1.49. Two toppings, $1.89. With a trip to the salad bar, just add 90¢.
ORDER FROM THE WAITRESS
FOR PIZZA OUT, IT'S PIZZA INN

PIZZA BY THE SLICE (1982), *In-store promotion*
PIZZA INNS OF AMERICA, *Client*
CHUCK JOHNSON, *Designer*
CHUCK JOHNSON, *Illustrator*
BOB DENNARD, *Art Director*

HOAGIES (1982), *Tent card promoting new sandwiches*
PIZZA INNS OF AMERICA, *Client*
GLYN POWELL AND BOB DENNARD, *Designers*
GLYN POWELL, *Illustrator*
BOB DENNARD, *Art Director*

PICK TALKERS (1982), *Cross-merchandising tools*
PIZZA INNS OF AMERICA, *Client*
BOB DENNARD, *Designer*
JAN WILSON, *Illustrator*
BOB DENNARD, *Art Director*

ROD DYER AND STEVE TWIGGER

A graduate of the School of Art at the Johannesburg Technical College, Rod Dyer worked for a number of advertising firms in South Africa before emigrating to New York and finally Los Angeles. He honed his skills as head of graphic design for the Charles Eames office and as art director for Capitol Records. The Rod Dyer Group Inc. is a design firm that services clients as diverse as aerospace, real-estate, and financial industries; restaurants; and record companies. The group also works on the visual marketing of motion pictures, including logo and advertising design and trailers. Born in Coventry, England, Steve Twigger also has an advertising background. As a graphic designer and art director in England he used a considerable amount of illustration for advertising records and films. Currently he is a senior designer with the Rod Dyer Group. Here the two discuss a variety of projects best suited to illustrative solutions.

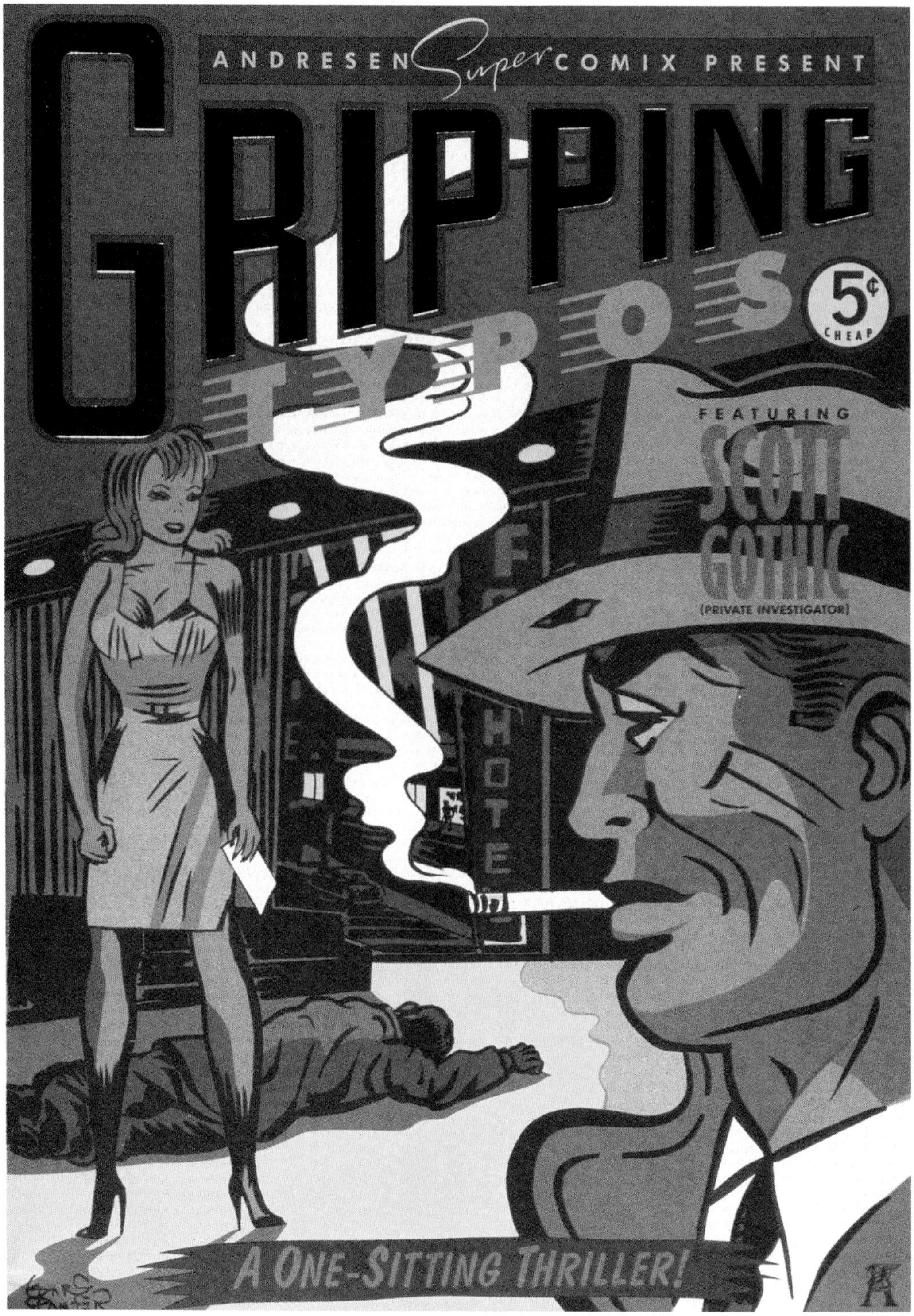
ANDRESEN Super COMIX PRESENT
GRIPPING
TYPOS
5¢
CHEAP
FEATURING
SCOTT GOTHIC
(PRIVATE INVESTIGATOR)
HOTE
A ONE-SITTING THRILLER!

TWO goons had tried to make me and my car look like the window display of a Melrose clothing store. A lot of people in this burg, including six ex-wives, might want to run me off the road for sport, but this was serious.
I didn't know it at the time, natch, but they were after the ad. They had been sent by an unspeakably evil speck of slime named Günter Gerhard Lange, an account exec at a flashy agency called Snowham, Stallom, Cheatam and Billum.
DA' BOSS'LL LOVE DIS...
DAT SHAMUS IS HISTORY, BOSS
WHAT?!!
Günter wanted the ad, the account, the whole enchilada. And he was none too pleased when his ensemble of walking chuck roasts came back without it.
GRRR
BUT, I'M YOUR BRUDDAH.
OOPS.
YOU FOOLS.

GRIPPING TYPOS (1986–87), *Promotion*
ANDRESEN PRINTING, *Client*
CLIVE PIERCY, *Designer*
GARY PANTER, *Illustrator*
ROD DYER, *Art Director*

Dyer on "Gripping Typos," a promotional piece for a Los Angeles typographer: The owner of Andresen Typography wanted a piece that would go to all the art directors and type buyers in town. But he wanted an institutional piece using classic photography—a solid, traditional-looking piece. I thought, if it arrived in the mail for me I would throw it away. I didn't care how beautiful the design was, it was a boring concept. So I came up with the idea of a Raymond Chandler approach: a comic book with Chandleresque characters involved in a typographic mystery. Though he liked the idea, he was leery at first. So I offered to present him with a visual proposal that involved a little writing and some sample drawings by Gary Panter. I convinced him that art directors have seen everything, and that to have appeal one has to knock their socks off. The piece, whatever it is, has to leave a lasting impression. He finally agreed. We proceeded to have a freelance writer do a story based on the adventures of Scott Gothic, which is the name of the typeface Andresen wanted to promote. It's now in its third printing; Drew Andresen then decided to produce T-shirts and sweatshirts as a giveaway incorporating the art in the book.

About the genesis of "Gripping Typos": I had seen some exciting art in *Raw* magazine [the avant-garde comics periodical], for whom Panter is a contributor. I also had a very old Dick Tracy comic book that had an incredible look. But I wasn't interested in just making a facsimile of the old; I wanted a new approach and a cartoonist who was artistic in a strange way. At the time Panter was finishing some work on the Pee-wee Herman show in Los Angeles and had time on his hands. We gave him the premise, and Clive Piercy [a former art director with Rod Dyer] made some rough layouts. David Lees, a freelance writer, was hired. Together they came up with the story; the writer wrote some dialogue and Gary basically illustrated the words, deciding which captions were most important. Other than leaving proper space for type we didn't bother them or change it at all. Panter, however, actually pulled back from his normal style, which is extraordinarily abstract, and gave us something that was a little more accessible but still very offbeat. The book was well received and ultimately did the job it was supposed to do.

Steve Twigger on the Jones Intercable and Jones Spacelink annual reports: Jones Intercable is a client in Denver, Colorado. Jones Spacelink, the newer company, is an offshoot of Intercable. The former sends information out through networks and the latter through satellite hookups that feed other cable systems. The two companies will always be brother and sister, so that was a design consideration from the start. Glenn Jones, by the way is a very progressive thinker and is open to good ideas, or what he calls "innovative positioning." He deals, however, with financial brokers, who are a conservative lot. And he communicates with them through institutional-looking annual reports that become pretty mundane after a while. He wanted to jump light-years ahead of his particular market, and with these pieces we took him right over the edge. The response from the brokers was incredible. People who normally wouldn't take the time to even open an annual report were taking time to go through this page by page and give us positive critiques.

I was introduced to Glenn via a videotape of him talking to shareholders, and I based the concept of the annual report on that speech. I took

Jones Intercable Inc. Annual Report (1987)
Jones Intercable Inc., *Client*
Steve Twigger, *Designer*
Brian Grimwood (*cover*), Ursula Brookbank (*pp. 2, 4*), Steve Twigger (*pp. 6, 7, 16*), and Monxo Algora (*p. 22*), *Illustrators*
Steve Twigger, *Art Director*

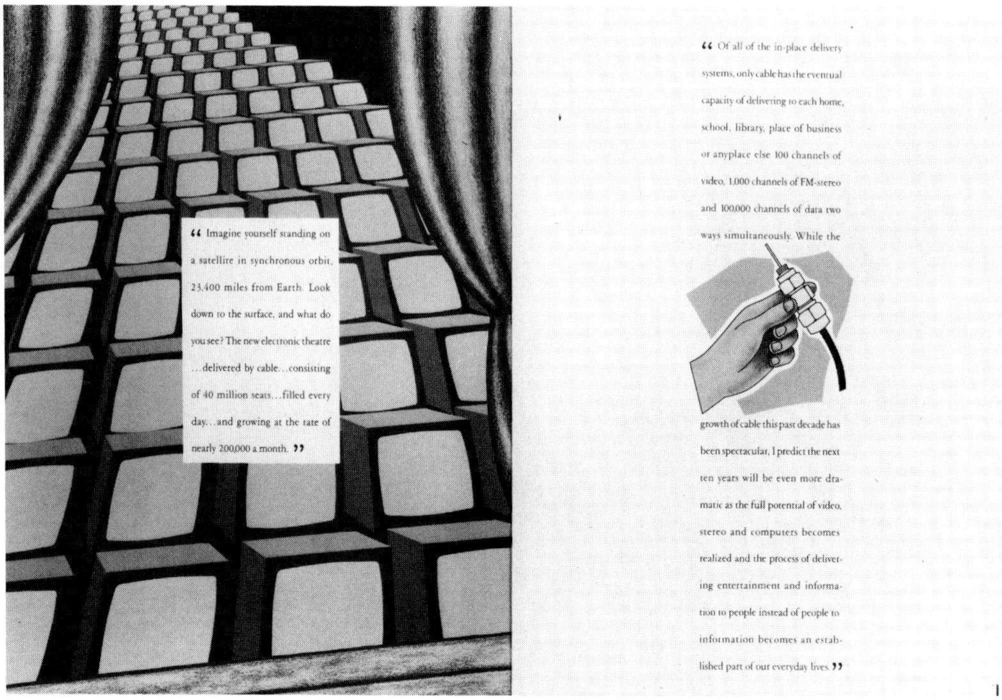
“Imagine yourself standing on a satellite in synchronous orbit, 23,400 miles from Earth. Look down to the surface, and what do you see? The new electronic theatre ...delivered by cable...consisting of 40 million seats...filled every day...and growing at the rate of nearly 200,000 a month.”
“Of all of the in-place delivery systems, only cable has the eventual capacity of delivering to each home, school, library, place of business or anyplace else 100 channels of video, 1,000 channels of FM-stereo and 100,000 channels of data two ways simultaneously. While the growth of cable this past decade has been spectacular, I predict the next ten years will be even more dramatic as the full potential of video, stereo and computers becomes realized and the process of delivering entertainment and information to people instead of people to information becomes an established part of our everyday lives.”

the salient points that were worth emphasizing and began to construct some illustrations. Since I worked as an illustrator in London for a while, I always think as an illustrator/designer/art director, which is ideal for a project of this kind where one gets free rein.

On working with illustrators: I love to use illustration wherever I can, and this seemed like a good opportunity. Jones was open for something new because the previous reports used trick photographs with computerlike spectrum bursts. And more important, their competitors all used similar photography. I presented the page-by-page roughs with some samples of various illustrators' work, but mostly did the preliminary sketches myself. I wanted to keep the drawings loose, so I selected Brian Grimwood because he's incredible and I had worked with him before in London. Originally I was going to do the cover myself, but Brian is so good that I couldn't resist using him. It's nice to do a sketch and give it to an illustrator that you trust and that you know will give it *life*. Illustration, I believe, can convey more feeling and is more communicative than a photograph. I used good photography in this piece to give stability and as documentary evidence; this gave me more leeway to go farther afield with the illustrations. More precisely, photography is to illustration as practice is to theory.

I used a number of illustrators for, among other things, practical reasons. Brian is great, but expensive, so I used him for the cover alone. I hired a local illustrator, Ursula Brookbank, who was relatively new to the business, because her natural style is so appealing. The computer art is by Monxo Algora, who moved to LA from Spain. I wanted all the artwork to be wed but also have separate identities. I achieved this to some extent by the selection of distinctive PMS colors for each. Though many illustrators worked on these pieces, the colors tie them together, as if they all happened at the same time. None of the illustrators were pleased that I was printing in flat color, which required them to do pre-separated art. I understand this because they were, in effect, working blind; they're proud of what they do and like to see a finished piece before handing it in. Because they didn't have a chance to see their color until the proof stage, they were nervous about how the piece would print. I too was nervous and had to trust my judgment.

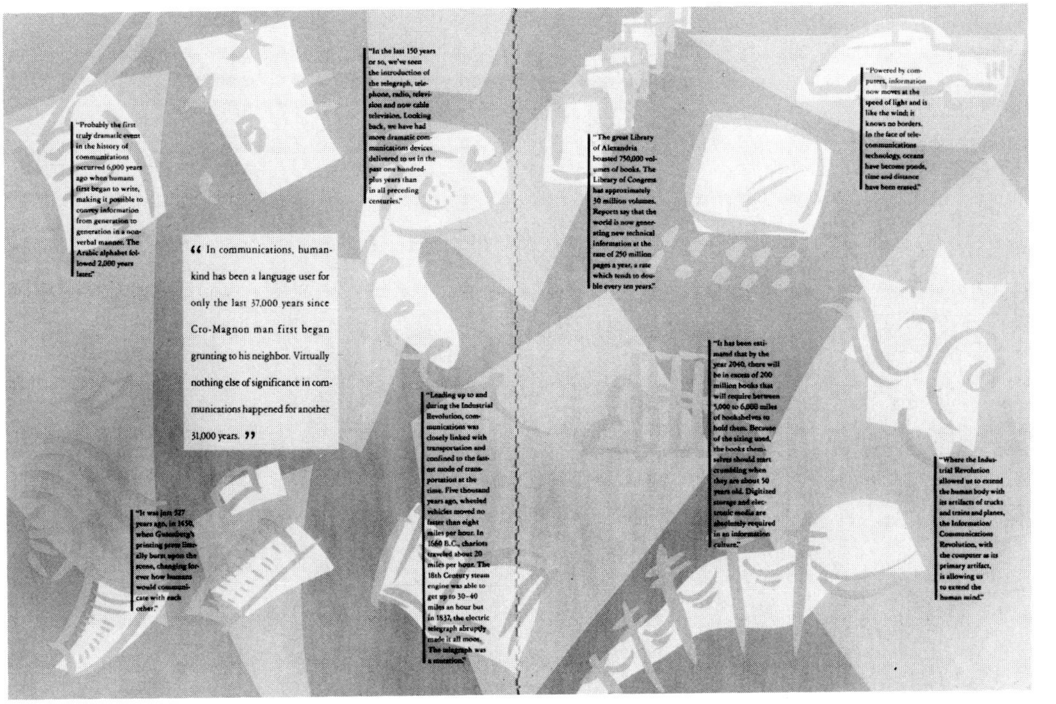
"Probably the first truly dramatic event in the history of communications occurred 6,000 years ago when humans first began to write, making it possible to convey information from generation to generation in a non-verbal manner. The Arabic alphabet followed 2,000 years later."
"In the last 150 years or so, we've seen the introduction of the telegraph, telephone, radio, television and now cable television. Looking back, we have had more dramatic communications devices delivered to us in the past one hundred-plus years than in all preceding centuries."
❝ In communications, humankind has been a language user for only the last 37,000 years since Cro-Magnon man first began grunting to his neighbor. Virtually nothing else of significance in communications happened for another 31,000 years. ❞
"Leading up to and during the Industrial Revolution, communications was closely linked with transportation and confined to the fastest mode of transportation at the time. Five thousand years ago, wheeled vehicles moved no faster than eight miles per hour. In 1660 B.C., chariots traveled about 20 miles per hour. The 18th Century steam engine was able to get up to 30–40 miles an hour but in 1837, the electric telegraph abruptly made it all moot. The telegraph was a sensation."
"It was just 527 years ago, in 1450, when Gutenberg's printing press literally burst upon the scene, changing forever how humans would communicate with each other."
"The great Library of Alexandria boasted 750,000 volumes of books. The Library of Congress has approximately 30 million volumes. Reports say that the world is now generating new technical information at the rate of 250 million pages a year, a rate which tends to double every ten years."
"Powered by computers, information now moves at the speed of light and is like the wind; it knows no borders. In the face of telecommunications technology, oceans have become ponds, time and distance have been erased."
"It has been estimated that by the year 2040, there will be in excess of 200 million books that will require between 5,000 to 6,000 miles of bookshelves to hold them. Because of the sizing used, the books themselves should start crumbling when they are about 50 years old. Digitized storage and electronic media are absolutely required in an information culture."
"Where the Industrial Revolution allowed us to extend the human body with its artifacts of trucks and trains and planes, the Information/Communications Revolution, with the computer as its primary artifact, is allowing us to extend the human mind."

JONES SPACELINK ANNUAL REPORT (1987)
JONES SPACELINK, *Client*
STEVE TWIGGER, *Designer*
BRIAN GRIMWOOD, URSULA BROOKBANK, STEVE TWIGGER, AND MONXO ALGORA, *Illustrators*
STEVE TWIGGER, *Art Director*

On doing his own illustration: Since I am an illustrator I wanted to have something of my own represented in this project. I basically took a piece of clip art showing a head and enlarged it on Xerox until the scan lines could be seen with the eye. I was just playing around, but it worked well.

Typographically speaking: I had great typographic influences in London—good, solid typographers from the old school, like the Swiss masters, who provided springboards to break the rules. If you know that your story looks correct on the page, that it's in the right hierarchy of importance, then you can start building around that structure. You know that whatever you do with it you'll still have a structure. The illustration and type tell a story. And maintaining integrity with the material is important so that it does not become design for its own sake.

On the relationship between art directors and illustrators in London: Working back home was a different ball game. Illustrators and designers are hired to illustrate and design. That's what they do. In fact, as a designer, a lot of times I would say to a client, "Well, the concept for the cover is that I'm going to use Brian Grimwood." And that would be a given. Then I would say to Brian, "This is what we have to convey, do it for me." I would provide the inspiration and then pull out of him what was needed, but ultimately trust him to be able to interpret that. Given that trust illustrators can create so much more freely. Here in Los Angeles an art director almost has to be the illustrator too, which kind of defeats the object. The usual scenario with a client might go: "I'd like to use so-and-so." "Well," they say, "what's it going to look like?" "I don't know," you say. "He hasn't done it yet." So you end up doing a facsimile illustration for the presentation. Then the illustrator gets that comp and he's scared to do anything else because that's what's been approved. I believe if you pay for an illustrator's talent, there's no sense in telling him exactly what to do.

On occasion the illustrator must adhere to the comp, but it depends on the client and the job. If it is a movie project, you've made ten refinements to the concept by the time you get around to giving it to the illustrator. In that situation freedom is not always possible.

LOUISE FILI

After working for Herb Lubalin for two years, Louise Fili became the art director of Pantheon Books, a job that has lasted over ten years. She annually directs more than two hundred titles. Some she designs herself; others are given out to freelance designers. Yet Pantheon Books, and its new Schocken Books imprint, have a distinctive style—one based on original typography and strong illustration. Here Fili describes some recent work for which illustration is either the basis of design or an element in the total puzzle.

On the transition from designer to art director: Before taking the job with Pantheon I had never art directed illustration or photography—or for that matter design, which is even harder. I always had a preconceived idea of what I wanted the design of a jacket to look like; to give that up to someone else produced some unforeseen results. I was less reliant on illustration, and most of my early covers were typographic. Today most of my work still begins with type. Often I will have a precise idea of how the type will look and select an illustrator whose style will go with that type.

On becoming more comfortable with illustration: Becoming an art director gave me more opportunities to work with illustration. As an independent designer there just isn't the same kind of flexibility—one has to make do with found-material and copyright-free art (like the kind found in Dover books). The challenge that comes from working with illustration is finding that perfect balance between the letterform and the image. I prefer to work more often with illustrators than photographers because I have much more creative and technical control.

About the Kafka series: This series exemplifies that balance. Here, however, I worked out the entire format before making the illustration assignment. I took an Anthony Russo drawing out of *American Illustration* and used it on the original comp; I knew that Russo would be the best illustrator for the job, but I also had other design priorities. These were the first books for Schocken, Pantheon's new imprint, and I wanted to establish a look that was both unusual and well suited to the subject matter. Though the series is published only in paperback, I wanted the books to look like they were a three-piece case. To achieve the spine I had the printer print from the edge of rice paper. I also wanted to print it on Speckletone, a matte stock. So I based my design on an old wood typeface, with a script that is no longer available from typesetters.

Like many of my typefaces I found the wood alphabet in an old book; but it was too condensed. I sent it out to my typesetter to have it

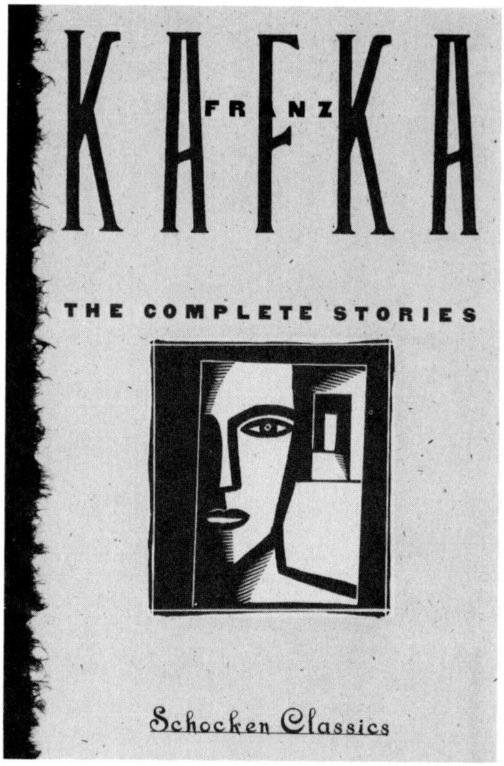
KAFKA
FRANZ
THE COMPLETE STORIES
Schocken Classics

expanded photographically to make it more readable. We also changed the position of the crossbar on the *A* because it was not harmonious with the rest of the letters. Often letters in the same alphabet do not work in juxtaposition with each other, and that's when manipulation is necessary.

On working with illustrators: Sometimes I provide a manuscript, but it depends on the illustrator—whether we've worked together before; how much I can trust them. Sometimes I will suggest exactly what I want, other times I will give *carte blanche.* Since there is nothing worse than to find an anachronism on a book jacket, I want to make certain that the illustrator has the right points of departure, then the rest is up to him or her. I showed Russo a sketch of what I was looking for: a simple, straightforward illustration that could work well in a small space—preferably done in scratchboard. I also gave him the manuscript to read, and for the *Kafka Diaries* I gave him pictures of the author. Since we had worked together before, I knew that his method was not to show me sketches but to do as many as three scratchboard finishes. They are all

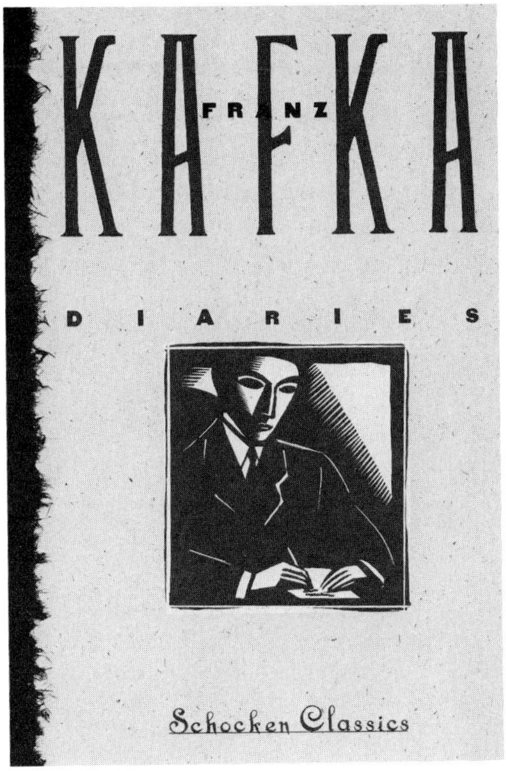
FRANZ
KAFKA
DIARIES
Schocken Classics

FRANZ
KAFKA
THE CASTLE
Schocken Classics

KAFKA SERIES BOOK COVERS (1988)
PANTHEON BOOKS, *Client*
LOUISE FILI, *Designer*
ANTHONY RUSSO, *Illustrator*
LOUISE FILI, *Art Director*

somewhat similar, but it's a luxury to have a selection. It is not difficult to choose the right one. I always know, because I'm looking for the most direct image.

Sometimes I reject the illustration entirely, but I try not to. I prefer to save an illustration, no matter what the circumstance. If I feel that the illustrator has really let me down, that's a different issue. But if I feel that they have done their job and there was some miscommunication, or the editor has been the problem, I suggest another direction.

On selecting an illustrator: I try not to use illustrators who are typecast as book jacket artists. In fact, I usually just look up at my wall. You see, I've been in my office for over ten years, and the wall is one big collage covered with hundreds of papers and artists' cards. When I'm looking for an illustrator I'll look up at the wall and will often find the right one. With Kafka I thought of Russo immediately because I knew that a color image was not appropriate (or affordable); something black-and-white was the answer, and that dictated which group of illustrators to focus on. Other times I flip through *American Illustration* until an idea hits me. If I cannot think of an illustrator in a day, I'm in trouble.

About the jacket for *Perfect Gallows*: This is a mystery, and the mystery genre is replete with clichés. It's odd that every young illustrator I meet wants to do a mystery or cookbook; those are the two most difficult kinds of jackets. I attempt to use artists who are not familiar with the form in the hope that they will bring something fresh to it. Robert Goldstrom, who did *Perfect Gallows*, usually does editorial and corporate work, but his meticulous style lends itself to the British mystery genre. And we have the perfect working relationship. I tell him exactly what I want, I give him the passage in the manuscript that should be illustrated, and he takes it a step further, thus making my idea work better than I had originally conceived.

With *Perfect Gallows* Goldstrom was to render a scene where a hanged man is found in a dovecote. And it took us a long time to figure out what a dovecote was—it's very British. In fact, it is a small domed shelter where doves are kept. Gold-

"Exciting, funny, and refreshingly nasty." —Martin Amis
DUFFY
DAN KAVANAGH
PANTHEON
INTERNATIONAL
CRIME

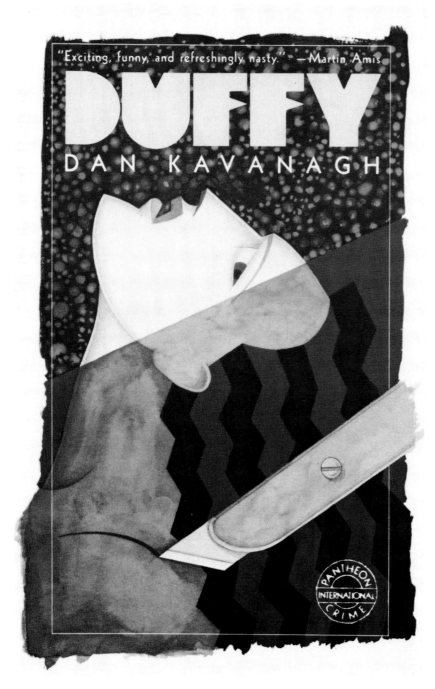

DUFFY (1985), *Book cover*
PANTHEON BOOKS, *Client*
LOUISE FILI, *Designer*
JOHN MARTINEZ, *Illustrator*
LOUISE FILI, *Art Director*

strom researched the thing extensively—which is something I expect my illustrators to do—and came up with a wonderful image. Curiously, his sketches are very primitive, so much so one would think he cannot draw. When he suggested the idea of the hanging man in the bird's eye, it seemed rather trite. But I trusted him, and the finished art bore out that trust.

About integrating type on the jacket: When I see a sketch, I make certain that there is room for type, and the illustrator will accommodate my needs. I hate it when type is just smacked on as an afterthought. With *Perfect Gallows* I asked Goldstrom to move down the window a bit. Since each word in the title had an equal number of letters I decided to use a condensed face with vertical red rules between each letter (a subtle allusion to hanging). I wanted a simple, bold typeface, but not just straight type—without the rules it would have been boring, and maybe even hard to read.

On encouraging illustrators to do their own type: Often illustrators are reluctant to do this, but when they do, the results are usually quite satisfying. I believe that most illustrators have an innate sense of typography just waiting to be unleashed. But for many who won't try, I will set the type and then have them render it. It never fails to make a stronger, seamless piece.

About the cover for *Duffy*: This and the sequel, *Fiddle City,* are very odd stories about a bisexual detective. They are gritty, raunchy, mass-market paperbacks. I had to come up with an image that was suitable but unusual given the constraints of the genre. John Martinez had done a book series for which he used a hard-edged, linear Art Deco approach, and he was tired of working in that style. He had been experimenting with a new, painterly style that was perfect for these covers. The illustration is very violent, echoing the book's theme. I designed the cover using the raw edge of his painting because it added to that sensibility. After the illustration came in, I designed the type. I drew from an Italian Futurist type, but I was playing off the knife—I wanted something that looked like cut paper. I used a standard face to balance it out. And balance is the key to making type and illustration work together.

PERFECT
GALLOWS
A NOVEL OF SUSPENSE
PETER DICKINSON

PERFECT GALLOWS (1987), *Book jacket*
PANTHEON BOOKS, *Client*
LOUISE FILI, *Designer*
ROBERT GOLDSTROM, *Illustrator*
LOUISE FILI, *Art Director*

PAT GORMAN

Manhattan Design, which not coincidentally is based in the heart of New York City, was founded in 1979 by illustrator-designers Frank Olinsky and Pat Gorman in an effort to have more creative and quality control over their projects. An early promotional piece, the Manhattan Design calendar of 1984, for which each month was interpreted through an illustration by a "New Wave" artist, evidenced the studio's pictorial interests. Along the same lines, Frank's conception for an illustrated Talking Heads lyric book allowed a broad range of painters, illustrators, and cartoonists to comment on and interpret these extraordinarily visual songs. Manhattan Design uniquely represents the look of contemporary culture, specifically through the identity materials done for MTV. The following traces the evolution of their most visible work, the MTV logo, and some collateral material as well.

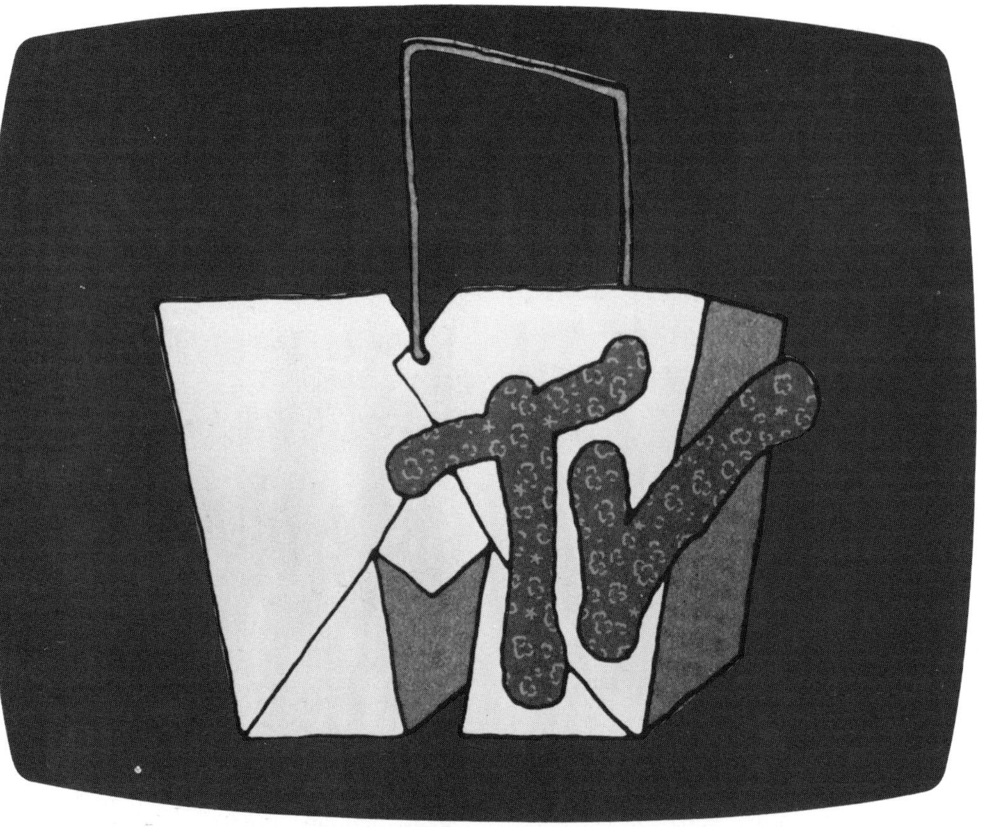

MTV
MUSIC TELEVISION

About the beginnings of Manhattan Design: I've always been addicted to comics and picture books; what is a good book without pictures? Certainly that's the reason why Frank and I got involved in this business. I had been trained as a painter, and so was Frank; but he was more on the edge of illustration than I, and it was therefore easier for him to make the transition to applied arts. Having done work for *New York* magazine and Paper Moon greeting cards, he was well on the road to becoming a substantial illustrator. For me, graphic design was not the main interest; rather set design became an important focus in my life. My transition occurred when I started doing theater posters for the shows on which I was working (incidentally many of my paintings are a combination of words and pictures). And I seriously crossed over to graphic design because I was not interested in just making pretty things. That's where Frank and I connect.

About the importance of content: For both of us the idea is the important thing, and a great idea is very often *not* pretty. Rather, in the beginning at least, a seminal concept is very often visually obnoxious simply because it's different.

How that "difference" relates to the MTV logo: The MTV logo was a great idea but was opposed at first by most of the people at the station, particularly the salesmen. Thanks to Bob Pittman, the brilliant man who "invented" MTV, as well as the support of several others, it finally passed.

Discussing their mandate for the logo: We were called in before the station had a name. Pittman told us that the logo could be anything—it could be a barfing dog if we wanted. So we knew that he wouldn't be opposed to a pictorial rather than a symbolic or typographic solution. And I really hate the current logos that have horizontal lines through them. From the beginning we had the idea that it should be something that could be animated, and the very first thing we came up with was a hand holding a musical note (it may look like a Disney cartoon hand, but at

Music Television

MTV
Music Television

FRESH SQUEEZED MUSIC (C. 1980–81), *Logo*
MTV, *Client*
PAT GORMAN, *Designer*
FRANK OLINSKY, *Illustrator*
MANHATTAN DESIGN, *Art Director*

(below)
LOGOS (C. 1980–81), *Rough sketches created at client's request*
MTV, *Client*
PAT GORMAN AND FRANK OLINSKY, *Designers*
PAT GORMAN AND FRANK OLINSKY, *Illustrators*

(opposite, top)
CHINESE NEW YEAR-TAKE OUT (1985), *Program identity for* MTV TO GO
MTV, *Client*
FRANK OLINSKY, *Designer*
FRANK OLINSKY, *Illustrator*
MANHATTAN DESIGN, *Art Director*

(opposite, bottom)
LOGO (1985)
MTV, *Client*
FRANK OLINSKY, *Designer*
FRANK OLINSKY, *Illustrator*
MANHATTAN DESIGN, *Art Director*

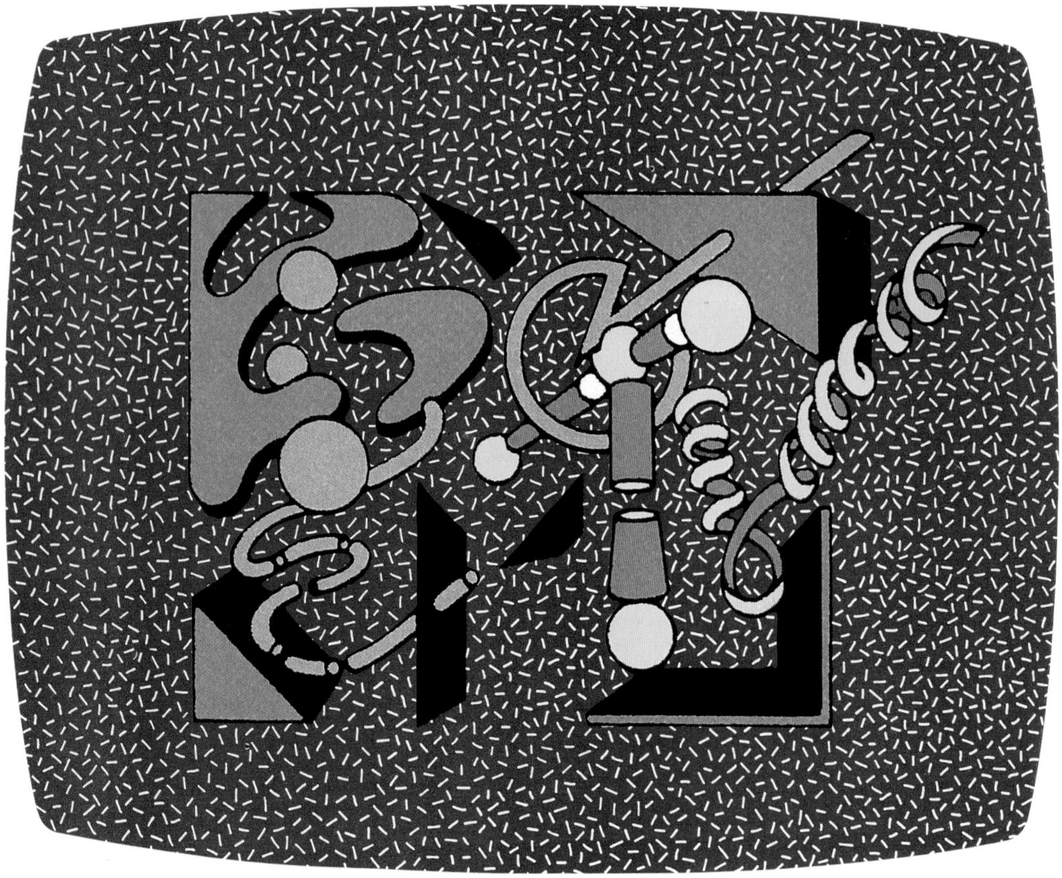

the time the Disney Channel did not exist). We took a photograph of Frank squeezing a tomato with a pencil sticking out—the idea was that it represented fresh-squeezed music and different stars would be doing it for different on-air spots. We were told that the idea was okay, but they needed to have call letters. Then after some discussion over whether to call it the Music Channel, the idea emerged that the station could be called M (for music) and TV (for television). We did MTV in handwriting with a rainbow pattern, which didn't work at all but nevertheless made us resolve to use illustration in the finish somehow.

We never considered a type logo because type alone is boring. It can be wonderful, of course, in the right hands, and some people have a distinct talent for it. Even Frank and I have designed several interesting typefaces for album covers. But *every* television station uses letters—ABC, NBC, CBS. We both loved the NBC peacock; it was the most interesting trademark on TV. And so was Speedy Alka-Seltzer and all that other visual stuff that influenced our childhood. What's television for, anyway? Pictures! Moreover, the station was about rock and roll, and letters alone would have appeared too stagnant.

The process, philosophically speaking: I don't think in terms of a problem. It's semantics really; a problem implies that there is a solution, whereas I don't believe one always exists. The term I prefer is *issue,* which suggests a subject of discussion. I also think that making design or a design element look pretty is a secondary phase—lots of people can do that very well, better than I. It takes a very different talent to make a fresh idea. And we wanted to do something that was equally as fresh as the unheard-of idea of a twenty-four-hour music video station.

The process, physically speaking: We had a business partner at the time who, not being a designer, sat down one day in the midst of the whole deadline process and drew the shape of an *M.* Frank was out of the office, and I wasn't too keen on it being exclusively done as letters, but she wanted to take a stab at it and I tried to guide her. All day long, back and forth, we worked at it. She wanted to have three giant letters, and I was opposed. At the end of the day I modified the *M* and scrawled a little *TV* onto it. When Frank came in and saw the rough logo for the first time, he said it was incredibly ugly—at which point our partner rolled it into a ball and threw it into the trash. Since I was the peacemaker, I retrieved it, smoothed it out, and convinced Frank that it was a good basic concept for discussion. He then took a large piece of paper and said, "If you're going to do this, you might as well have a decent-looking *TV.*" Then came a moment of inspiration: Frank and I looked at each other—as if we had the same brain for fifteen seconds—and said that the *M* could be a screen and then images could be projected on it. The *M* could be an object—it could be a cake, or anything we wanted to make it.

The messenger was on the way to pick up our sketches for the review by the station execs, and we were not really prepared to let it out. So, very fast, we set to work and did about fifteen to twenty sketches, many of which were adopted for use in the first animation of the man landing on the moon. And we sent along a stack with the crumpled original.

I was amazed that the client actually could decipher all the visual mishmash, but they came back to us with, "We kind of like it, but we think maybe the *TV* should be big and the *M* should be small." To which we replied it could not be done that way and showed them, and they said, "Okay, we see that doesn't work, but we don't think people will recognize the big *M* as part of the *TV,* so why don't you make a graffitied *M* to go with the *TV* and put it all over the big *M*?" We sent them a sketch of that idea, but it looked so obscene that they backed down. After running through their objections, they decided that they liked it. And since we had some more time, we could show how it could be three-dimensionally tilted in space and used with other variations.

The higher-higher-ups, however, were still unconvinced that our small studio could do this work and commissioned more conventional firms to do some sketches. They said that they wanted a Herb Lubalin-like solution—or something as memorable as the CBS eye. But predictably the firms they went to came up with things with boring musical notes, which was our first idea; and it was just too obvious. Incidentally, we've never since used musical notes or instruments to symbolically depict music.

On some of the many MTV variations: After the logo became established, we consulted on various MTV stage sets, especially for New

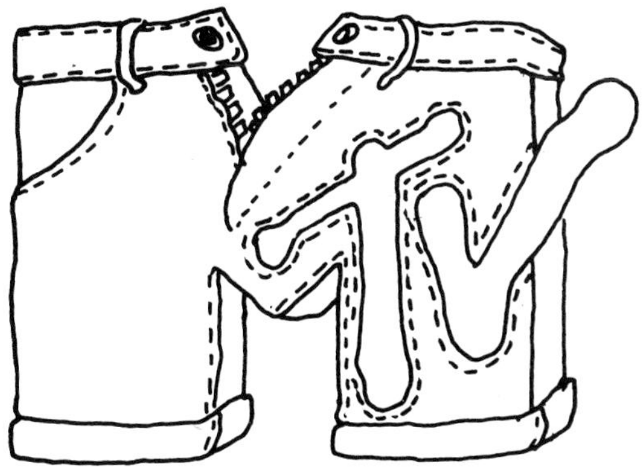

Logo (1983–87)
MTV, *Client*
Pat Gorman, *Designer*
Pat Gorman, *Illustrator*
Manhattan Design, *Art Director*

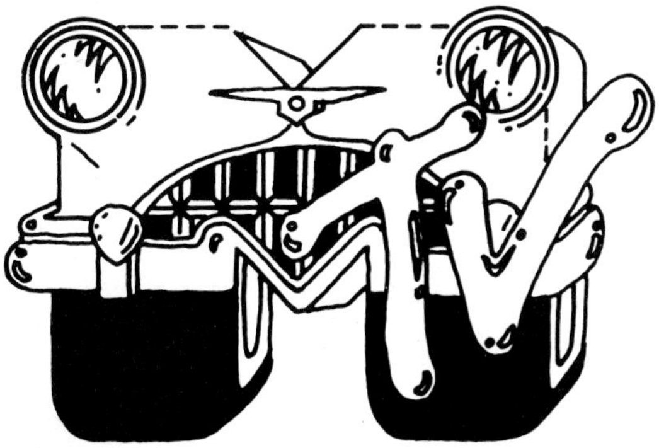

Logo (1983–87)
MTV, *Client*
Pat Gorman, *Designer*
Cheri Dorr, *Illustrator*
Manhattan Design, *Art Director*

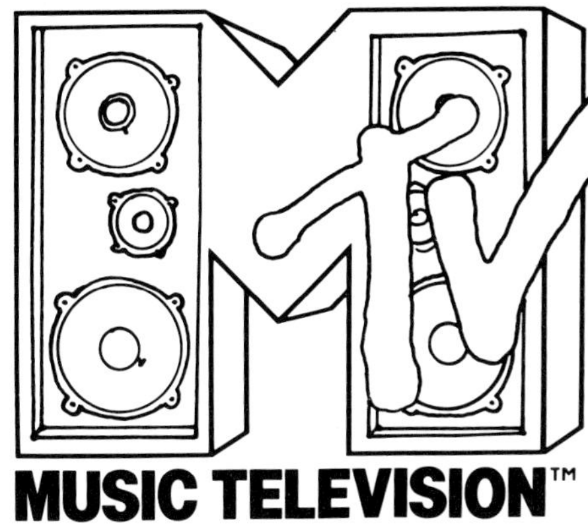
MUSIC TELEVISION™

Logo (1983–87)
MTV, *Client*
Frank Olinsky, *Designer*
Frank Olinsky, *Illustrator*
Manhattan Design, *Art Director*

(opposite)
Futuristic "Boomerang" MTV (1986), *Logo identity*
MTV, *Client*
Pat Gorman, *Designer*
Pat Gorman, *Illustrator*
Manhattan Design, *Art Director*

Happy Birthday

MTV's First-Birthday Logo (1983),
Animation and print identity
MTV, *Client*
Frank Olinsky, *Designer*
Frank Olinsky, *Illustrator*
Manhattan Design, *Art Director*

Year's eve; one year we used a giant pink sneaker with a clock on the side, while the next was an elaborate scaffolding with a projection screen. In the beginning the logo was used rather conservatively because people didn't always understand what to do with it, and the station had a difficult time drawing in viewers and wanted to build a solid identity. But as time went on we were allowed to be more adventuresome, and developed many variations, including jerky black-and-white animation that characterizes some of the on-air look. The animation companies were the first to catch on and started doing their own versions.

About the thrill of animation: I learned early on that one can do incredible things in a video studio without really being a true animator. We weren't really animators, but when we had ideas that required immediate attention we did the animation ourselves, just to see if they would work. And our approach, which is to make virtues out of primitive flaws, is diametrically opposite to the union guys', who are trained to make everything look perfect. In fact they resisted some of our ideas because they could not believe we actually wanted the result to be so crude. We convinced one technician, however; he allowed

FRACTURED FACES (1988), *Twenty-second video identity*
MTV, *Client*
PAT GORMAN AND MANHATTAN DESIGN, *Designers*
VARIOUS ILLUSTRATORS, INCLUDING MARK MAREK AND JOHN VAN HAMMERSVELD
MANHATTAN DESIGN, *Art Director*

us in a studio, locked the doors so that no one would see that we were turning the dials ourselves, and then Frank and I went crazy, making incredibly messed-up Ms. When we began there was no "paint box" technology (that came later), but we did learn about those incredible machines that distort and rotate art in space. Being rather knowledgeable means that we can take full advantage of all the possibilities.

About "Fractured Faces": The idea for this MTV on-air animation was to make an *M* out of a number of different, bizarre faces, which were sliced in four sections and, like a children's game, recombined to make a new face (or *M*). We asked sixteen illustrators, including John Van Hammersveld, Mark Marek, Lynda Barry, and Steven Guarnaccia, to contribute. I gave them a grid to follow—showing where the eyes, nose, and mouth should fall—but most ignored it and did their own thing. And I threw in a few photographs at the beginning so the viewer would think that it was something normal.

On working with freelance illustrators: We approach new illustrators as if we are the new kids on the block wanting to make friends. You either get into a fight or give them a job. And the artists we work with become a kind of extended family. Hence, we never call an illustrator in on a project that we would not want to do ourselves. Illustrators working with us know that they will have a good time and do a piece that will be far beyond what they usually do.

PETER HARRISON

Pentagram was one of the first international graphic design firms, with founding offices in London, then New York and San Francisco. (It is also well represented in this book; see the sections on Kit Hinrichs and Susan Hochbaum). From its inception, Pentagram has taken the Modern design sensibility to its next evolutionary stage in the areas of product, packaging, corporate communications, and graphic design. Peter Harrison, Colin Forbes, and Woody Pirtle are the three New York principals. Here Harrison discusses his penchant for illustration as applied to the difficult problem of designing unconventional corporate annual reports.

On his current preference for illustration: On the whole we've gone more to illustration than ever before, primarily because of our need to change the look of annual reports. Good photography has become such a convention that it's difficult to differentiate oneself from the others. Even with superb photography the result looks predictable. Second, illustration allows us to present abstract and symbolic ideas more effectively than photography, and so aids in getting more complex ideas across.

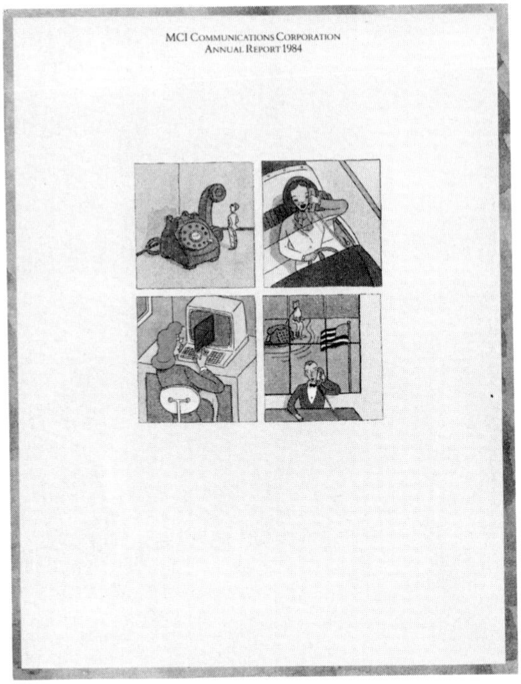
MCI Communications Corporation
Annual Report 1984

Concerning the *1985 MCI Communication Corporation Annual Report:* This was a case when I used David Suter, a *New York Times* regular who is essentially known for his acute symbolism, to illustrate a series of quotes by the CEO of MCI on directions they were taking for future growth. We decided to make the illustrations like political cartoons; and the drawings were strong and gritty. I must admit that I wasn't totally happy with the outcome, partly because we had a difference of opinion with the client. I wanted the drawings to be in black-and-white (which is Suter's strong suit). They wanted them in color. We did them in color, and I still believe they should have been monochromatic.

Not all clients like this approach. In fact it is risky in this area of annual reports to try new things. In the case of MCI we took a big risk, and the result is we don't do their annual reports anymore. Perhaps it was this approach, or maybe they had wanted a change of designer anyway. The annual-report business is legendary for its ebbs and flows.

MCI Communications Corporation Annual Report 1985
"The Information Age isn't coming.
It's here! MCI will play an increasingly
central role in delivering the services and
technologies of the Information Age to
American business and industry."
William G. McGowan

The 1984 MCI report: We actually used illustration once before for them in a much more successful way; it was a huge map of the United States rendered by Steven Guarnaccia. As a foldout, it actually showed every place MCI had established a business center. It was extremely detailed and game-like, which most readers enjoy—full of extraordinary little vignettes, all literally relating to MCI's growing network.

Background of the Bell South annual report: This was the company's first annual report after the Bell system divested to become regional companies. Its purpose was to focus reader attention on where and who Bell South is. The South is a strong region with a lot of economic clout: we commissioned James McMullan and used his drawings in a journalistic manner, as

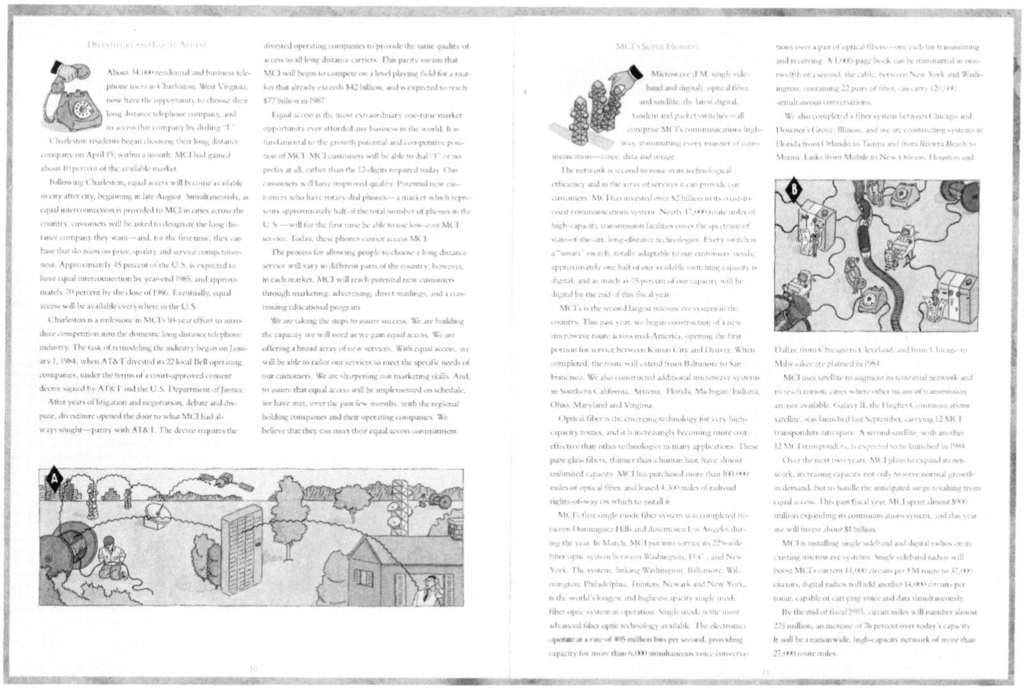

MCI COMMUNICATIONS CORPORATION
ANNUAL REPORT (1984)
MCI, *Client*
SUSAN HOCHBAUM, *Designer*
STEVEN GUARNACCIA, *Illustrator*
PETER HARRISON, *Art Director*

MCI COMMUNICATIONS CORPORATION
ANNUAL REPORT (1985)
MCI, *Client*
SUZANNE MORIN, *Designer*
DAVID SUTER, *Illustrator*
PETER HARRISON, *Art Director*

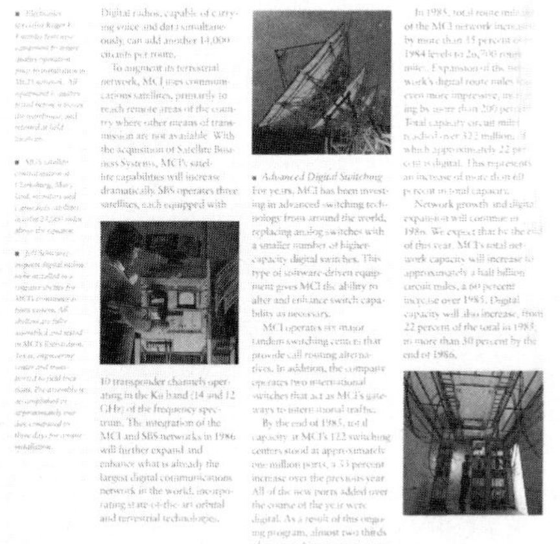

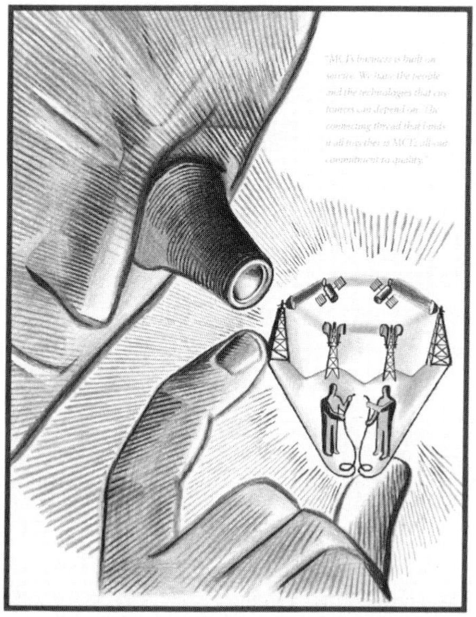

though he had done a sketchbook trip of the region. We had drawings of a town, a river, and a farm and included little side notes giving demographic information and growth rates. The drawings were intended to offer a commercial story—a visual dialogue, so to speak.

On the format of the report: We alternated information about the company with the regional pages; for example, one spread was about the South while the next was about what Bell South was doing. Jim did both versions as sketchbook pages.

We thought of using landscapes in the initial stage, but photographs were envisioned. For example, one idea was to show a photo of a winding road passing a farmhouse, with hills in the background and a caption saying something like, "Underneath this road, every day of the week, travel 27 billion telephone messages. Because buried under this road is a fiber optic cable." This was the kind of sharp contrast we wanted to convey. We prepared both the photographic and illustrative treatment using some sketches Jim had done, and the client preferred the illustrative version.

About working with the illustrator: I'd say it was a good designer-illustrator relationship. I prefer not to lead the illustrator too much, so we'd talk and I'd roughly sketch out what we had in mind—just enough to give him direction so that he could come up with his own ideas. We decided on certain sights because of their pictorial potential. Since we didn't begin the job until November, and March is the frantic deadline for annual reports, we didn't have time to send Jim on location. Instead, after we got the client to agree on the approach, we hired a photo researcher to get a representative selection of scrap from which Jim could work. Jim did roughs which we would Fed Ex down to the client for discussion like whether the scale was okay. It was actually a pretty effective way of working.

On the typographic treatment: The type, in a funny way, is akin to a postage stamp on a postcard. We knew we would have to include some text, so the illustrations were composed to accommodate the minimalist shapes. In fact, they are all slightly different shapes so that they integrate well with the drawing.

The result: The relationship with the client was fine, considering the job was done in such a scramble, but there were the attendant crises. There were some production problems owing to the large quantity, and bits and pieces could have been resolved more satisfactorily with more time. But it came out the way I wanted it to. And they recieved over two thousand laudatory letters from

BellSouth Corporation
1984 Annual Report
BELLSOUTH

people. The response was so good that we reprinted a number of the drawings on better paper, and Jim signed and numbered a couple hundred. If there was any problem with the project it was that people inside Bell South wanted to see themselves as more high-tech and cutting-edge than these romantic illustrations about the "sleepy South" might suggest.

About the Warner Communications project: Pentagram had a series of annual reports for this client, and they seem to be pleased with our approach [see also the section on Susan Hochbaum]. This one is based on the company's twenty-fifth anniversary, and my idea was to have a section that was a mini-scrapbook history focusing on the significant events of the day, beginning in 1962. We asked the Los Angeleno artist John Van Hammersveld to come East for a day or two, and we did some mock-ups which I showed to Steve Ross at Warner, who gave us the go-ahead. Then, of course, we had to gather all the various components, which was not easy to do. We had to get the client to attach relative importance to the images so we could proceed with the size relationships. John came back to New York to work this out.

Bell South Corporation
Annual Report (1984)
Bell South Corporation, *Client*
Suzanne Morin, *Designer*
James McMullan, *Illustrator*
Peter Harrison, *Art Director*

July '84
stopped to sketch this thoroughbred playfully kicking his heels in the kentucky bluegrass
Between 1984 and 2000, the South's population will grow by over eleven million people, one third of the growth of the entire nation. Its immense reservoirs of fertile land, clean air and water provide the basis for a quality of life unexcelled in the United States.
McMullan

Savannah, Georgia... a handsome town of brightly colored houses and abundant flowers
June '84
McMullan
The quality of life in the South continues to be a magnet. Jobs, the heartbeat of a growing economy, will be created at the rate of 375,000 per year through the end of the century. Abetted by real personal income growth of over three percent per year, four million new households will be formed in that period.

This was a design team effort. I worked with Harold Burch, who was the project designer. Together we would come up with the ideas and decide upon the direction, and then we would go ahead and develop roughs. John worked very well with us: he did the roughs; I reviewed them with Harold; and then we got them up to the client for an okay. Not all annual reports are as frenetically paced as this, but this one was on a tight schedule. John had to work in the office to make

WARNER COMMUNICATIONS INC.
1987 ANNUAL REPORT
WARNER COMMUNICATIONS, *Client*
HAROLD BURCH, *Designer*
JOHN VAN HAMMERSVELD, *Illustrator*
PETER HARRISON, *Art Director*

WARNER COMMUNICATIONS INC. 1987 ANNUAL REPORT
'87
1962 - 1987

the process most efficient. After a few minor changes, he returned to LA to do the finishes, leaving space for type.

We wanted to make the type actually become the illustration. However, since we did not have time to do color comps before this went into mechanical, I had no way of checking; so we had problems with readability. But the client loved it, although he too regretted that the legibility wasn't fully refined.

FILMED ENTERTAINMENT

Throughout its history, Warner Bros. Records, the largest of the WCI Record Group labels, has developed and produced some of the most influential artists in American pop music.
Recordings from such diverse artists as Frank Sinatra, Jimi Hendrix, The Doobie Brothers, Neil Young, Fleetwood Mac, Paul Simon, Van Halen, Prince, and Madonna have not only established new directions for American music but also have had tremendous world wide impact. What has characterized Warner's long term success has been its willingness to experiment and take risks with artists and their repertoire, often developing and supporting an artist or a project over a long period of time before achieving ultimate success.
Guided through the past two decades by Mo Ostin, Warner Bros. artists consistently top the charts in rock, pop, country, and black music.
DOORS
JACKSON BROWNE
When Jac Holzman founded Elektra Records with $600 in 1950, he envisioned a label that would specialize in the folk music of the world. In its early years, the label fulfilled that vision with releases from Judy Collins and Phil Ochs as well as the influential Explorer series on Elektra's home for "serious" music, Nonesuch Records. As the Sixties grew in ever less predictable ways, so did Elektra, signing artists such as Love, Tim Buckley, the Butterfield Blues Band, and the Doors.
Elektra became part of WCI in 1970, and soon after, David Geffen's Asylum Records merged with Elektra. During this decade, the company discovered some of its most popular artists including Jackson Browne, the Cars, the Eagles, and Linda Ronstadt.
Today, under the leadership of Bob Krasnow, the company's strength continues to be the discovery and development of a wide-ranging group of artists, from Anita Baker to the Kronos Quartet.
In the annals of America's pop music industry, Atlantic Records is legend. Established as an independent jazz and blues label forty years ago by Ahmet Ertegun, his brother Nesuhi, and Jerry Wexler, Atlantic Records has produced artists whose contributions have shaped the direction of American music. The long list includes rhythm and blues pioneers Ray Charles, The Drifters, Aretha Franklin, and Otis Redding; jazz greats John Coltrane, Charles Mingus, Ornette Coleman, and The Modern Jazz Quartet; and rock superstars Crosby, Stills and Nash, Led Zeppelin, and Cream. Today, with such multi-platinum performers as Foreigner, AC/DC, Genesis, and Phil Collins, Atlantic Records is still headed by Ahmet Ertegun. The label continues to combine commercial success with artistic vision.
NEIL YOUNG
ARETHA FRANKLIN

MIKE HICKS

Humor plays a large part in the house "style" of Mike Hicks's Hixo Design firm in Austin, Texas. Although he rejects the idea of a singular style in favor of a job-by-job approach, he blends the conceptual sensibility of an advertising man with the visual wit of a designer in developing campaigns for myriad real-estate and retail clients. Despite the various typographic, illustrative, and photographic approaches, the Hicks touch is nevertheless unmistakable. Here he discusses some disparate projects for a bookstore chain, three real-estate development firms, and an adult novelty toy designed to compete head to head with the Pet Rock.

About the bovine campaign for Bookstop: The president of this discount retail book company gave us only one requisite: he wanted to stress Bookstop's "unheard of selection and price." Well, what is more obvious than to play with the word *unheard?* It logically follows that *heard* becomes *herd,* so we just did word associations to come up with the cow motif—a herd of cows. Oddly enough, the campaign was very successful. Indeed Bookstop became one of the fastest-growing chains in the U.S. They compete with the big chains like Dalton's and Waldenbooks, but the main difference is that Bookstop is a more spontaneous company: they are smaller and are not constrained by a giant bureaucracy. They can move quicker on many fronts. Moreover, they apparently have a better sense of humor than the other companies. Regardless, they did not come to us to be offbeat, they just wanted to sell a lot of books.

Bookstop's in-house posters were designed to be pasted on crates positioned as locators at the ends of aisles. Therefore they are illustrated in the style of classic fruit crate labels. They were produced so quickly—literally overnight—that they had to be color Xeroxed instead of printed. Ultimately, though, they were printed. We wanted them to appear out of context by establishing a premise that seemed reasonable, then injecting an image that was off the wall. One would expect that the fiction poster, for example, would indeed show a Hollywood-type man and woman in passionate embrace; instead we have the cow licking the woman's face. The same sensibility was later applied to the newspaper advertising.

The importance of marketing in the design process: Marketing is an inherent aspect of design—at least at Hixo it is. And before I can even think about a design problem—whether or not to employ a photographer or illustrator or what type to use—I must understand who the message is aimed at. I believe that most people in the eighties (and there will surely be more in the nineties) are very leery about advertising, and that the public is more educated, and therefore fairly sophisticated, because it has been exposed to so many advertising messages. So in terms of Bookstop we are not making hype. We are saying, "Of course our prices are low, of course we have a greater selection than the competition." But more important, we are emphasizing, "If *you* owned a bookstore isn't this the way you would want to relate to the people who buy your books?" Even if the prices aren't better, and in some cases they are not, the customers will be loyal over time because they like the *style* of this company. With a generic product like books, the venue where one buys speaks as much to one's life-style as the book one actually purchases. We are attempting to establish a tone that consumers can positively respond to for the aesthetics and humor. Restaurants and clothing stores do the same thing; in fact, we are like the Banana Republic of book emporia.

About three distinct real-estate prospectuses: Our style varies wildly. Some pieces look extremely corporate while others are completely off the wall. The work ranges from brochures for hospitals to menus for hot dog stands. Our rationale is: do what is correct for the client. For Great Hills Corporate Center, an office building with adequate but not luxury accommodations, we devised a little booklet and audio tape of the "Three Best Stories You Ever Heard," pegged, of course, to the idea of a three-story building. For Legend Oaks, another, more elegant office complex, we did something very elaborate with multi-colors and multiple embosses and had Dugald Stermer render a number of Audubonesque drawings of the flora and fauna around the site. For The Exchange on Wall Street, a small office building, we sent out boxes with little gifts: a dollar, a lure, and a knife. In terms of marketing it is amazing that you can be working in the same industry—in the same market even—and have radically different conceptual approaches. People do not come to us asking for a carbon copy of what we've done before; and that's to our advantage because we are not a traditional design group.

About the covers for the *Good Health School:* I had Michael Schwab do some covers for this marketing piece for the Seton Hospital

Fiction
BRAND
NOVELS
HOLSTEIN PACKING CO.
CHILDREN'S
BRAND
BOOKS
HOLSTEIN PACKING

BOOKSTORE CRATE LABELS AND CATALOGUES (1987), *Christmas direct-mail and in-store promotion*
BOOKSTOP INC., *Client*
TOM POTH, *Designer*
JOHN WILSON, MELINDA MANISCALCO, AND HARRISON SAUNDERS, *Illustrators*
TOM POTH, *Art Director*

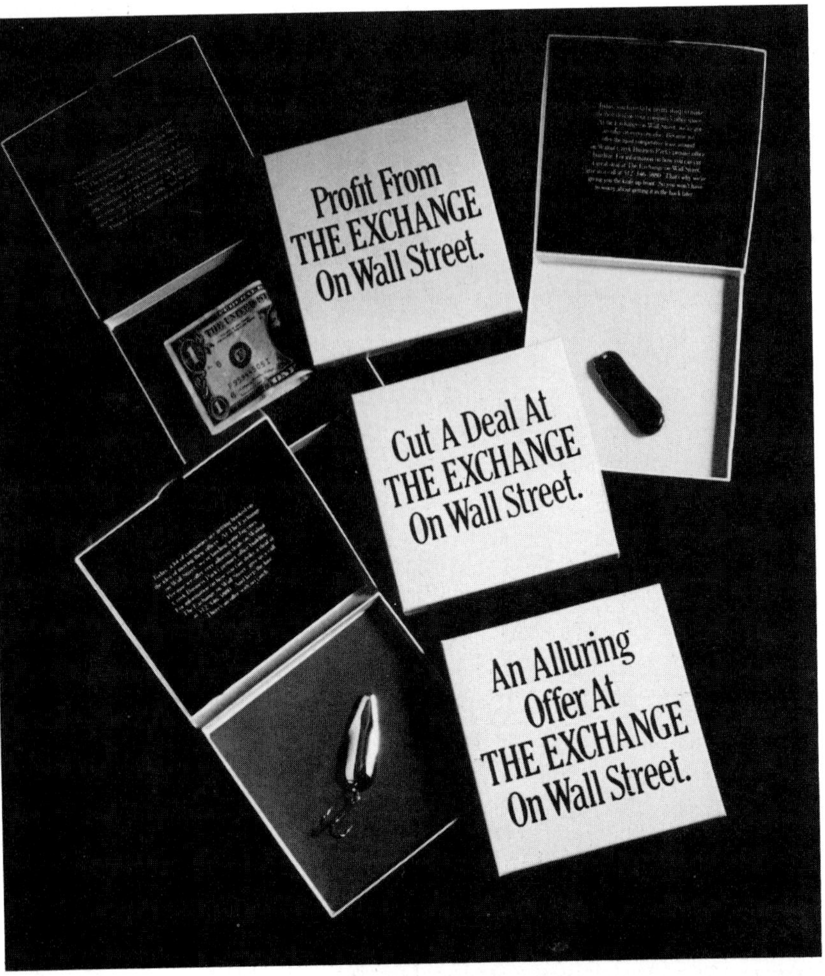
Profit From
THE EXCHANGE
On Wall Street.
Cut A Deal At
THE EXCHANGE
On Wall Street.
An Alluring
Offer At
THE EXCHANGE
On Wall Street.

THE EXCHANGE ON WALL STREET (1987), *Direct-mail piece to the brokerage community to stimulate leasing*
JASPER FEDERAL SAVINGS, *Client*
TOM POTH, *Designer*
TOM POTH, *Art Director*

GREAT HILLS CORPORATE CENTER (1986), *Direct-mail promotional brochure and tape*
LANDMARK ASSOCIATES, *Client*
MIKE HICKS, *Designer*
DUANA GILL, *Illustrator*
MIKE HICKS AND DUANA GILL, *Art Directors*

complex, which is owned by the Sisters of Charity of Saint Vincent de Paul in Saint Louis. The idea behind the magazines is to get people to associate this hospital with health rather than illness. The publications are mailed gratis to a quarter of a million people in Austin, providing them with information on health issues and schedules for regular health classes. Even if one never attends any of the classes the magazine is a real benefit. And chances are when a person takes ill, he will choose to go to Seton because of the rapport established through *Good Health.*

Every six issues we redesign it, select an artist—Schwab did the first group—and develop a style. For the magazines shown here we told Schwab the subject—what images we thought would probably work, like two people walking a dog or doing aerobic exercises. Then we got black-and-white sketches and fiddled with them back and forth until they were right. Schwab sent us black-and-white finishes and we selected our own color.

Schwab also rendered the poster for a bicycle race to benefit the cardiac research lab at the hospital. There are countless bicycle posters around; the one thing Schwab and I wanted to do was abstract the image so that it did not conform to the conventional ones. We talked about showing it from above, but for some reason his first sketch showed two people from a side view. I was insistent that it be done from above, but that had its problems too: at first the rider looked somewhat like a bug, and it took a minute or two to figure out what was going on. Adding the shadow made it less oblique. Since it is a street race I also wanted the yellow stripe. I thought that running the shadow over the stripe would contribute to a more compelling composition.

On a preference for drawing: Photography is not convincing unless one is dealing with tightly composed images. I favor illustration because it is not as literal, can be more stylized, and is often easier to print. With illustration I can focus on what I want and feel is important; with photography too much energy is devoted to fiddling with backgrounds. Of course anything illustrated is not as credible as a photograph, but then a lot of things we do, do not require that kind of journalistic credibility.

Empathizing with illustrators: I was an illustrator for seven years, so I know what it is like to do the twelve-hour illustration. I'd rather give illustrators enough leeway so if they are actually going to make a contribution to the process, they can. The trick for a designer or art director is to develop some kind of rapport with or respect for an illustrator. Schwab, for example, likes to control everything about his projects. In fact, he prefers not to work with designers at all. Ordinarily I don't care to work with people like that because I like to be in control too. But it becomes moot if I have confidence that the illustrator can do a great job. The problem comes when my interest may not be the same as the illustrator's. Some artists are prejudiced about working outside big markets and think they can turn in a bad job because Austin is off the beaten track, where no one is going to see their work anyway. So it's harder for me to push for a great job than it is for a big-city art director with national exposure. National-quality illustrators have a history of being high-handed with clients who are not in the major markets. I usually tell them from the beginning to forget that this is Austin and just do a world-class job.

About the semi-precious Texas Diamond: We were on a crash schedule to come up with a package and write the copy for a product to be marketed as a Christmas gift. Conceived by two former fraternity brothers whose parents owned a coal mine, it was the Texas version of the Pet Rock—a piece of anthracite coal that was to be a diamond in the rough. The budget was meager (they wanted to sell it retail for $7.95), and so we did all the illustration in the studio. We lifted the basic image from an old high school art clip book—the section on Future Farmers of America, with little images of farmers, cheerleaders, and so on. We redrew most of it and made the lettering out of the cowboy's rope. We were not paid, however, for half of what was owed, making this one of our least financially successful projects. But if the idea doesn't jell, we will own it. At the very least it provided some good samples.

LANTANA

LANTANA & LEGEND OAKS (1987), *Promotion*
PEYTON COLLINS & CO. *Client*
MIKE HICKS AND DUANA GILL, *Designers*
RICK KRONGER, DUGALD STERMER, AND JOHN WILSON, *Illustrators*
MIKE HICKS AND DUANA GILL, *Art Directors*

SETON CARDIAC CLASSIC (1987), *Poster*
SETON HOSPITAL, *Client*
MIKE HICKS, *Designer*
MICHAEL SCHWAB, *Illustrator*
MIKE HICKS, *Art Director*

SETON
CARDIAC
CLASSIC
APRIL·5
8

THE SETON CARDIAC CLASSIC. SUNDAY, APRIL 5, 1987 IN DOWNTOWN AUSTIN. THE LAST STAGE OF THE WORLD-CLASS BRANDERS JEANS TOUR OF TEXAS. BENEFITTING THE SETON CENTRAL TEXAS HEART INSTITUTE.

SETON GOOD HEALTH SCHOOL
SETON GOOD HEALTH SCHOOL
SETON GOOD HEALTH SCHOOL
SETON GOOD HEALTH SCHOOL
SETON GOOD HEALTH SCHOOL
FEB/MAR
OCT/NOV

SETON GOOD HEALTH SCHOOL (1987–88), *Magazine covers*
SETON HOSPITAL, *Client*
MIKE HICKS, *Designer*
MICHAEL SCHWAB, *Illustrator*
DUANA GILL, *Art Director*

TEXAS DIAMOND (1988), *Humorous gift product for Texas Market*
TEXAS DIAMOND, *Client*
MIKE HICKS, *Designer*
TOM POTH, HARRISON SAUNDERS, AND MIKE HICKS, *Illustrators*

TEXAS
Diamonds
SOLID INVESTMENT
LONE STAR QUALITY
TEXAS
Diamonds
GENUINE

KIT HINRICHS

A distinctive stylist, Kit Hinrichs is a master of the "more is more" school of design. Whether for Potlatch Corporation, Royal Viking Line, or The Nature Company, his work is a quilt of visual surprises, exhibiting not only an obsession with graphic diversity but a painterly sense of composition. A San Francisco–based partner in the internationally known design firm Pentagram, he deals with a wide range of design problems. Here he speaks about two projects: *Vegetables*, a celebration of fresh and succulent produce in colorful pictures, history, folklore, nutrition, and recipes; and Simpson Paper's *Dimensions '85: Predictions*, an alluring potpourri of paper and printing samples. Both seamlessly wed illustration to typographic design.

About his early career: When I left college [Art Center College of Design], illustration was one of the hats I wore to make a living. Very early, as a struggling designer with my partner, Tony Russell, the integration of design and illustration within our work was a necessity because we rarely had budgets large enough to buy outside art. Tony designed and I did the illustrations. It's something I don't do anymore, primarily because I'm just not good enough—I certainly wouldn't hire me. At the same time that experience enabled me to understand the illustration process and allows me to communicate comfortably with the illustrators with whom I now collaborate.

On the process of working with illustrators: I am a glutton for visual stimuli and find myself continually looking through magazines, newspapers, annual reports, promotions, and design annuals to make notes for future needs. I often conceive of an idea and then draw upon these "notes" for the appropriate person or persons to work with in creating it. I don't just award an assignment to whomever is "hot" at the moment; nor do I have a blank piece of paper and say to an illustrator, "Here's the manuscript, just do anything you'd like." From the beginning I design a piece with a specific idea in mind that takes into account who the illustrator will be and what the illustration should convey. I usually communicate the concept to the illustrator in a rough sketch, which enables us to begin at a common reference point and then build from there.

The interdependency of designer and illustrator makes for a uniquely fragile relationship. Ideas and opinions must be carefully balanced. Their roles are complementary, not hierarchical. Together they can achieve a result that neither could achieve alone.

On the importance of drawing skills for a designer: Whether or not my own drawing is used for finished art isn't important, but the skill to draw gives me a third eye, the ability to see a total picture. It allows me to compose differently from someone without drawing ability. I can visually articulate ideas during a meeting that are understandable to both our client and the illustrator. It's an invaluable communication asset. Indeed, I always communicate my initial concept through a drawing, be it a poster, catalog, or book; it's all done first as thumbnail sketches.

About *Vegetables*: This book was conceived around the history, folklore, recipes, and unique visual properties of vegetables. The wealth of material led me to structure the book into four sections. As with most publishing ventures, there was a limited budget for original art, so many pieces of art and all the vignettes were created in-house by our staff. I took what budget there was and asked a number of friends and associates in the field if they would do a drawing for me for a set price. They were all very charitable and delivered some terrific illustrations. It was an opportunity for them to experiment and it enhanced the energy level of the book. I decided to combine both photography and various styles of illustration because I knew it would result in a richness that could not be achieved by a single consistent style. I also used various paper stocks and production techniques to distinguish the four individual sections. The intent was to surprise and delight the reader every time the page is turned. In a book of this size (140 pages), with a subject perceived to be rather commonplace, you have to work to keep people interested beyond page 4.

On the book's layers of imagery: Working with a combination of photography, original illustration, and found-art (engravings, archival material, etc.) is not new to me; I have been refining this eclectic approach for many years. Thank goodness for public domain! As I work with historical material, I better understand how the various design elements enhance an individual piece. The photography grounds everything, gives the book its necessary consistency. As long as you have that reality base, you can play off it with all kinds of other images. One consistent photographic style made it possible to use twenty-one very different illustrators without jarring or confusing the reader.

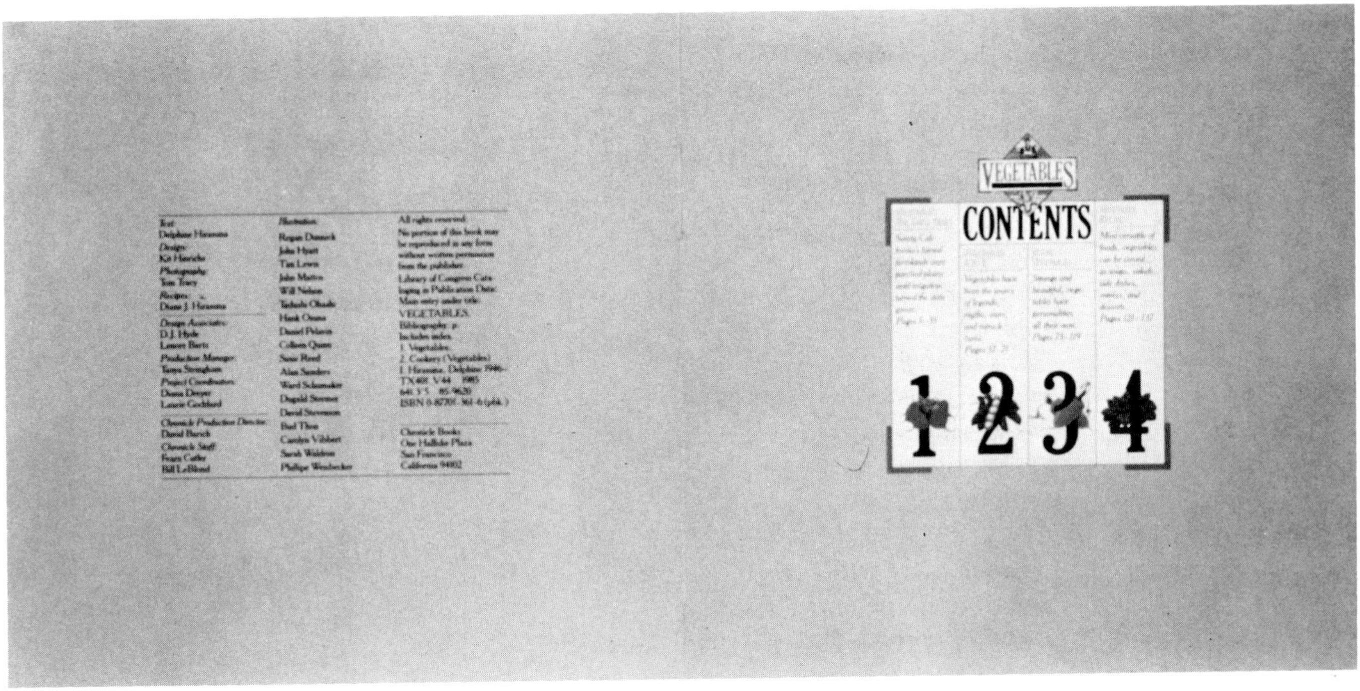

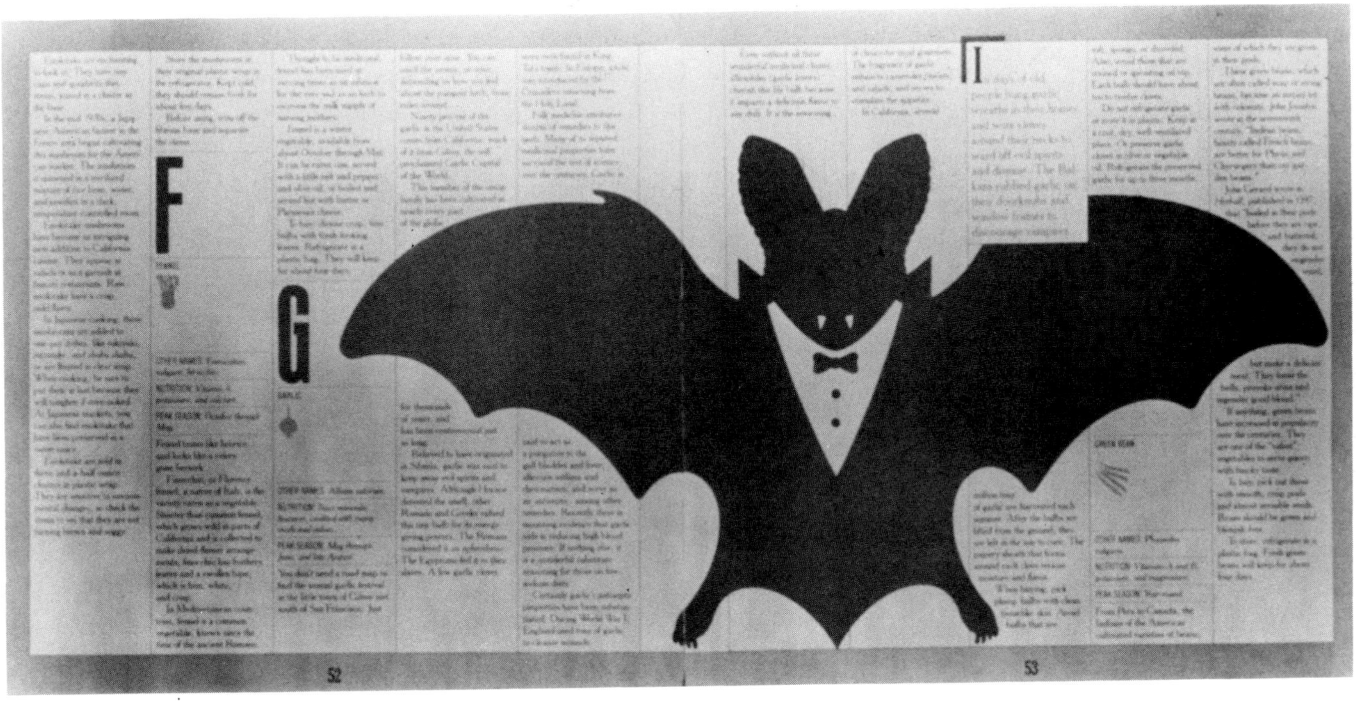

VEGETABLES (1985), *Spreads*
CHRONICLE BOOKS, *Client*
KIT HINRICHS, LENORE BARTZ, AND D. J. HYDE, *Designers*
KIT HINRICHS, *Art Director*

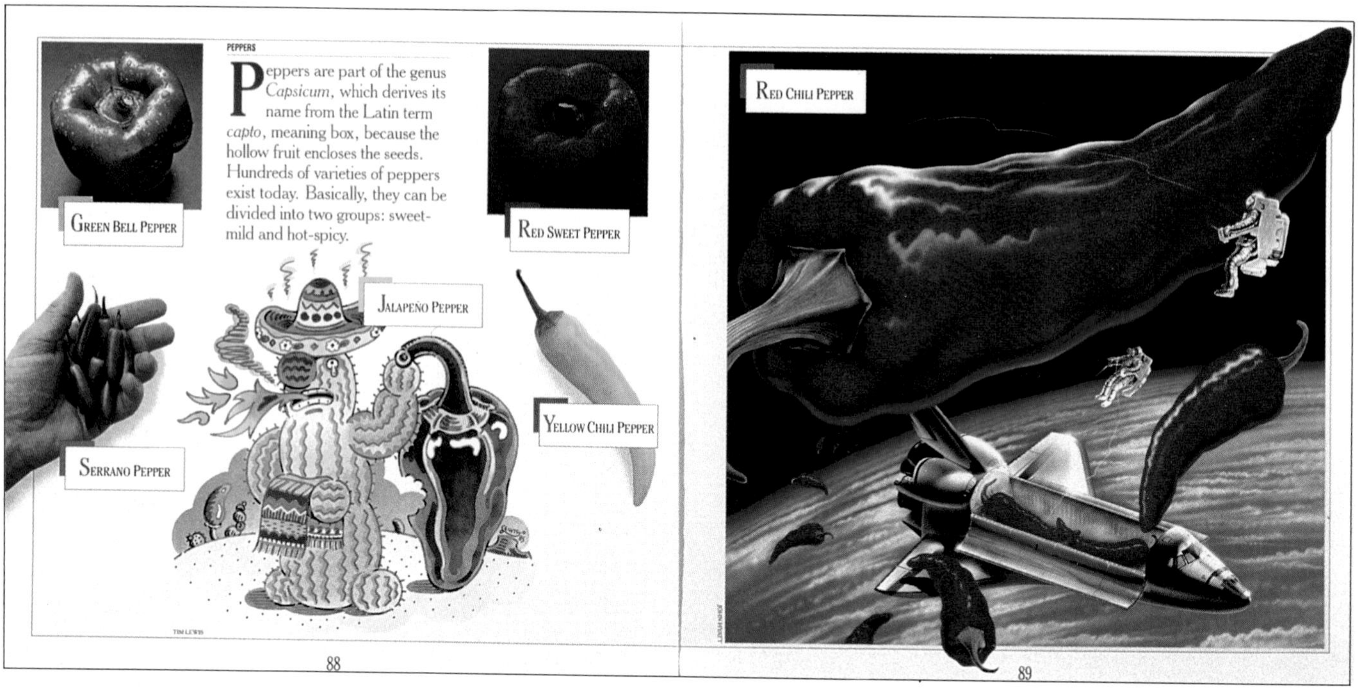
PEPPERS
Peppers are part of the genus *Capsicum*, which derives its name from the Latin term *capto*, meaning box, because the hollow fruit encloses the seeds. Hundreds of varieties of peppers exist today. Basically, they can be divided into two groups: sweet-mild and hot-spicy.
GREEN BELL PEPPER
RED SWEET PEPPER
JALAPEÑO PEPPER
YELLOW CHILI PEPPER
SERRANO PEPPER
RED CHILI PEPPER
88
89

PUMPKIN
CALABAZA SQUASH
BUTTERNUT SQUASH
COCOZELLE SQUASH
SCALLOP SQUASH
CROOKNECK SQUASH
WEISBECKER
102
103

On the marriage of design elements and illustration: Typography is another omnipresent design element. I used Cheltenham Oldstyle because it felt appropriate with the overall styling of the book. It is an "accessible," friendly typeface—not too elegant, but not too funky—and it conveyed the character and personality of the book perfectly. To further anchor the design, I echoed certain design and typographic elements throughout, including silhouette images, box rules, initial caps, and box corners. All this is well orchestrated: from large to small images, old to new, complex to simple, photograph to illustration, headline to body text.

LETTUCE
Lettuce has been the most popular salad ingredient since ancient times. Cool and refreshing, it has an unimposing flavor that does not become tiresome. Lettuce grows readily all over the country, but California is the nation's leading producer, harvesting more than two million tons of lettuce each year.
BUTTERHEAD LETTUCE
CHINESE LETTUCE
ROMAINE LETTUCE
LOOSELEAF LETTUCE
ICEBERG LETTUCE
104
105

VEGETABLES (1985), *Spreads*
CHRONICLE BOOKS, *Client*
KIT HINRICHS, LENORE BARTZ, AND D. J. HYDE, *Designers*
KIT HINRICHS, *Art Director*

About "Dimensions '85": Every year Simpson Paper Company commissions a different designer to conceive and produce its corporate "think piece." Though many paper promotions are geared primarily toward current style and technique, Simpson believes its promotions must have strong editorial content. We decided quickly on exploring the idea of predictions—not only those of Nostradamus but also the more ordinary, everyday questions about the future: Will it rain tomorrow? Will I fall in love with a tall, dark, rich stranger? and so on. With this premise we defined unusual areas for prediction and selected individuals who are known for particular expertise: George Orwell (*1984*); Casey Stengel (Who'll win the World Series?); Charles Richter (predicting earthquakes); and so on. All the major illustrations are portraits of these individuals across from the devices used to make their predictions. The subject often dictated the style: Stengel is done as a baseball card, and Frank Lloyd Wright as a blueprint; Henry Ford is a car-parts assemblage. Noteworthy is the double meaning of many of the portraits. Before recognizing Wright's face, for example, one sees that the subject of the drawing is architecture. Sometimes the finished illustration suggested the stock it should be printed on, or unusual methods of reproduction. For example, the scratchboard art of Doug Smith echoed the style of the 1930s and 1940s for the portrait of George Orwell. When the artwork was received it cried out for its own reproduction technique, in this case, thermography.

On how to effectively combine diverse graphic styles: *Predictions*, like *Vegetables*, had a visual complexity where the range of the imagery from page to page was so wild that a structured format was necessary. We therefore imposed a comparatively rigid pacing to the book, alternating between large bleed images and small silhouette images and using mini-page inserts that introduce the reader to a new story and a different paper.

The value of illustration as part of the design puzzle: Illustration teases the mind and demands more involvement of the reader. For me, illustration is the best tool for projecting ideas and concepts. Photography represents what things are. Illustration allows us to imagine what they *might* be.

DIMENSIONS '85—CHARLES RICHTER (1985), *Promotion*
SIMPSON PAPER CO., *Client*
KIT HINRICHS AND FRANCA BATOR, *Designers*
DAVE STEVENSON, *Illustrator*
KIT HINRICHS, *Art Director*

DIMENSIONS '85—PERFESSER STENGEL (1985), *Promotion*
SIMPSON PAPER CO., *Client*
KIT HINRICHS AND FRANCA BATOR, *Designers*
GARY OVERACRE, *Illustrator*
KIT HINRICHS, *Art Director*

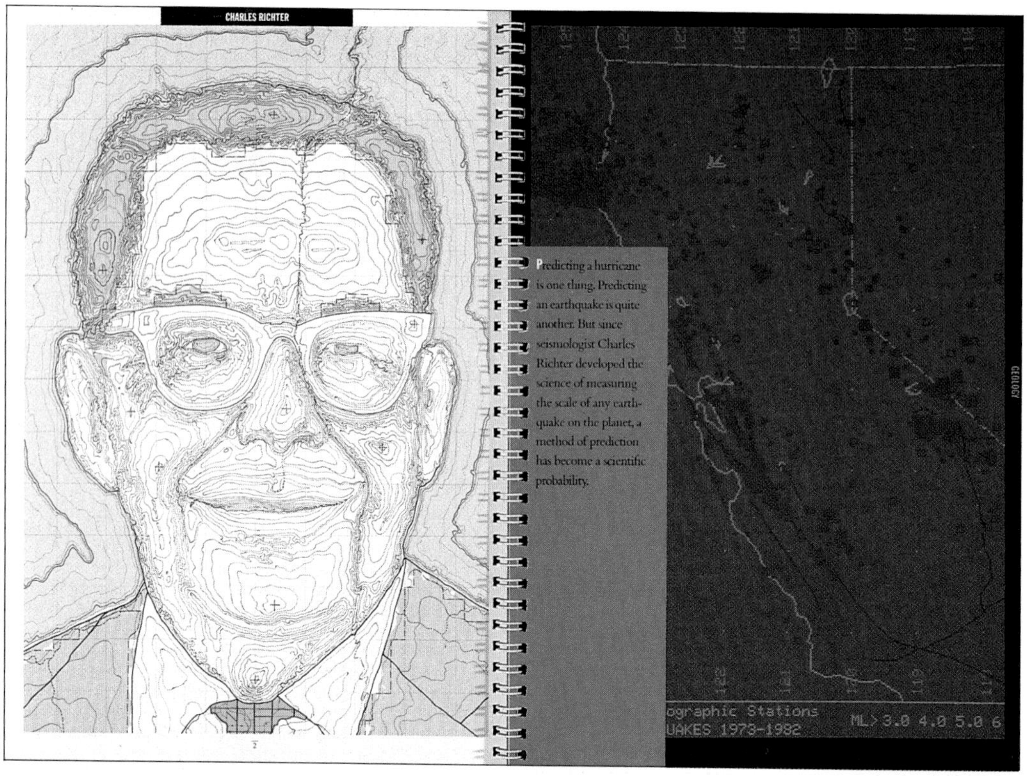
CHARLES RICHTER
Predicting a hurricane is one thing. Predicting an earthquake is quite another. But since seismologist Charles Richter developed the science of measuring the scale of any earthquake on the planet, a method of prediction has become a scientific probability.
ographic Stations
UAKES 1973-1982
ML> 3.0 4.0 5.0 6
GEOLOGY
2

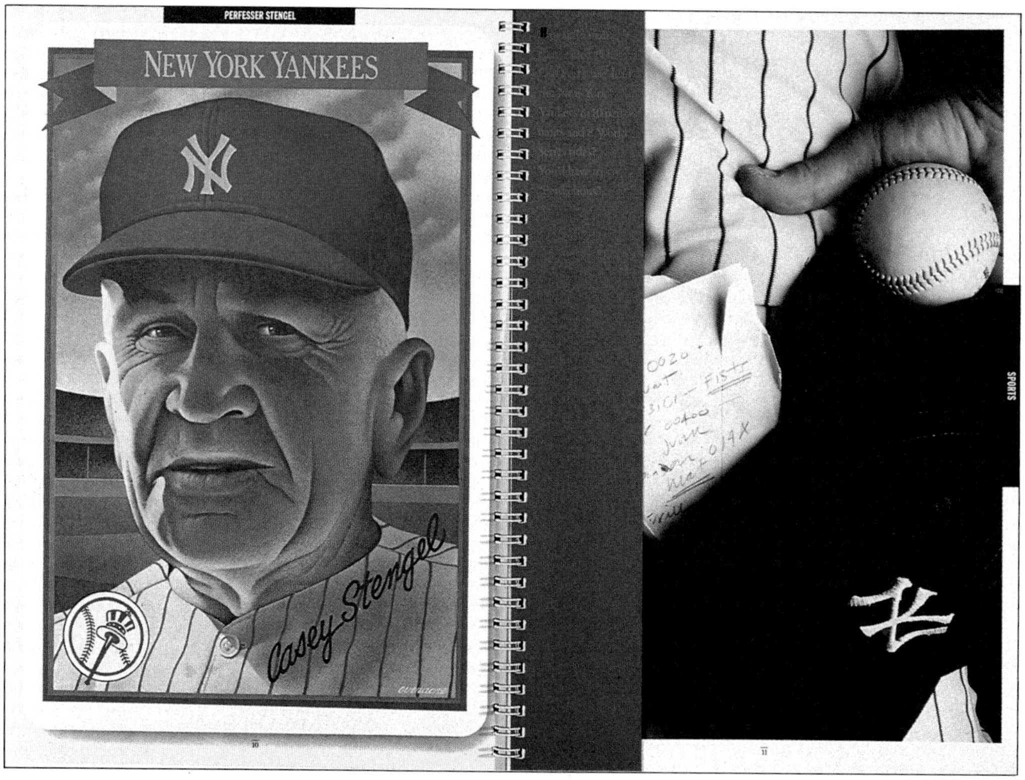
PERFESSER STENGEL
NEW YORK YANKEES
Casey Stengel
SPORTS

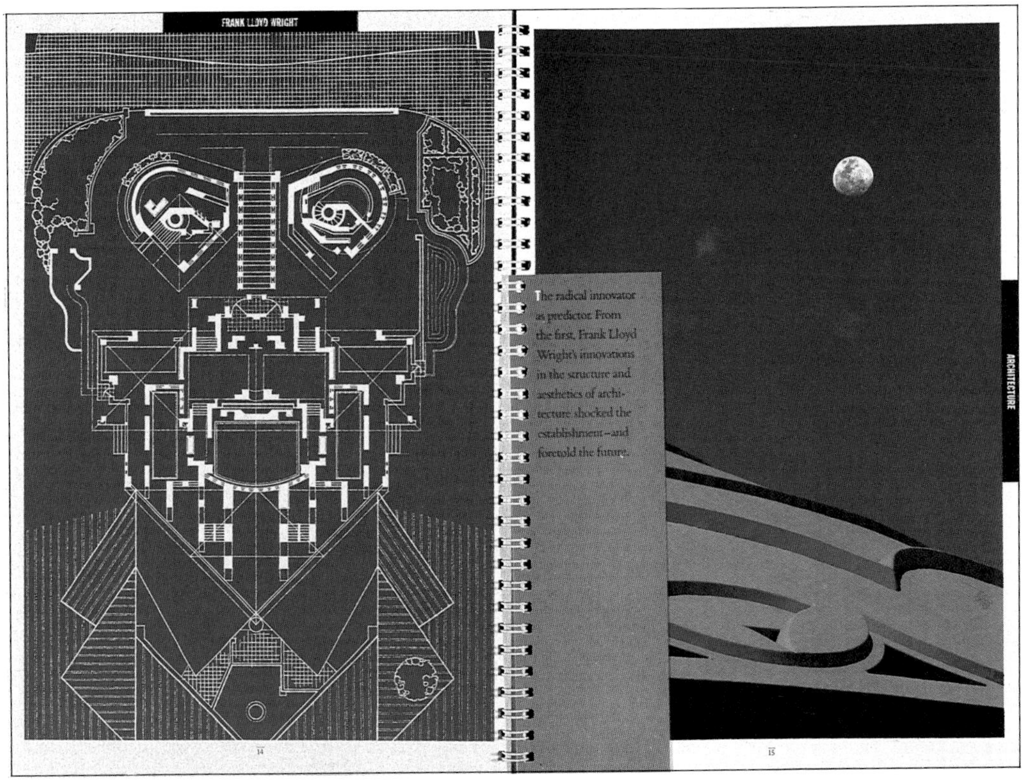

FRANK LLOYD WRIGHT
The radical innovator as predictor. From the first, Frank Lloyd Wright's innovations in the structure and aesthetics of architecture shocked the establishment—and foretold the future.
ARCHITECTURE
14
15

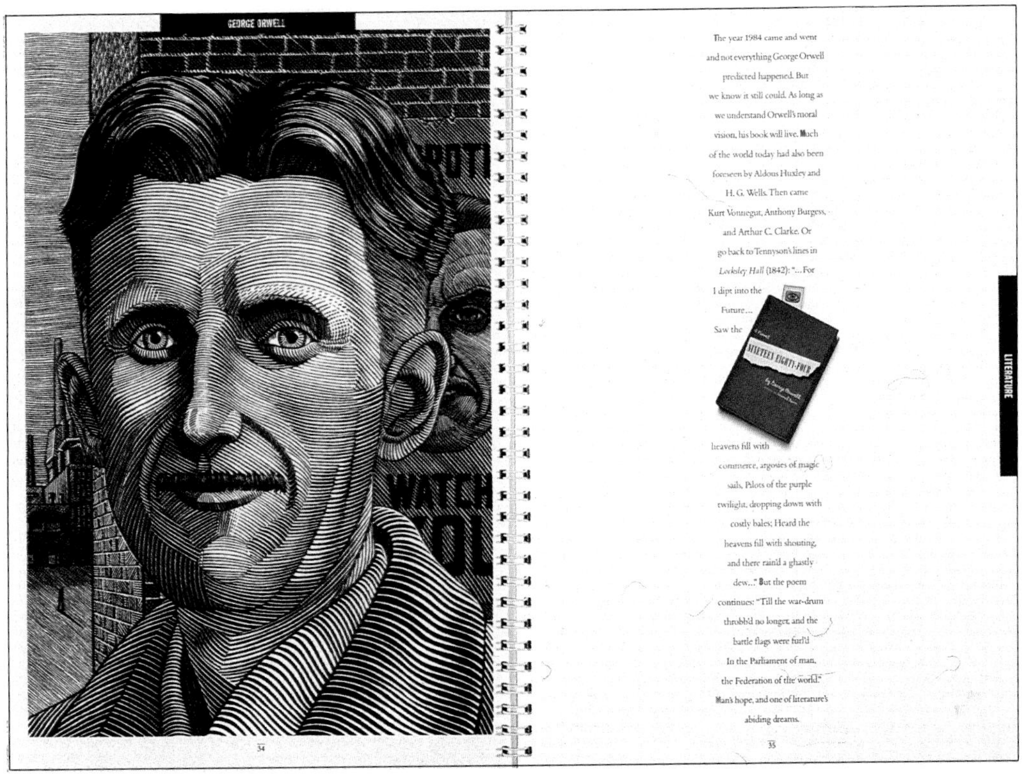

GEORGE ORWELL
The year 1984 came and went and not everything George Orwell predicted happened. But we know it still could. As long as we understand Orwell's moral vision, his book will live. Much of the world today had also been foreseen by Aldous Huxley and H. G. Wells. Then came Kurt Vonnegut, Anthony Burgess, and Arthur C. Clarke. Or go back to Tennyson's lines in *Locksley Hall* (1842): "...For I dipt into the Future... Saw the heavens fill with commerce, argosies of magic sails, Pilots of the purple twilight, dropping down with costly bales; Heard the heavens fill with shouting, and there rain'd a ghastly dew..." But the poem continues: "Till the war-drum throbb'd no longer, and the battle flags were furl'd In the Parliament of man, the Federation of the world." Man's hope, and one of literature's abiding dreams.
LITERATURE
34
35

DIMENSIONS '85—FRANK LLOYD WRIGHT (1985), *Promotion*
SIMPSON PAPER CO., *Client*
KIT HINRICHS AND FRANCA BATOR, *Designers*
DAVE STEVENSON, *Illustrator*
KIT HINRICHS, *Art Director*

DIMENSIONS '85—GEORGE ORWELL (1985), *Promotion*
SIMPSON PAPER CO., *Client*
KIT HINRICHS AND FRANCA BATOR, *Designers*
DOUGLAS SMITH, *Illustrator*
KIT HINRICHS, *Art Director*

SUSAN HOCHBAUM

Each of Pentagram's three offices (in London, New York, and San Francisco) is staffed with talented partners and associates who tend to their own clients and employ different methodologies. Though this acclaimed design firm maintains a consistently clever, inventive, and often witty sensibility, each participant has a personal style—or no style—as dictated by the commission. Susan Hochbaum is an associate who works with Peter Harrison, a partner in the New York office (see page 192). Although the two sometimes work in a direct collaboration, more often Harrison acts as adviser, with Hochbaum as designer. Such is the case with the work discussed here: Hochbaum was responsible for designing the pieces and selecting and commissioning the illustrations. The examples reveal various unique applications of illustration for projects, including a corporate annual report, restaurant identity, record company logo, and paper promotion.

About the unusual design for Warner Communications' annual report: Pentagram began doing their reports in 1980 to push the limits of what an annual report could look like. In 1984, a year in which profits were low and the company wanted to present a conservative image, we did a book using formal black-and-white photographic portraits. Then, in 1985, the company's performance turned around, which gave us a chance to do something a little more adventurous than they were accustomed to—something that would reflect the energy and vitality of the business. The fact is, illustration can be particularly well suited for a corporation that trades in multiple forms of entertainment. How else can you get Clint Eastwood and Bugs Bunny on the same stage? Illustration allows you to juxtapose multiple realities in the same image. Warner supplied us with good, bad, and mediocre photographs; 3D objects, such as videos, film cans, records, books, fiber optic cables; and publicity shots of their various stars and cartoon characters. The challenge was to tie all that disparate material together. Collage seemed to be a good solution.

On selecting the illustrators: Huntley and Muir are two women illustrators who live and work in London. Someone in our London office had worked with them before, but this was the first time that we in New York went overseas for talent. They had an affinity for the entertainment business, having done a few rock videos in England.

About the illustration process: Since Clint Eastwood is Warner's biggest box office draw, his picture was going to have to be prominent. He refused to be photographed for the book, so we were left with a terrible black-and-white publicity photo. Huntley and Muir's approach was perfect for manipulating and transforming this kind of material. Starting with a photograph, they usually "degrade" it—their term for the process by which they use multiple Xeroxes and other techniques. We brought them to New York to discuss what materials were important. We talked about a format; that it might be a theater set with

Warner Communications Inc.
1985 Annual Report

something happening on stage. I basically gave them as much freedom as possible. I don't expect artists to carry through my sketches to the letter. I try not to give concepts to illustrators unless the client insists on a particular idea. In this case we gave them the visual material in an order of importance, and they went back to London to create this magical world. I saw only very rough sketches; we just talked about the ideas on the phone. It was one of the most painless and satisfying projects I've ever done.

On the design process: I did rough page layouts to determine how many images were needed. And there was a form to follow based on Warner's four lines of business; each section (i.e., "Movies and Television") opens with a double-page spread that summarizes what goes on in a specific corporate division and is followed by two or three small images. I asked for handwritten scribbles to use as titles, and I didn't plan the color breakdown until I saw what they were doing. In fact, the color copy blocks came from seeing the finished work. I must say that the design was certainly in part inspired by the images, which is a much better method than pushing an illustration to fit a design. The images were so

Publishing

Warner Communications Inc.
1985 Annual Report
Warner Communications, *Client*
Susan Hochbaum, *Designer*
Sue Huntley and Donna Muir, *Illustrators*
Susan Hochbaum and Peter Harrison, *Art Directors*

14:59:27:01

rich and complex that a simple type treatment was necessary to avoid any competition between the art and the words. My tendency is usually to let the art dominate and use the other design elements to support that.

The cover was the most difficult part. It always is. For years Warner insisted that they didn't want *anything* on the cover; in fact, for the first five years the covers were solid gray with "Warner Communications Inc." and the year set in type. As I said, 1985 was a good financial year, and putting an image on the cover was a way to make that announcement. The idea was to find an integrated image for all the divisions—the head, representing the human senses, unites everything.

Warner's response and responsibility: It was very well received even by the conservative financial community. A lot of credit has to go to Warner for being so open-minded. Never has a portrait of the chairman of the board looked like the one we used. Moreover, the designer cannot take full credit for a piece like this—without a client with some vision it just can't be done.

About the booklet for the '21' Club: This is a very old and famous New York restaurant. Back in the twenties it was a speakeasy; and, though open to the public, it always had the allure of being a private men's club. Indeed celebrities do have private tables, and it can be very hard to get a reservation. When Marshall Cogan bought it he wanted to retain the tradition and at the same time attract more business people, women, and a younger clientele. The restaurant was given a facelift, and our job in the printed material was to update without losing the sense of history. The first project we did was a 4-inch by 6-inch hand-bound history of the restaurant designed as a promotion piece to encourage people to join a private breakfast club.

The idea came from two books published for '21' in the thirties that included essays and drawings by patrons of the club. In this case the design solution was obvious. All the drawings and cartoons in the book are part of the restaurant's collection. Then we were asked to redesign all the menus, matchbooks, and other collateral material and, ultimately, things like '21' cigars, jams and jellies, and so on.

Concerning the restaurant's identity problem: Two aspects of the identity needed to be addressed for use on menus and other printed material. The first was the logo, an italic script we changed to a more elegant typeface. We gave it single rather than double quotation marks and put the whole thing in a square. The second was their trademark jockeys which line the stairway of the brownstone building on West Fifty-second Street. The horse and jockey were key to their public image, and it made sense to continue using them in graphic form. To create the new emblem we drew inspiration from old English horse pictures in the manner of George Stubbs, and decided that Paul Davis would be perfect for the job. He has the right blend of realism and personal vision. Though he's more concerned with design these days, and not in the habit of taking illustration assignments, he was convinced to do it. We told him that the horse and jockey were essential, and discussed the need to maintain an old and new feeling; but basically we did not give him any artistic direction. And the result is perfect.

About the Jump Street logo: I got involved with this job through Steven Guarnaccia, my husband. Jump Street Records was a new label started by a splinter group from a company that had used Steven's work for *their* label. Steven came up with the Jump Street character, and we decided that it would be fun to use it in various poses and positions. So on the letterhead he appears right side up, on the envelope he's upside down, and on the business card he's jumping over a record. We decided Steven would hand-draw the logotype, which would give it the same character as the drawing. Though I designed their first album cover, and was the art director on this identity project, the inspiration really came from the illustration.

On working together as a husband-and-wife team: I met Steven when I gave him an assignment, and we can continue to work together because we respect each other's talents. He knows I trust him and I know that he trusts me.

About the Mead Paper Company promotion: Mead and Gilbert came out with a new line of coated and uncoated papers, and decided to do a joint promotion directly to art directors and designers. The idea was to publish a small

THE '21' CLUB
21 WEST 52 STREET · NEW YORK

'21'

THE '21' CLUB HISTORY BOOK AND MENU (1987), *Promotional material for private breakfast club; collateral material for restaurant*
THE '21' CLUB, *Client*
SUSAN HOCHBAUM, *Designer*
Various Illustrators
SUSAN HOCHBAUM AND PETER HARRISON, *Art Directors*

book (6 inches by 6 inches) for the big marketing push in September. The concept, therefore, is a celebration of that month, with each day a humorous or serious September event—everything from the Bald Is Beautiful convention to Henry Hudson discovering the Hudson River. It offered a broad range of image possibilities, and the chance to show photography and illustration reproduced through various printing techniques on a number of different papers. There was very little budget for art, so I gave the artists as much artistic freedom as possible. I got some fantastic results. I do feel bad about not offering proper recompense, but all the illustrators responded well because they got a sample that went to thousands of potential clients.

About the Chase/Global identity kit: This was not so much an illustration problem as one of identity. Chase/Global, a division of Chase Manhattan Bank, wanted a program that stressed the idea that what they provide is a real relationship—you know, a human being at the other end of the telephone who signifies reliability, partner-

September 1862: 11 O. Henry born
Oh Henry!
Oh Henry!
Candy made the Home Made way

SEPTEMBER (1988), *Promotion for a new line of papers*
MEAD AND GILBERT PAPERS, *Client*
SUSAN HOCHBAUM, *Designer*
Various Illustrators
SUSAN HOCHBAUM AND PETER HARRISON, *Art Directors*

ship, and guidance. So we came up with the hand as a symbol of reaching out; and it is used in many different contexts, with the illustration varying from drawing to photography. Unfortunately the client responded best to the realistic rather than the abstract versions.

JUMP STREET

About the disappointments with this project: For one of the brochures I chose an illustrator whose strength was portraits and still lifes. I wanted to give him a chance to develop ideas, but we were under terrible time pressure, and he wasn't used to working that way. Sometimes it's great to have artists do what they are not used to doing because they can get a fresh solution. But in this case it was hard to predict the results, and ultimately they were not what they could have been. I wish we had had the chance to implement the idea of the hand, but Chase/Global ran out of money and began doing the work internally. That often happens. We set up a system, turn it over, and lose control over what gets produced.

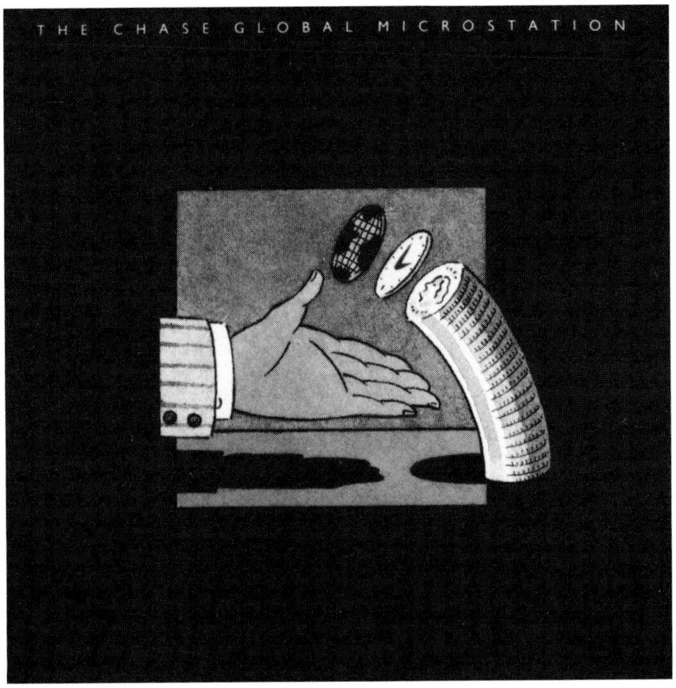
THE CHASE GLOBAL MICROSTATION

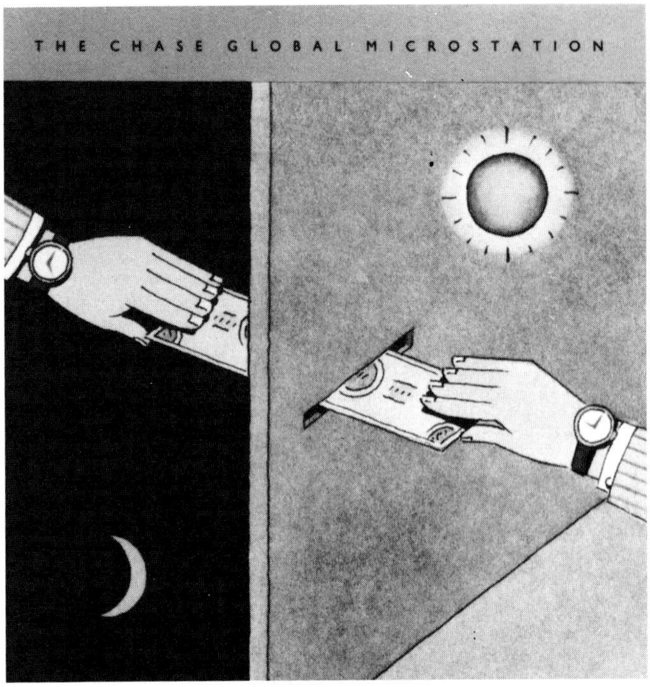
THE CHASE GLOBAL MICROSTATION

JUMP STREET
JUMP STREET RECORDS, INC.
200 WEST 72 STREET, SUITE 66
NEW YORK, NY 10023
JUMP STREET RECORDS, INC., 200 WEST 72 STREET, SUITE 66, NEW YORK, NY 10023, (212) 873-1248

MICROSTATION DISK PACK (1986), *Demonstration disk mailed to potential customers*
CHASE/GLOBAL, *Client*
SUSAN HOCHBAUM, *Designer*
STEVEN GUARNACCIA, *Illustrator*
SUSAN HOCHBAUM AND PETER HARRISON, *Art Directors*

JUMP STREET IDENTITY (1987)
JUMP STREET RECORDS, *Client*
SUSAN HOCHBAUM, *Designer*
STEVEN GUARNACCIA, *Illustrator*
SUSAN HOCHBAUM, *Art Director*

PAULA SCHER

For some art directors illustration is the centerpiece of design, worked around rather than fiddled with. For others illustration is an integrated component, controlled for maximum impact. Paula Scher's album covers for CBS Records represent the latter. Former art director for CBS (from 1975 to 1982), and currently a principal of the New York design firm Koppel and Scher, she is decidedly a hands-on practitioner, directing illustration like a cop directs traffic. Yet her grip is never so tight as to strangle creativity or surprise. Rather, the key to Scher's ability to get good results from illustrators is a skill at articulation: not only of the problem, but in most cases of the solution. Add to that her ability to draw (she studied to be an illustrator) and one has an exemplary art director. Here Scher describes the process behind some of her most provocative record jackets.

On the trouble of selling illustration over photography: Literal imagery is easier to present than nonliteral imagery. It is much easier for marketing people at a record company or publishing house to respond positively to a photograph, because it is *real.* Something conceptual and cerebral is more difficult for them to grasp, and they want the most immediate response. If the consumer has to think to get it, they assume the consumer will be turned off. Conceptual photography is also difficult to sell because it requires some thought too. However, if tomorrow some agency were to do a sensational advertising campaign based on conceptual illustration, and it was phenomenally successful, everyone would rush to copy it. In the sixties there was an abundance of good conceptual advertising; hence there was a surge in conceptual illustration and design that continued through the seventies until the economy crumbled and the MBAs became a powerful force with their belief in demographics, marketing surveys, and the philosophy that visual ideas are threatening.

On using illustration: I am not very interested in what might be called mood-oriented illustration, where style triumphs over content. Neither am I interested in the "salable" illustration of the moment—why feed the clichés?

There are fundamental differences between an editorial art director (which I am when I design magazines) and a record cover art director. In the former situation I generally give the illustrator an article and a space to fill. The illustrator basically solves the problem without my conceptual interference. At CBS, however, I rarely gave an illustrator a job that I didn't preconceptualize, because I sold it to the company before the sketch stage. I realized that showing sketches would result in too many questions and changes. It was always best just to put forth my idea and give them a finish later—hopefully so late that there was no time for revisions.

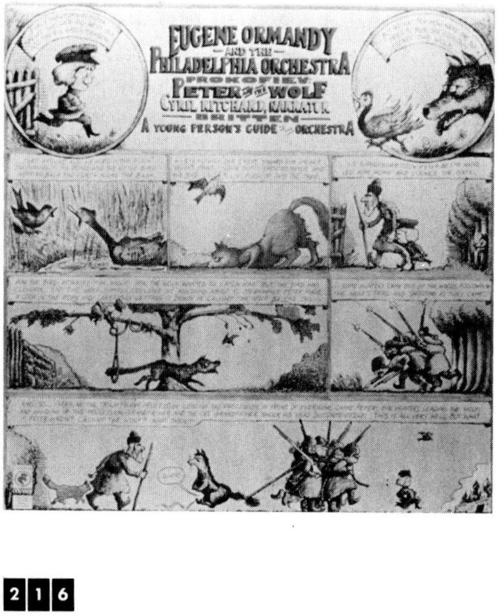
EUGENE ORMANDY
AND THE
PHILADELPHIA ORCHESTRA
PETER AND THE WOLF

About the *Peter and the Wolf* album: Although not all my work shows it, I am most interested in the visual pun and the double entendre, because covers should have different levels of comprehension. However, *Peter and the Wolf* doesn't have one. Instead I developed a children's book–comic strip style of illustration that tells the story of the ballet and encourages the child to read along or at least follow the pictures. The illustrator is Stan Mack, who had already illustrated a children's book I had written [and now does a weekly comic strip, "Real Life Funnies," in the *Village Voice*]. I hired him because, while many illustrators have trouble thinking sequentially, Stan generally works in a comic strip form and is comfortable breaking information up into narrative scenes. Moreover, his are not cuddly-cute children's book illustrations; they are livelier, and even a little nastier. He created a wonderfully eerie scene, for example, when the wolf eats the duck and a quack comes from his stomach.

The drawings continued on the back cover to accommodate the whole story. We worked out how many frames were needed, then Stan did the drawings, and together we edited the copy. The typography is hand-drawn in the tradition of [Winsor McCay's] *Little Nemo,* to maximize the effect of the comic genre. Every decision was purposeful, nothing was arbitrary.

On intuition versus reason: Color is the only area in which I am consistently intuitive. Design decisions, in terms of how I select an illustrator or how I am going to handle the type, are generally intellectually based. Despite the fact

KALINNIKOV
SYMPHONY NO.1 IN G MINOR
STATE ACADEMIC ORCHESTRA
YEVGENY SVETLANOV, CONDUCTOR
McMullan
MELODIYA

KALINNIKOV (1976),
Record album cover
CBS RECORDS, *Client*
PAULA SCHER, *Designer*
JAMES MCMULLAN, *Illustrator*
PAULA SCHER, *Art Director*

PETER AND THE WOLF (1976),
Record album cover
CBS RECORDS, *Client*
PAULA SCHER, *Designer*
STAN MACK, *Illustrator*
PAULA SCHER, *Art Director*

that I can be a decorative designer, working with a wide range of period typefaces and so on, my work is much more reasoned than one might think.

About the record cover for *Kalinnikov*: This is romantic Russian music from the Czarist period. I gave the job to Jim McMullan because he can do lush watercolors, and I thought he would create a romantic scene. But it wasn't enough for him. He felt that my idea was too trite.

Jim and I worked together a lot and have a good rapport. If he didn't like my thinking he often suggested that another illustrator render the idea. Sometimes I could convince him to do it hoping that the result would be a happy surprise for both of us. In this case he could have done a very nice vignette, as I envisioned, but he thought that it lacked focus as a cover. He wanted to include something that was more indicative of the music and so researched an ornate period of Russian decorative art, which inspired the flower border shown here. He then thought that the border was too static and made the vignette burst out of the border and drip around it so that the romantic part of the image gets a little stormy on the top and counteracts the ornateness at the bottom. I think the painting turned out very well, though Jim doesn't—in fact he thinks the type made it work. Actually, he doesn't like this cover at all.

Yardbirds Favorites (1977),
Record album cover
CBS Records, *Client*
Paula Scher, *Designer*
David Wilcox, *Illustrator*
Paula Scher, *Art Director*

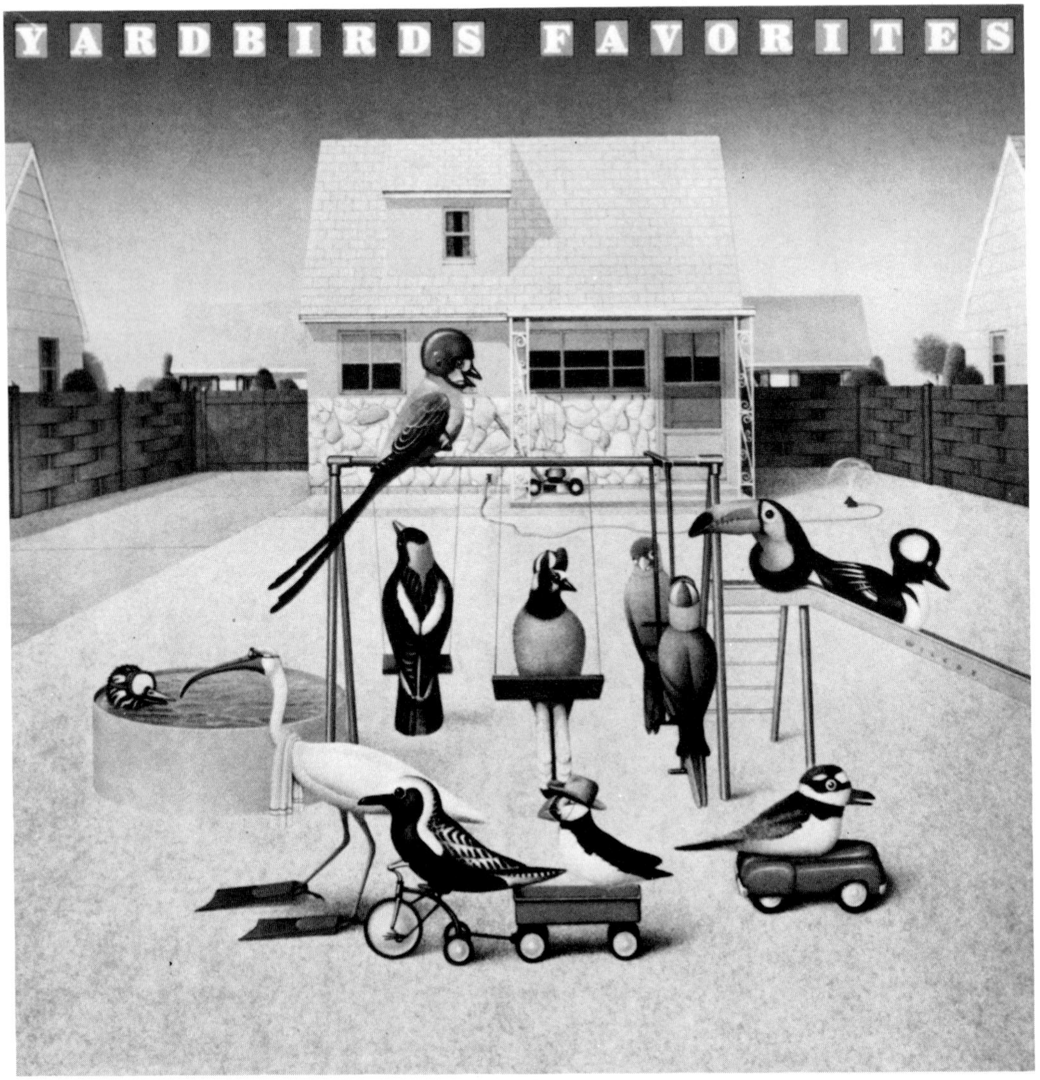
YARDBIRDS FAVORITES

On type and image: There are few instances where I think about typography before the illustration is completed. Most of the time I find out as much about the music as possible. Then I call up an illustrator whose sensibility is appropriate to the preconceived subject matter. The illustrator does the art, and my problem is figuring out how to get the damn type on there. I get better work if the illustrator is not worrying about type constraints. In fact, every time I've asked an illustrator to leave room on the top for type, the result has been a cover with type on the top and illustration on the bottom—very boring and not a terrific way to approach design.

The *Kalinnikov* cover was actually a typographic nightmare. Jim left me no place at all to position type. I selected a typeface (Windsor) that was not from the same period as the painting, but it was condensed with a series of curves that seemed to work nicely with the configuration within the art. When I began to repeat what was going on in the watercolor by creating one curve for the big type that said *Kalinnikov,* and then made these sweeps with other pieces of typography, it began to complement the painting and flowed out nicely from the border. Making it work involved hours of trial and error, during which time the instinctive part of me took over. Sometimes one just has to try different things, and sometimes they are disastrous failures. Sometimes you make a lousy cover, you put it in the drawer, you forget about it and go on to the next

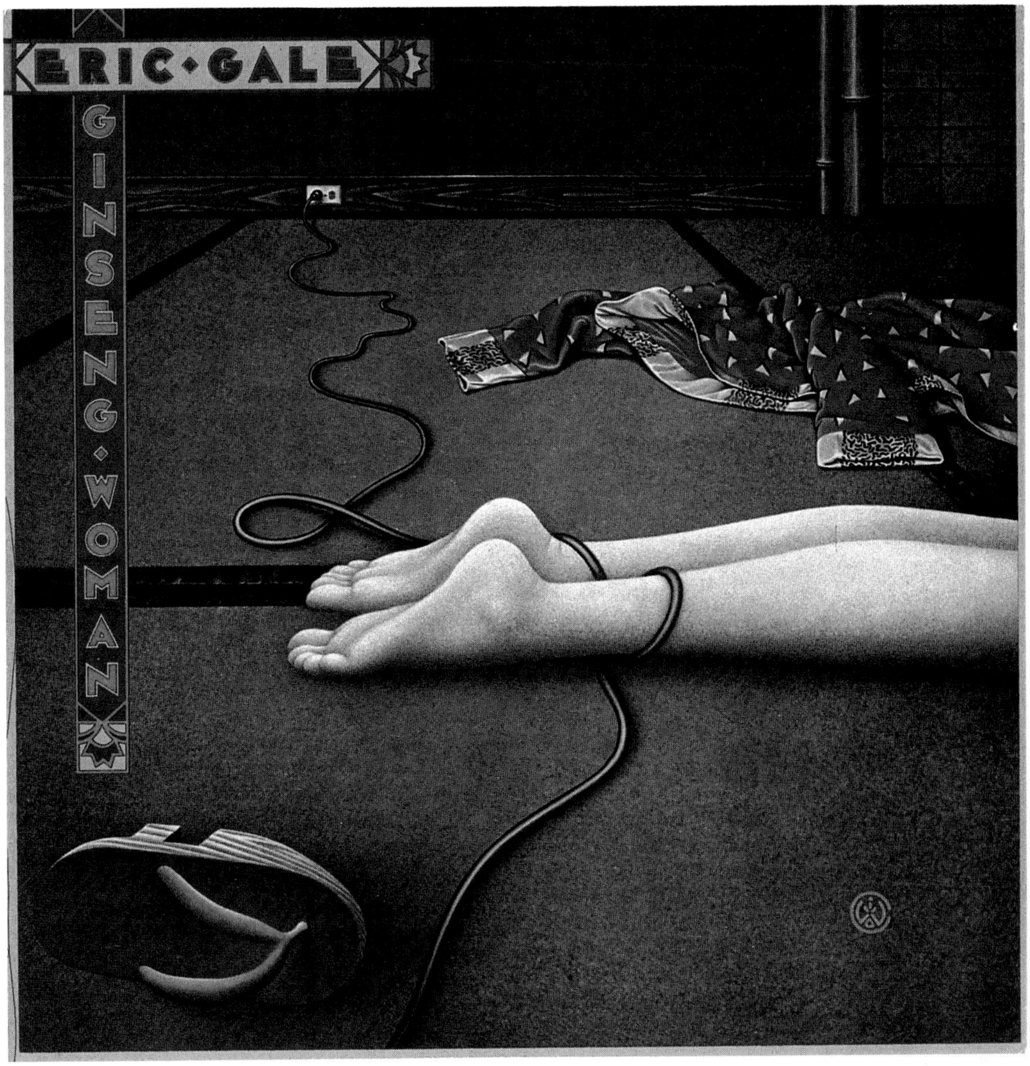
ERIC•GALE
GINSENG•WOMAN

GINSENG WOMAN (1977),
Record album cover
CBS RECORDS, *Client*
PAULA SCHER, *Designer*
DAVID WILCOX, *Illustrator*
PAULA SCHER, *Art Director*

one. But if you don't take the risks, you don't create anything new. If you stay with what you know, you don't grow. I always thought the type made this cover look Hawaiian. Maybe it's really Don Ho's greatest hits.

About the Yardbirds record cover: I have done around fifteen covers with David Wilcox; he's a surrealist painter who paints on masonite and manipulates color so that it's usually dark and bizarre. The Yardbirds cover is actually more pastel than most of his work. I love to use him on ridiculous visual puns, which this certainly is. *Yardbirds Favorites* is just a literal, and foolish, play on the rock group's name showing birds playing in the backyard of a suburban house like the one I grew up in. David precisely rendered all the details—the walkway, lattice work, even the sprinkler—so that this extremely dumb idea did not become a cartoon but is nevertheless absurd.

The type was put in squares because that is the nature of suburbia: a yard is an enclosure and suburban blocks are nice little grids. The face is called Whitin Black and is a familiar stencil on baby blocks.

The expected thing for the Yardbirds cover would have been to use an artist like Elwood Smith because he draws a lot of funny animals. I hate that logic. Turning things around is what's exciting about illustration. Illustration is terrific because it can represent something that doesn't exist. It's about creating the Great Surprise. Now, if I come up with a cartoony idea like this with a cartoonist, it's no longer a surprise. I wanted a detailed and explicit rendering of a stupid idea; the surprise made it work.

GOOGIE AND TOM COPPOLA
Shine the Light of Love
WILCOX

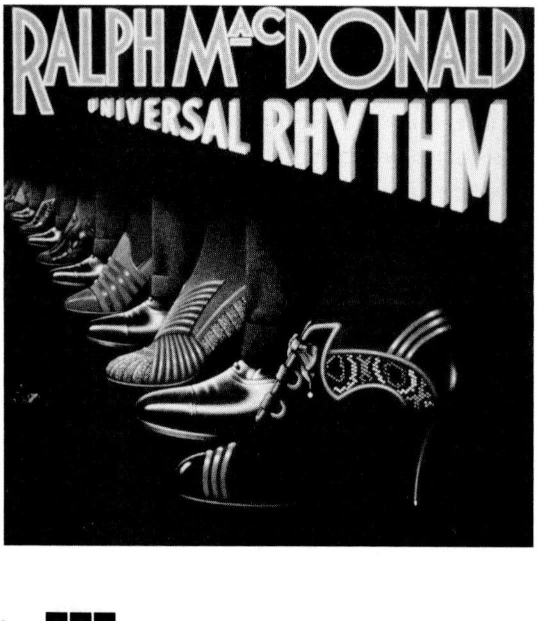
RALPH MacDONALD
UNIVERSAL RHYTHM

Concerning the *Ginseng Woman* cover: Recording artists usually have cover approval, and musician Eric Gale wanted to dedicate this cover to his Asian wife; hence the title *Ginseng Woman,* which, of course, dictated the oriental motif. This was a controversial cover. The National Organization of Women petitioned against it because they believed the image suggested violence to women. That was not my intent. Gale plays an electric guitar, symbolized by the green electric cord. The album title reminded me of *Lady from Shanghai* or *Shanghai Lil,* the kind of seamy genre scene that in this case suggests a mysterious Eastern setting. The art is pure Wilcox-style, mottled on masonite so that the masonite comes through, producing the dark, dramatic hues.

The scale was wrong in the sketch. The legs were too far back, the thong was too small. We pulled up the thongs and moved the legs, making the whole thing very mysterious. The type design was based on Japanese stamps.

About the *Shine the Light of Love* album: Tom and Googie Coppola were born-again Christians doing a religious album, and they wanted a religious cover. My problem was to create something that was spiritual enough to satisfy the Coppolas but did not put off CBS records, which was marketing the record as R&B. The title, *Shine the Light of Love,* inspired me to take the idea to the extreme by having David Wilcox make everything in the painting in the shape of a heart, even down to the doorknob, the wood grain, and the smoke in the heart-shaped ashtray. The idea is corny, but because of the obsessiveness it becomes good.

On the album for *Universal Rhythm*: This is the only cover Wilcox and I did together where I designed the type before the image was completed. It had to do with my obsession with the great French poster artist A. M. Cassandre. I wanted to make shapes that integrated the typography and have the illustration make sense with the type. But the genesis of the album is funnier than that.

Ralph MacDonald, a famous jazz drummer with

Endless Beach

ENDLESS BEACH (1981), *Record album cover*
CBS RECORDS, *Client*
PAULA SCHER, *Designer*
ELWOOD SMITH, *Illustrator*
PAULA SCHER, *Art Director*

SHINE THE LIGHT OF LOVE (1978), *Record album cover*
CBS RECORDS, *Client*
PAULA SCHER, *Designer*
DAVID WILCOX, *Illustrator*
PAULA SCHER, *Art Director*

UNIVERSAL RHYTHM (1979), *Record album cover*
CBS RECORDS, *Client*
PAULA SCHER, *Designer*
DAVID WILCOX, *Illustrator*
PAULA SCHER, *Art Director*

whom I had worked on projects before, gave me a long dissertation on the history of rhythm, from the tom-tom to the teletype, and how it is a great communicator, et cetera. I really thought he wanted me to do a cover that explained this whole history, which, obviously, would have been a boring nightmare. But when he finished his 45-minute spiel he said, "Just do something nice that a little white girl like you would like." Whew! I decided to do a fantastic line of shoes—all stiff and regimented. Normally, one would illustrate rhythm with dancing feet . . . well, this was just the opposite. The idea was not to be perverse but to be surprising and create a tension between the letterforms and the image. Ironically, the predesigned type never sat properly on the illustration.

About the *Endless Beach* album: Here's where I used Elwood Smith, a terrific cartoonist, because this Beach Boys–type music screamed for a raucous beach scene. Now you may think that it is too predictable and contradicts my own need to have counterpoints, but in reality what we did was complicate the scene so much that it became totally absurd. I told Elwood that he could include whatever disgusting thing he wanted to say about beach music. There's even dog-doo on the cover—right in front with all the steam. The art is so jammed with stuff that the company didn't even notice it. Had I chosen David Wilcox to do this cover, all this disgusting stuff would have been too real, too offensive, and not funny at all.

INDEX

Italicized numbers refer to pages with artwork